Communications
in Computer and Information Science   **1166**

Commenced Publication in 2007
Founding and Former Series Editors:
Phoebe Chen, Alfredo Cuzzocrea, Xiaoyong Du, Orhun Kara, Ting Liu,
Krishna M. Sivalingam, Dominik Ślęzak, Takashi Washio, Xiaokang Yang,
and Junsong Yuan

Editorial Board Members

More information about this series at http://www.springer.com/series/7899

Hein Venter · Marianne Loock ·
Marijke Coetzee · Mariki Eloff ·
Jan Eloff (Eds.)

Information
and Cyber Security

18th International Conference, ISSA 2019
Johannesburg, South Africa, August 15, 2019
Proceedings

 Springer

Editors
Hein Venter (iD)
University of Pretoria
Pretoria, Gauteng, South Africa

Marianne Loock (iD)
University of South Africa
Florida, Gauteng, South Africa

Marijke Coetzee (iD)
University of Johannesburg
Auckland Park, Gauteng, South Africa

Mariki Eloff (iD)
University of South Africa
Pretoria, Gauteng, South Africa

Jan Eloff (iD)
University of Pretoria
Pretoria, Gauteng, South Africa

ISSN 1865-0929   ISSN 1865-0937   (electronic)
Communications in Computer and Information Science
ISBN 978-3-030-43275-1   ISBN 978-3-030-43276-8   (eBook)
https://doi.org/10.1007/978-3-030-43276-8

This Springer imprint is published by the registered company Springer Nature Switzerland AG
The registered company address is: Gewerbestrasse 11, 6330 Cham, Switzerland

Preface

ISSA 2019 is the annual conference for the information security community that continues on the successful recipe established in 2001. The conference is held under the auspices of the Academy for Computer Science and Software Engineering at the University of Johannesburg, the School of Computing at the University of South Africa, and the Department of Computer Science at the University of Pretoria.

ISSA 2019 was held on August 15, 2019. The conference has evolved each year in various ways. For the first time the conference was hosted at the premises of the University of Pretoria. We believe that the quality and relevance of the information presented by industry practitioners and academics has also evolved over the years, as have the opportunities for senior research students to present their research to a critical and representative audience. This year university students were allowed to register for the conference for an unprecedented 200 ZAR per person in order to make the conference extremely accessible to students.

Conferences have become a major focus area – and often a money spinner – in many industries, so at any time a number of conferences are always being advertised in similar fields such as information or cyber security. What sets the ISSA conference apart is that it is not intended to generate a profit for an organization and it does not encourage marketing of products and services through presentations. Instead, the proceeds from registration fees are reinvested to ensure that the conference evolves each year. In exchange for their investment in the conference, sponsors are afforded an opportunity to present company-specific information that has a bearing on the conference themes and presentations submitted by potential speakers are sent through a vigorous double-blind review process, managed by a team of respected international experts in information security.

We trust that the annual ISSA conference will continue to be recognized as a platform for professionals from industry as well as researchers to share their knowledge, experience, and research results in the field of information security on a South African, but also on an international level.

To ensure ongoing improvement, every year we encourage input from all those interested in the field of information security, particularly those who are actively seeking to progress the field, to take part and share their knowledge and experience.

August 2019

Hein Venter
Marianne Loock
Marijke Coetzee
Mariki Eloff
Jan Eloff

Conference Focus

Information security has evolved and in the last few years there has been renewed interest in the subject worldwide. This is evident from the many standards and certifications now available to guide security strategy. This has led to a clearer career path for security professionals.

The Internet of Things (IoT) together with advances in wireless communications, have brought new security challenges for the information security fraternity. As these IoT devices become more available, and more organizations attempt to rid their offices of "spaghetti", the protection of data in these environments becomes a more important consideration. It is this fraternity that organizations, governments, and communities in general look to for guidance on best practice in this converging world.

Identity theft and phishing are ongoing concerns. What we are now finding is that security mechanisms have become so good and are generally implemented by companies wanting to adhere to good corporate governance, that attackers are now looking to the weak link in the chain, namely the individual user. It is far easier to attack them than attempt to penetrate sophisticated and secure corporate systems. A spate of ransomware is also doing the rounds, with waves of viruses still striking periodically. Software suppliers have started stepping up to protect their users and take some responsibility for security in general and not just for their own products.

The conference therefore focused on all aspects of information and cyber security and invited participation across the information security spectrum including but not limited to functional, business, managerial, theoretical, and technological issues.

Invited speakers talked about the international trends in information security products, methodologies, and management issues. In the past, ISSA has secured many highly acclaimed international speakers, including:

- Pieter Geldenhuys, Vice-chair of the Innovation Focus Group at the International Communications Union, Geneva, Switzerland: "BUSINESS UNUSUAL: Strategic insight in creating the future. Leveraging the value of the Hyper-connected world."
- Wayne Kearney, Risk & Assurance Manager at Water Corporation, Australia: "Why are management shocked with all the "PHISH" caught? A case study in perspective."
- Prof. Dr. Sylvia Osborn, Associate Professor of Computer Science, The University of Western Ontario, Canada: "Role-based access control: is it still relevant?"
- Prof. Dr. Steve Marsh, Associate Professor at University of Ontario, Canada: "Trust and Security - Links, Relationships, and Family Feuds."
- Alice Sturgeon manages the area that is accountable for identifying and architecting horizontal requirements across the Government of Canada: "An Identity Management Architecture for the Government of Canada."
- Dr. Alf Zugenmaier, DoCoMo Lab, Germany: "Security and Privacy."
- William List, WM List and Co., UK: "Beyond the Seventh Layer live the users."

- Prof. Dennis Longley, Queensland University of Technology, Australia: "IS Governance: Will it be effective?"
- Prof. TC Ting, University of Connecticut and Fellow of the Computing Research Association, USA.
- Prof. Dr. Stephanie Teufel, Director of the International Institute of Management in Telecommunications (iimt) at Fribourg University, Switzerland.
- Rich Schiesser, Senior Technical Planner at Option One Mortgage, USA, and Rick Cudworth, Partner at KPMG LLP, International Service Leader, Security and Business Continuity – Europe, Middle East and Africa.
- Dario Forte, CISM, CFE, Founder, DFLabs, and University of Milan, Italy.
- Reijo Savola, Network and Information Security Research Coordinator, VTT Technical Research Centre of Finland, Finland.
- Mark Pollitt, Ex Special Agent of the Federal Bureau of Investigation (FBI) and Professor at the Daytona State College, Daytona Beach, Florida, USA.
- Prof. Joachim Biskup, Professor of Computer Science, Technische Universität Dortmund, Germany.
- Dr. Andreas Schaad, Research Program Manager, SAP Research Security & Trust Group, Germany.
- Prof. Steven Furnell, Head of the School of Computing and Mathematics (Faculty of Science and Technology), University of Plymouth, UK.
- Prof. Matt Warren, School of Information and Business Analytics, Deakin University, Australia.
- Christian Damsgaard Jensen, Associate Professor, Institute for Mathematics and Computer Science, Technical University of Denmark, Denmark.
- Prof. Rebecca Wright, Director of DIMACS, Rutgers University, USA.

The purpose of the conference was to provide information security practitioners and researchers worldwide with the opportunity to share their knowledge and research results with their peers. The objectives of the conference were defined as follows:

- Sharing of knowledge, experience, and best practice
- Promoting networking and business opportunities
- Encouraging the research and study of information security
- Supporting the development of a professional information security community
- Assisting self-development
- Providing a forum for education, knowledge transfer, professional development, and development of new skills
- Promoting best practice in information security and its application in Southern Africa
- Facilitating the meeting of diverse cultures to share and learn from each other in the quest for safer information system

Organization

Conference General Chairs

Hein Venter	University of Pretoria, South Africa
Marijke Coetzee	University of Johannesburg, South Africa
Marianne Loock	University of South Africa, South Africa
Mariki Eloff	University of South Africa, South Africa
Jan Eloff	University of Pretoria, South Africa

Organizing Committee

Mariki Eloff	University of South Africa, South Africa
Marijke Coetzee	University of Johannesburg, South Africa
Marianne Loock	University of South Africa, South Africa
Hein Venter	University of Pretoria, South Africa
Jan Eloff	University of Pretoria, South Africa

Program Committee

Reinhardt Botha	Nelson Mandela University, South Africa
Marianne Loock	University of South Africa, South Africa
Mariki Eloff	University of South Africa, South Africa

Publication Chair

Hein Venter	University of Pretoria, South Africa

Honorary Committee

The following member is an Honorary Committee member of the ISSA conference. This committee member is honored for his effort as one of the founding members of the ISSA conference in 2001. The current conference committee feels obliged to honor him as such.

Les Labuschagne	University of South Africa, South Africa

On behalf of the general conference chairs, we would like to extend our heartfelt appreciation to all the Conference Committee members and chairs for their hard work in organizing ISSA 2019! Without your continuous hard work and efforts, ISSA 2019 would not have been possible. Again, we thank you!

Review Committee

A rigorous double-blind refereeing process was undertaken by an international panel of referees to ensure the quality of submissions before acceptance. Authors initially submit abstracts to determine if the paper meets the goals and fits into the theme of the conference. The ISSA Program Committee assesses each submission for relevance and fit. Authors are then notified whether their abstracts were accepted, and if so, invited to submit a full paper for peer review. The task of a reviewer is often a thankless task, however, without them this conference would not be possible. The ISSA Organizing Committee would like to extend their heartfelt thanks to the list of reviewers below whom include leading information security experts from around the world.

On the due date, authors submit full papers, anonymized by the authors for the double blind review process. Each paper goes through an administrative review and is assigned to at least three reviewers selected from an international panel of reviewers, in order to confirm that the paper conforms to the specifications and quality for the conference. If a paper does not meet the requirements, the author is asked to make the required changes as indicated by reviewers and asked to resubmit the paper, or to consider submitting the paper to another conference.

A Review Committee is invited to participate, consisting of both local and international experts in the field of information security. A process is followed by the Program Committee to allocate papers to reviewers based on their area of expertise. Reviewers are subject matter experts, of which over 50% are international. Reviewers usually have five or six categories that they are willing to review against. Each reviewer will establish the number of papers they can review in a specific time period and are allowed to bid on the papers they want to review. An automated process allocated papers to each reviewer according to their preferences.

Each paper is reviewed by a minimum of two reviewers (but mostly by three reviewers) in a double blind review process. Papers are reviewed and rated on a 5 point system with 1 being poor and 5 being excellent as follows:

- Originality (1 to 5)
- Contribution (1 to 5)
- Overall quality (1 to 5)
- Reviewer's confidence (1 to 5)
- Overall evaluation (calculated by an algorithm as a number in the range −5 to 5, where a negative score of −5 would indicate an extremely strong reject, 0 would indicate a borderline paper, and 5 would indicate an extremely strong accept)

Reviewer's confidence in their own rating is also taken into account by the algorithm that calculates the overall evaluation. Reviewers are also encouraged to make anonymous suggestions to the author(s) of the paper.

Based on the overall evaluation (−5 to 5), a paper with 0 or below points can be recommended for a poster/research-in-progress session and a 3 to 5 point paper can be put in the "best paper" category. An acceptance rate of between 25% and 35% is maintained for the conference. In 2019 the acceptance rate was 35%.

Authors are notified of the outcome of the review process which includes the anonymous suggestions and recommendations of the reviewers. Authors then have to submit the final version of the paper that will then be included in the formal conference proceedings. This proceedings is the official version of the proceedings. An unofficial version of the proceedings was distributed on USB flash drives during the conference. All USB proceedings from all previous ISSA conferences are also available at www.infosecsa.co.za/past.

Name	Company/Affiliation	Country	
Hanifa Abdullah	University of South Africa	South Africa	
Ikuesan Adeyemi	University of Pretoria	South Africa	
Alapan Arnab	Private	South Africa	
Sampson Asare	University of Botswana	Botswana	
Frans Blauw	University of Johannesburg	South Africa	
Hettie Booysen	Private	South Africa	
KP Chow	University of Hong Kong	Hong Kong	
Evan Dembsky	University of South Africa	South Africa	
Vasiliki Diamantopoulou	University of the Aegean	Greece	
Moses Dlamini	University of Pretoria	South Africa	
Lynette Drevin	North-West University	South Africa	
Jaco du Toit	University of Johannesburg	South Africa	
Eduardo Fernandez	Florida Atlantic University	USA	
Stephen Flowerday	University of Fort Hare	South Africa	
Evangelos Frangopoulos	University of South Africa	Greece	

Steven Furnell	University of Plymouth	UK
Lynn Futcher	Nelson Mandela Metropolitan University	South Africa
Stefanos Gritzalis	University of the Aegean	Greece
Marthie Grobler	CSIRO Data61	Australia
Bertram Haskins	Nelson Mandela University	South Africa
Barry Irwin	Rhodes University	South Africa
Christian Damsgaard Jensen	Technical University of Denmark	Denmark
Jason Jordaan	DFIRLABS	South Africa
Maria Karyda	University of the Aegean	Greece
Hennie Kruger	North-West University	South Africa
Grace Leung	University of Johannesburg	South Africa
Candice Louw	University of Johannesburg	South Africa
Tayana Morkel	University of Pretoria	South Africa
Francois Mouton	Council for Scientific and Industrial Research	South Africa
Martin Olivier	University of Pretoria	South Africa
Rolf Oppliger	eSECURITY Technologies	Switzerland
Jacques Ophoff	University of Cape Town	South Africa
Mauricio Papa	University of Tulsa	USA
Guenther Pernul	University of Regensburg	Germany

Rayne Reid	Nelson Mandela Metropolitan University	South Africa	
Karen Renaud	University of Glasgow	UK	
George Sibiya	CSIR	South Africa	
Stephanie Teufel	University of Fribourg	Switzerland	
Kerry-Lynn Thomson	Nelson Mandela Metropolitan University	South Africa	
Aleksandar Valjarevic	Vlatacom Research and Development Institute	Serbia	
Dustin van der Haar	University of Johannesburg	South Africa	
Johan Van Niekerk	Nelson Mandela Metropolitan University	South Africa	
Brett van Niekerk	University of KwaZulu-Natal	South Africa	
Alf Zugenmaier	University of Munich	Germany	
Wynand van Staden	University of South Arica	South Africa	

Contents

Information Security Cost Reduction Through Social Means

Sunthoshan G. Govender[✉], Elmarie Kritzinger,
and Marianne Loock

University of South Africa (UNISA), Pretoria 0001, Gauteng, South Africa
32393113@mylife.unisa.ac.za,
{kritze,loockm}@unisa.ac.za

Abstract. As data breaches in mid-sized to large organizations become more frequent and more public, there is a need to focus less on technological solutions to information security management and more on sociological solutions. In this paper cost saving information security initiatives are identified and a framework is proposed for organizational and behavioral change in technical human resources, to better address information security concerns.

Keywords: Information security · Security culture · Security cost

1 Introduction

Information security breaches have received significant publicity and become more frequent. Studies conducted by IBM and Kaspersky indicate that even though the cost per breach has been reduced incrementally with the adoption of better technology, organizational structures and awareness, the number of breaches has risen [1–3]. This implies that the overall cost to protect an organization has and will continue to increase.

The factors that are considered as remediation to the major data breach vectors are a combination of social (structural and awareness) and technical (product and service acquisition). With the increased likelihood of breaches, technical solutions are increasingly employed to reduce risk. However, these solutions incur significant cost for the solutions themselves as well as the scarce information technology (IT) human resources required to manage, maintain, monitor and administer these solutions. Improved behavior and understanding of information security risk and technology in IT employees is key. Models such as defined in [4] describe metrics to understand the effect of culture on information security, but in this article, a social alternative with practical application activities is proposed to reduce risk and thereby reduce the cost of information security management in organizations. The proposed model consists of five key activities or programmes an organization can embark on to improve behavior and culture in respect of information security.

© Springer Nature Switzerland AG 2020
H. Venter et al. (Eds.): ISSA 2019, CCIS 1166, pp. 1–14, 2020.
https://doi.org/10.1007/978-3-030-43276-8_1

2   Information Security Culture

Organizations need information systems to survive and prosper and thus need to be serious about protecting their information assets. Many of the processes needed are largely dependent on human cooperative behavior [5]. The definitions of information security focus on the technology that supports the cause as opposed to the people [6]. Employees, whether intentionally or through negligence, are the greatest threat to information security, often due to a lack of knowledge [7].

The vast majority of security breaches originate from human actions and the potential reasons for this are as follows [5]:

- People are poorly trained and have poor security awareness.
- People are not motivated to perform at the required level.
- People are malicious and deliberately expose the organization to risk.
- People are aware of the problem of security but, as managers and employees, make poor decisions.

As a result, people, their behavior, attitude, and therefore culture must become an integral defense in information security [8].

Establishing an organizational sub-culture of information security, which is a fragmentation of overall organizational culture, is key to managing (mitigating) the human factors involved in information security breaches. As the scope of connected devices becomes greater and more information is shared between future internet technology, the context of how organizations secure these devices becomes more important [9]. Organizations will be unable to do business without access to their information resources. However, protecting any information resources often has no direct return on investment. Securing information resources does not, as a rule, generate income for an organization [10]. Business people are therefore rarely interested in how their information resources are protected [4].

Organizations are cognizant of the importance of information security and infor-mation assurance to the value of their business. As a result, they are moving to respond to the threat in a more context-aware manner. Context awareness allows information security managers to address information security risk from a contextualized and focused perspective [11]. One of the key methods is by organizations creating or elevating chief information officer positions to senior planning roles, removing the position from the IT department, and integrating security planning and policy devel-opment into the strategic management process [12]. However, the problems related to creating a security culture are not always solved by a top-down management approach. The way in which employees interact with technology and the controls that need to be in place for information security are complex. Differences in individual's personalities and cognitive abilities impact the effectiveness of any security program [13]. Fur-thermore, personal bias and experience will have an effect on people's perception of risk, thus affecting the security decisions they make [13]. Knowledge and the involvement of employees are key to securing an organization. If the security culture of an organization is not strong, then even minimal technology security measures will become inadequate [14].

2.1   The Human Factor of Information Security Culture

Studies have shown that the establishment of an information security culture in the organization is necessary for effective information security [15]. However, the security culture cannot be assessed in isolation from the overall corporate culture [16]. Culture may not be uniform throughout an organization but may be split into sub-cultures. Sub-cultures can be observed in different job levels, functions and roles within an organization, resulting in differences in attitudes, beliefs, and values among the members of an organization [17]. Differing sub-cultures may be fully aligned with corporate culture, somewhat aligned with corporate culture or completely incongruent with corporate culture [18]. Sub-cultures within an organization can be problematic and can negatively affect performance when they have different priorities and agendas [19].

In organizations, the information security culture is usually managed through basic awareness and training programs. These usually deal with simple issues and are generally not assessed to provide an honest view of the actual learning taking place. Furthermore, these awareness programs are usually focused on general staff, without a focus on management and, more importantly, the technical IT staff. A security culture is far more important amongst IT staff in an organization compared to general staff, as these IT staff members manage and implement security controls. Sub-cultures are formed within the IT department, reducing the concentration of security efforts but focusing on the technical specifics of each environment. In addition, technical staff do not consider security as a primary concern even though technical actions that support information security management, such as patching, updates, application enhancement, and upgrade equipment lifecycle management, are implemented by them. It has been established that technical security measures are key to information security management success [20, 21].

Considering that technical staff have a greater influence on factors that support information security management, it would be reasonable to contend that enhancing the information security behavior and values of these technical staff members would improve information security [22, 23] and in turn reduce information security cost.

3   Information Security Cost

The economics of information security are of significant interest to senior management and leadership in organizations [24]. In all businesses, cost-benefit justifications for information security investments are important [25]. There has always been a difficulty in quantifying an organization's cost for information security in a comprehensive and comparable way, and information security professionals need to be able to articulate their value in economic terms [26]. Using economic and business administration principles helps to quantify information security management costs [25].

In 2013, PricewaterhouseCoopers reported a decline in hiring cybersecurity staff; at the time, Kaspersky Lab research found 58% of companies admitting their IT security was under-resourced in at least one area of staff, systems or knowledge [29]. In a 2018/19 survey it was reported that 53% of organizations have a cybersecurity skills shortage [28].

Therefore cybersecurity cost is still a significant issue that must be considered. A balance between technology and the human resources to support, manage, and administer those technologies must be found to provide an economically viable option for the protection of information within an organization.

3.1 What Determines Information Security Cost?

Cavusoglu et al. [29], propose a set of organizational pressures that influence information security control and therefore information security cost. Mimetic pressure is related to the actions taken by an organization based on action taken by others such as competitors. Coercive pressure is related to internal organizational or cultural expectations. Normative pressure is related to adapting behavior based on input from the organization's business or provider network, including business partners, trade, and professional associations. Investment in information security is traditionally considered based on assessment, risk analysis or institutional need, e.g. complying with the Sarbanes-Oxley Act.

Comparing information security spend across industry peers or based on standardized regulation is also not possible as there is no common definition or accounting methodology to assist in normalizing the cost [30]. Information security cost is also transversal in nature within an organization as budgets may be split amongst multiple functions such as IT, risk, fraud, physical security, compliance, and legal. Increased levels of security standards, e.g. card payment standards or compliance-related controls, may also drive up costs.

Other models for determining information security investment include the following:

- Faisst et al. (2007) as explained in [25] present a traditional return-on-investment model.
- Gordon and Loeb [31] present risk reduction through aligned resource allocation, strategies to limit security incident impact and a model to quantify business value of information security value for future investment.
- Longstaff et al. [32] propose a hierarchical model to assess the security risks of IT.

3.2 Why Determine Information Security Cost?

Tsiakis and Stephanides [33], state that the immediate, short-term and long-term economic impact of information security risk has a direct impact on driving quantification of information security management cost. The conundrum of estimating information security management cost is exacerbated by present technology trends which introduce hybrid technology models of cloud and on-premises infrastructure and business applications [27].

Brecht and Nowey [25], offer a concise framework that illustrates the key drivers for information security cost (Fig. 1), but these drivers do not clearly align with accounting practices of attributing cost to functional areas within an organization. The difficulty in attributing cost for information security also lies in actions that are taken to manage information security risk. If, for example, risk is reduced by implementing stricter programing guidelines or using infrastructure such as a firewall, where does the cost lie - with the application development or network infrastructure teams or within the budget of the information security program?

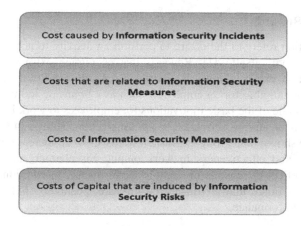

Fig. 1. Key drivers of information security cost [25]

As information security management is a cross-functional discipline, the justification for the existence of the program must therefore clearly be quantified. This ability to understand the economic impact of information security on an organization allows for long-term planning from a strategic investment perspective [7].

4 Motivation, Positive Reinforcement and Reward

Motivation is a complex process driven by personal, socio-psychological, and contextual factors that interact with one another [34]. Motivation is influenced internally and externally, which implies that psychological and environmental factors impact the motivation of people [43]. There are three high-level types of motivation [36]:

- Intrinsic motivation – motivation due to a person's interests in a task and therefore a drive to pursue completion of the task.
- Autonomous motivation – motivation due to a person's understanding of the value or importance of executing a task.
- Introjected motivation – motivation due to a person's need to complete a task to prove themselves, where the person does not necessarily value the task.

One of the key external drivers of motivation is reward. In a variety of forms, rewards are often utilized to influence individuals and improve their performance [37, 38].

Positive reinforcement is a practice to stimulate and strengthen new behavior by adding rewards and incentives instead of eliminating benefits [39]. Positive reinforcement can be actioned in an organization by rewarding staff with fringe benefits, promotion opportunities, verbal and written praise or remuneration. Rewards can be classified into two categories, viz. intrinsic and extrinsic. Intrinsic reward refers to something intangible such as praise and acknowledgement, whereas extrinsic rewards include salary, promotion, freedom in office, and job security. Both types of rewards are closely associated with employees' accomplishments within an organization [40].

4.1 Extrinsic Reward

Extrinsic motivation refers to the desire to perform an activity to achieve an outcome other than the activity itself [41]. Rewards that encourage extrinsic motivation in workers are termed extrinsic rewards. Extrinsic rewards are therefore rewards that provide something tangible for an employee, such as a bonus or additional leave. [42] and [43] state that one of the basic motivations for employees to work is salary and that personal income is positively correlated to job satisfaction. Studies [44–46] in the US and Taiwan have shown that strong extrinsic rewards show an increase in productivity, output, alertness, and effectiveness in work output. Eisenberger and Aselage, [38], found a positive effect of rewards on creative performance. In additional studies [47, 48], it was also found that extrinsic rewards are positively linked to material improvement in performance.

4.2 Intrinsic Reward

Intrinsic reward is related to non-financial motivation and can be verbal or written praise, work delegation, empowerment or acknowledgement [49, 50]. These rewards are simple to execute but have a positive impact on an employee's performance [40]. Studies show [51, 52] that intrinsic reward helps employees feel appreciated, feel a sense of common purpose within an organization, and feel like they are part of the organization. This leads to improved work performance, more satisfied customers and increased commitment of employees to the organization [53, 54].

5 Information Security Remediation Factors

In the study conducted by Ponemon [1], 20 factors were considered as remediation for security breaches. Of these factors, 12 were considered to have an effect of decreasing the cost of a breach whereas 8 were considered to increase the cost. These cost-reducing factors were as follows:

- Having an incident response team
- Extensive use of encryption
- Employee training
- Business continuity management processes
- Participation in threat analysis and sharing
- Use of security analytics services
- Extensive use of data loss prevention products, policies and processes
- Data classification
- Cybersecurity insurance
- Having a chief information security officer appointed

- Board level involvement in information security spend
- Having a chief privacy officer appointed.

The cost-increasing factors were as follows:

- Provision of ID protection
- Consultant engaged after the breach
- Rush to notify after the breach
- Lost or stolen devices
- Extensive use of mobile platforms
- Compliance failures
- Extensive cloud migration
- Third-party/outsourced management.

Figure 2 shows the cost-reducing factors, six of which are socially influenced (human, managerial or structural) and six of which are technically influenced. Therefore, concentrating the information security management effort on these twelve factors will provide the best information protection at the lowest cost.

Fig. 2. Social and technical security cost-reduction factors

For each of the six technical factors, there is a requirement for some human intervention and response for these factors to be successful. The technical factors may include management, participation, configuration, administration, continuous monitoring and evaluation, and periodic ad hoc processes to remediate [55, 56]. Since this human interaction is social in nature, people's behavior and values within an organization have a direct influence on whether these actions supporting information security management are successful. Improving the values and behavior of technical resources (e.g. server and network administrators, application developers, desktop support specialists and email and file-server administrators) that support information security remediation requirements will also assist in reducing the risk of information security breach incidents. In effect, developing and enhancing the socially relevant factors creates a stronger foundation for success of the technical factors.

6 Proposed Framework

Organizations determine the information security landscape using several methods such as ISO 27001 assessments, risk assessments, or longer-term strategy defined by a security architecture program. The outcomes of these assessments or programs are supported by the selection of products and/or solutions that fit the information security and business needs. Information security products and solutions are complex in nature and require many technical inputs to function appropriately or effectively within the organization. Products and solutions purport to be autonomous and self-running but in reality, require significant human input and intervention in order to function in a valuable way for the business. Figure 3 describes the relationship between generalized common information security evaluation methods and the reliance on human resources to run, manage, monitor and maintain information security systems that are identified through these methods. Security tools are not always managed by the security function within the organization and staff that do manage these solutions are from alternative functional areas within the IT department, i.e. application development, infrastructure, end user computing or networks. The motivation and behavior for these IT staff members to consider security first is generally incongruent with their motivation for their primary job responsibilities. The effect of what staff consider additional work to their primary job responsibility is a lower motivation to consider their information security responsibilities as important.

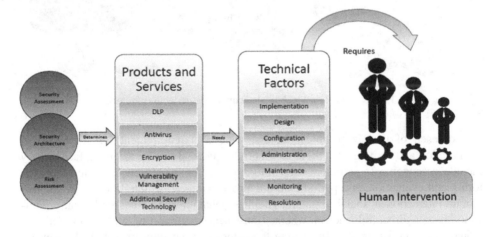

Fig. 3. Human intervention in information security capability

The model in Fig. 4 proposes five pillars of cultural change that are applicable in redefining the values and behaviors of IT staff members which will develop and enhance the socially relevant factors that lead to information security cost reduction. The effect of improving IT employees' information security culture is twofold: firstly, staff will be motivated within their job functions to consider information security a priority and secondly, the enhancement of information security cultural aspects will allow for long-term value for the organization and create the foundation for information security practices to become a prioritized norm. The model proposes 5 practical streams of activity that can be applied to enhance the information security culture of IT staff. The model is not interdependent, and an organization may execute each pillar independently of each other or select to execute the necessary pillar that may be relevant to that organization.

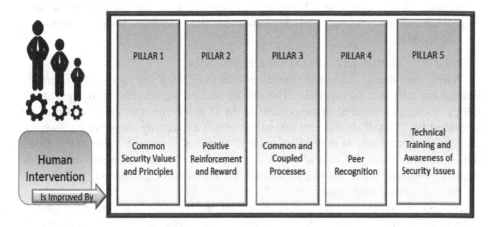

Fig. 4. Five pillars of information security culture enhancement model

The five pillars for the enhancement of information security culture in IT staff are as follows:

Pillar 1 -Common security values and principles

Information security management is the responsibility of different functional areas within an IT department. The areas are generally managed with a focus on the functional discipline and consider cross-functional responsibility a secondary matter. This pillar informs the creation of common security values and principles that need to be shared amongst each IT discipline. The value of security must be embodied and communicated with the common view to distribute responsibility of information security amongst all role players. The principles of information security must become part of the IT principles of the organization and should not be considered a stand-alone discipline. IT security as a concept must be supported and championed by executive and senior management, and structures and roles must be developed to support these common values and principles.

Pillar 2 - Positive reinforcement and reward

Organizational accomplishment is dependent on values and behaviors. Positive reinforcement often leads to improved behavior, and forming this into consistent and repeatable behavior embeds it into the culture of the organization. Positive reinforcement may also be supported by reward to enhance values and behavior through less social mechanisms. Positive reinforcement and reward are generally supported by three constructs to make them effective in an organization:

- They must be earned. IT staff should be supported for making good security decisions, living the values and principles, and emphasizing the security processes. Rewards may be awarded for consistent and continual adherence to positive security behavior.
- They must be quick. IT staff should get immediate feedback and recognition for their adherence to the positive values of information security in the organization.
- They must be frequent. The organization should consider smaller, more frequent rewards. When values and behavior are supportive of the information security program, short-term communication to those staff members involved should be commonplace.

Pillar 3 - Common and coupled security processes

When considering technical implementation, IT staff are generally internally focused on their area of expertise. The impact of layering security onto 'their' technology is rarely considered in the context of the IT disciplines that they support or are supported by. IT staff should understand the effects of security monitoring, blocking, patching and processes as they affect each IT discipline in the IT value chain. Information security managers should develop and socialize 'common-thread' information security processes where the impact of each IT discipline is transparent.

Pillar 4 - Peer recognition

As noted in Sect. 4 several studies show that peer recognition is one of the greatest motivators in the workplace. In the context of information security management, organizations should consider implementing a peer recognition program that is managed and controlled by the IT staff themselves. Peer programs that are managed by the staff and supported by senior management foster an environment of recognition and reward that is perceived to be less biased than those driven by management. Through this process, staff will be informed of the positive value that their peers, in all IT disciplines, are inputting into information security management and may be motivated to follow suit. Staff will also be able to see the impact of their contribution to information security and this in turn will create a more consistent information security behavior profile, thereby supporting the overall information security culture.

Pillar 5 - Technical training and awareness of security issues

Security awareness and training programs in organizations focus predominantly on the general user. While this is useful, it was established in Sect. 3 that the key factors to the success of information security management and the reduction of information security costs are the technical factors of security products and solutions. IT staff should receive significant technical training in the security solutions that are implemented and be made aware of technical security issues that are prevalent. IT staff should understand the scope of products selected and how these can be leveraged to support the information security values and principles. IT staff should also understand their value in threat remediation through patching and vulnerability management. Threat analysis and aggregated information from security analysis resources and information security staff should be shared with general IT staff. Lastly, information security awareness and training are rarely targeted at senior and executive management. As most governance best practices place data breach responsibility with the accounting officer of an organization, a greater focus on information security awareness and training for senior and executive management should be part of the cultural enhancement program.

7 Future Work

The model proposed in Sect. 6 is a theoretical model that needs to be tested through practical application. The behavioral concepts, which are the foundation upon which the model is created have been tested from a general social dynamics perspective. However, an evaluation needs to be conducted on the impact of these concepts in changing an information security culture.

8 Conclusion

Information security data breaches are becoming larger and more frequent. The reporting on such events is part of mainstream media reports, making people and organizations much more aware of these threats. Organizations have focused their security management efforts on technology at significant cost and complexity. They have, however, neglected incorporating information security into the culture of the IT staff members that support these technologies. The framework proposed in this research considers focusing on building the correct behaviors and values in IT staff members to better support information security management.

References

1. Ponemon: Cost of data breach study. Ponemon Institute Research Study (2017)
2. Verizon: 2017 Data breach investigation report, 10th Edn. (2017). http://www.verizonenterprise.com/verizon-insights-lab/data-breach-digest/2017/
3. Kaspersky Lab: Damage control: the cost of security breaches, IT security risks special report series (2016)
4. Van Niekerk, J.F., Von Solms, R.: Information security culture: a management perspective. Comput. Secur. **29**, 476–486 (2010)
5. Garret, C.: Developing a security awareness culture - improving security decision making. SANS Institute InfoSec Reading Room (2004)
6. Drake, P., Clarke, S.: Social aspects of information security. IGI Global (2009)
7. Mitnick, K.D., Simon, W.L.: The Art of Deception: Controlling the Human Element of Security. Wiley, Hoboken (2002)
8. Rotvold, G.: How to create security culture in your organization, Homepage of Information Management (2018). http://content.arma.org/IMM/NovDec2008/How_to_Create_a_Security_Culture.aspx
9. Colace, F., et al.: A context-aware framework for cultural heritage applications. In: Proceedings - 10th International Conference on Signal-Image Technology and Internet-Based Systems, SITIS 2014, p. 469 (2014)
10. Wylder, J.: Strategic Information Security. CRC Press, Boca Raton (2004)

11. Casillo, M., Colace, F., Pascale, F., Lemma, S., Lombardi, M.: A tailor made system for providing personalized services. In: Proceedings of the International Conference on Software Engineering and Knowledge Engineering, SEKE 2017, pp. 495–500 (2017)
12. Bodin, L.D., Gordon, L.A., Loeb, M.P.: Evaluating information security investments using the analytic hierarchy process. Commun. ACM **48**(2), 78–83 (2005)
13. Parsons, K., McCormac, A., Butavicius, M., Ferguson, L.: Human factors and information security: individual, culture and security environment. Government Research Paper edn. Australian Government, Department of Defence, Defence Science and Technology Organization (2010)
14. Siponen, M.T.: Five dimensions of information security awareness. Comput. Soc. **31**, 24–29 (2001)
15. Eloff, M.M., Von Solms, S.H.: Information security management: an approach to combine process certification and product evaluation. Comput. Secur. **19**(8), 698–709 (2000)
16. Ruighaver, A.B., Maynard, S.B., Chang, S.: Organizational security culture: extending the end user perspective. Comput. Soc. **26**, 56–62 (2007)
17. Hampden-Turner, C., Trompenaars, F.: The Seven Cultures of Capitalism. Piatkus, London (1994)
18. Martin, J., Siehl, C.: Organizational culture and counterculture: an uneasy symbioses. Am. Manag. Assoc. **12**(3), 52–64 (1983)
19. Furnham, A., Gunter, B.: Corporate culture: diagnosis and change. In: Cooper, C.L., Robertson, I.T. (eds.) International Review of Industrial and Organizational Psychology. Wiley, Chichester (2003)
20. Crossler, R.E., Johnston, A.C., Lowry, P.B., Hu, Q., Warkentin, M., Baskerville, R.: Future directions for behavioral information security research. Comput. Secur. **32**(February), 90–101 (2013)
21. Hsu, J., Shih, S.-P., Hung, Y.W., Lowry, P.B.: How extra-role behaviors can improve information security policy effectiveness. Inf. Syst. Res. **26**(2), 282–300 (2015)
22. D'Arcy, J., Hovav, A.: Deterring internal information systems misuse. Commun. ACM **50** (10), 113–117 (2007)
23. Vance, A., Lowry, P.B., Eggett, D.: A new approach to the problem of access policy violations: increasing perceptions of accountability through the user interface. MIS Q. **39**(2), 345–366 (2015)
24. Mecuri, R.T.: Analyzing security costs. Commun. ACM **46**(6), 15–18 (2003)
25. Brecht, M., Nowey, T.: A closer look at information security costs. In: Böhme, R. (ed.) The Economics of Information Security and Privacy, pp. 3–24. Springer, Heidelberg (2013). https://doi.org/10.1007/978-3-642-39498-0_1
26. Scholtz, T.: Articulating the business value of information security. Technical report, Gartner Inc. (2011)
27. Kaspersky Lab: Cyber security for business – Counting the costs, finding the value (2015)
28. Oltsik, J.: The cybersecurity skills shortage is getting worse (2019). https://www.csoonline.com/article/3331983/the-cybersecurity-skills-shortage-is-getting-worse.html. Accessed 28 Mar 2019
29. Cavusoglu, H., Cavusoglu, H., Son, J., Benbasat, I.: Institutional pressures in security management: direct and indirect influences on organizational investment in information security control resources. Inf. Manag. **52**(4), 385–400 (2015)
30. Asen, A., Bohmayr, W., Deutscher, S., Gonzalez, M., Mkrtchian, D.: Are you spending enough on cybersecurity? (2019). https://www.bcg.com/publications/2019/are-you-spending-enough-cybersecurity.aspx. Accessed 26 Mar 2019
31. Gordon, L., Loeb, M.: The economics of information security investment. ACM Trans. Inf. Syst. Secur. (TISSEC) **5**(4), 438–457 (2002)

32. Longstaff, T., Chittister, C., Pethia, R., Haimes, Y.: Are we forgetting the risk of information technology. IEEE Comput. **33**(12), 43–51 (2000)
33. Tsiakis, T., Stephanides, G.: The economic approach of information security. Comput. Secur. **24**, 105–108 (2005)
34. Kanfer, R., Chen, G., Pritchard, R.D.: Work Motivation: Past, Present and Future. Routledge, New York (2012)
35. Kozlowski, S.W.: The Oxford Handbook of Organizational Psychology, vol. 1. Oxford University Press, Oxford (2012)
36. Hendijani, R., Bischak, D.P., Arvai, J., Dugar, S.: Intrinsic motivation, external reward, and their effect on overall motivation and performance. Hum. Perform. **29**(4), 251–274 (2016)
37. Bartol, K.M., Durham, C.C.: Incentives: theory and practice. In: Cooper, C., Locke, E. (eds.) Industrial and Organizational Psychology. Blackwell, Oxford (2000)
38. Eisenberger, R., Aselage, J.: Incremental effects of reward on experienced performance pressure: positive outcomes for intrinsic interest and creativity. J. Organ. Behav. **30**(1), 95–117 (2009)
39. Catania, A.C.: Positive psychology and positive reinforcement. Am. Psychol. **56**(1), 86–87 (2001)
40. Wei, L.T., Yazdanifard, R.: The impact of positive reinforcement on employees' performance in organizations. Am. J. Ind. Bus. Manag. **4**, 9–12 (2014)
41. Deci, E.L., Koestner, R., Ryan, R.M.: Extrinsic rewards and intrinsic motivation in education: reconsidered once again. Rev. Educ. Res. **71**(1), 1–27 (2001)
42. Linz, S.J., Semykina, A.: What makes workers happy? Anticipated rewards and job satisfaction. Ind. Relat. **51**(4), 811–844 (2012)
43. Malik, M.A.R., Butt, A.N., Nam Choi, J.: Rewards and employee creative performance moderating effects of creative self-efficacy, reward importance, and locus of control. J. Organ. Behav. **36**, 59–74 (2015)
44. Liu, Y.: Reward strategy in Chinese IT industry. Int. J. Bus. Manag. **5**(2), 119–127 (2010)
45. Hübner, R., Schlösser, J.: Monetary reward increases attentional effort in the Flanker task. Psychon. Bull. Rev. **17**(6), 821–826 (2010)
46. Schuster, J., Weatherhead, P., Zingheim, P.: Pay for performance works: the United States postal service presents a powerful business case. Worldat Work J. **15**(1), 24–31 (2006)
47. Cerasoli, C.P., Nicklin, J.M., Ford, M.T.: Intrinsic motivation and extrinsic incentives jointly predict performance: a 40-year meta-analysis. Psychol. Bull. **140**(4), 980–1008 (2014)
48. Garbers, Y., Konradt, U.: The effect of financial incentives on performance: a quantitative review of individual and team-based financial incentives. J. Occup. Organ. Psychol. **87**(1), 102–137 (2014)
49. Sonawane, P.: Non-monetary rewards: employee choices & organizational practices. Indian J. Ind. Relat. **44**(2), 256–271 (2008)
50. Howard, J.L.: The use of non-monetary motivators in small business. Entrep. Exec. **13**, 17–29 (2008)
51. Shiraz, N., Rashid, M., Riaz, A.: The impact of re-ward and recognition programs on employee's motivation and satisfaction. Interdisc. J. Contemp. Res. Bus. **3**(3), 1428–1434 (2011)
52. Gohari, P., Ahmadloo, A., Boroujeni, M.B., Hosseinipour, S.J.: The relationship between rewards and employee performance. Interdisc. J. Contemp. Res. Bus. **5**(3), 543–570 (2013)
53. Sarwar, A., Khalid, A.: Impact of employee empowerment on employee's job satisfaction and commitment with the organization. Interdisc. J. Contemp. Res. Bus. **3**(2), 664–683 (2011)
54. Elloy, D.: Effects of ability utilization, job influence and organization commitment on employee empowerment: an empirical study. Int. J. Manag. **29**(2), 627–632 (2012)

55. Bojanc, R., Jerman-Blazic, B., Tekavcic, M.: Managing the investment in information security technology by the use of a quantitative model. Inf. Process. Manag. **48**, 1031–1052 (2012)
56. Takemura, T., Komatsu, A.: An empirical study on information security behaviors and awareness. In: Böhme, R. (ed.) The Economics of Information Security and Privacy, pp. 95–114. Springer, Heidelberg (2013). https://doi.org/10.1007/978-3-642-39498-0_5

A Management Decision Support System for Evaluating Information Security Behaviour

Dirk Snyman$^{(\boxtimes)}$ and Hennie Kruger

School of Computer Science and Information Systems, North-West University,
11 Hoffman Street, Potchefstroom 2531, South Africa
{dirk.snyman, hennie.kruger}@nwu.ac.za

Abstract. Information security management is a difficult task in organisations. Owing to skills shortages and the like, there are relatively few managerial staff that possess the required expertise to confidently make security decisions. The purpose of this paper is to present a decision support system that can analyse, and provide insight into, information security behaviour in an organisation, all the while supporting management decision-making for organisational factors. Behavioural threshold analysis is employed by the system to predict eventual information security behaviour for different groupings in an organisation. The decision support system that is presented here, which is the first of its kind, can be helpful in understanding the current state of organisational information security behaviour, and what can be done to improve upon the current state. After intervention measures the system may be used to test whether these measures had the intended positive effect. The system is discussed in terms of the different information areas that are used to allow insight into the security behaviours. A critical reflection provides an analysis of the contributions and limitations of the system.

Keywords: Information security · Decision support system · Behavioural threshold analysis

1 Introduction

The management of information security challenges within organisations have become of paramount importance in the contemporary landscape of reliance on information systems [1]. Traditional organisational structures often fail to address the potential impact that information security breaches might have. Organisations fail to employ preventative measures before an incident occurs, and after an incident has occurred they fail to correctly manage the aftermath.

Information security has three aspects that need to be considered in order to successfully provide for these abovementioned eventualities [2]. These are *technical aspects*, *organisational aspects*, and *behavioural aspects*. The management of these aspects needs to be well balanced and receive equal attention if an organisation is to attempt to ensure the information security of their stakeholders.

Technical aspects include the myriad of technological protection measures that are put in place to protect an organisation, such as anti-virus software, firewalls,

© Springer Nature Switzerland AG 2020
H. Venter et al. (Eds.): ISSA 2019, CCIS 1166, pp. 15–27, 2020.
https://doi.org/10.1007/978-3-030-43276-8_2

encryption, authentication systems, etc. This aspect is difficult to manage due to its inherent complexity in the implementation thereof, as well as the scalability of such implementations as an organisation grows and its needs changes [3]. However, even with the level of complexity, technical aspects remain the more straightforward to manage of the three, due to the availability of best practises (as set out in standards, e.g. ISO/IEC/SANS27002), and the successes of strategies that are used by other organisations. Shao, Siponen and Pahnila [4] presents information on how security decision-makers base their decisions on the example set by others.

The remaining two aspects, i.e. *organisational*, and *behavioural*, prove more challenging to manage. This is due to their relative unstructured nature in comparison to the technical aspects. *Organisational aspects* of information security typically refer to the influence that the organisational structure (usually including organisation size, physical location(s), management structures) of an organisation has on information security management. More specifically the organisational aspects in this context also refer to management decision-making under uncertainty with regards to information security policy and practise. Information security has been recognised as difficult to quantify when compared to traditional business and organisational analyses of risk versus reward trade-offs [3, 4]. This means that quantitative analysis, that is used by management to inform decisions, does not perform well as it does not incorporate the intangible aspects of information security. To further complicate matters, when management have (eventually) made decisions on how information security is to be promoted within the organisation, *behavioural aspects* come in to play. This relates to the attitudes and behaviours of the members of the organisation when working with information systems and how they go about security topics like password management and incident reporting. Policies and best practices are often not clearly communicated and therefore not followed by the members of the organisation. They are sometimes ignored or circumvented in favour of individual preference or to reduce so called red tape [5]. In the context of information security, behavioural aspects are often referred to as human aspects.

While the above-mentioned standards do provide some direction for the management of organisational and behavioural factors, the guidance that they provide are still mostly of a technical nature and do not prescribe specifics due to the unique requirements of each organisation. This leaves management, and by extension the organisation itself, at the mercy of an almost trial and error approach to information security management of the human aspect.

In an attempt to address the abovementioned shortcomings for managing both organisational and behavioural factors in information security, this paper reports on the development of a management decision support system (i.e. software program). The aim of the system is to provide managers with insight into the behavioural aspects of information security in their organisations, as well as provide concrete solutions on how these aspects may be addressed.

The decision support is based on a behavioural threshold analysis approach to measure the attitude of members of an organisation and, based on the analysis of these attitudes, can predict eventual behaviour of the group in terms of information security challenges. This will then allow a manager to make informed decisions on remedial actions that guide the information security behaviour of members of an organisation, e.g. through security awareness programs.

The remainder of this paper is structured as follows: Sect. 2 highlights related literature pertaining to the information security challenges that are faced by management, as well as literature on the information security behaviour model that is applied in the system. In Sect. 3, the software is described in terms of its features and insights it provides, and in Sect. 4, a critical reflection on the novelty and utility of such a computerised implementation is presented. Finally, conclusions and possibilities for future work is discussed in Sect. 5.

2 Background

As stated in Sect. 1, the management of information security in organisations faces many challenges. In order to formalise some of the challenges that are relevant to this research, i.e. organisational decisions (relating to) and behavioural factors, a twofold discussion is presented in this section, namely management issues and behavioural issues.

2.1 Management Issues in Information Security

A cursory look at information security literature confirms that the problems that are faced by such decision-makers are not a new occurrence and the same kinds of problems are universal across different types organisations. The (re)occurrence of some common themes in literature indicate that managing information security remains a troubled area. Some of these common themes include the following:

Top management buy-in [2, 6] – The support from the higher echelons of management often has a make-or-break influence on the information security of an organisation. Top management sets the tone for the company's outlook on security. They approve funding, support initiatives, and contribute to the overall security culture (see Sect. 2.2) in the organisation.

Managing human factors [1, 4, 7] – The human factor (and the effective management thereof) remains one of the key components in any organisation's information security strategy and include topics such as information security behaviour.

Budget constraints – Limited funding constrains decision-makers in the security controls that they can put in place [8]. Limited controls mean that some of the avenues of attack remain unprotected. Decision-making under this level of uncertainty is an assuredly difficult task.

Management confidence and skill - When confronted with decisions in terms of information security management, many organisational decision-makers are not confident in their ability to manage the possible threats and countermeasures appropriately [5]. This may be due to the sheer number of possible avenues that attackers can use to exploit systems and leave organisations and their data vulnerable. Well-trained and experienced information security analysts and managers are currently difficult to recruit. This skills shortage is a global phenomenon [9] which is still the case today.

These are only some of the management issues seen in literature, but the pervasiveness thereof highlights its importance and the relative ineptitude of organisations to effectively provide for it.

2.2 Behavioural Issues in Information Security

This sub-section highlights security behaviour in general as well as a model to quantify behaviour in this context.

2.2.1 Information Security Behaviour

Behaviour, in the context of information security, usually denotes the actions that the members of an organisation take when confronted with computerised systems and the interaction with security safeguards [10]. These actions (which are mostly negative actions) can be either deliberate, or unintentional in nature, but both types of actions have the potential to put an organisation at risk. As herding behaviour suggests [4], individuals do not commonly form attitudes (and the resulting behaviours) on their own in isolation. Being exposed to the behaviour of others, influences the way in which one behaves. This interaction of individuals within an organisation informs an information security culture which is the collective outlook (guided by norms, attitudes and behaviours) of the members of the organisation. The nature of how behaviour propagates between individuals allows negative behaviour to permeate the culture. In order to prevent this occurrence, the security culture of an organisation may be directed by implementing security awareness programs.

Security awareness programs have the main goal of influencing the attitudes of organisation members in such a manner that their behaviour is ultimately positively influenced [11]. Such programs usually focus on practical advice and guidelines to emphasise positive behaviour in specific security scenarios, often called security focus areas, e.g. incident reporting, working with e-mail attachments, etc. Selecting appropriate focus areas for inclusion in an awareness program helps to keep the associated costs low and prevents security fatigue due to overexposure to known focus areas [12, 13].

2.2.2 Model for Measuring Information Security Behaviour

In order to understand group dynamics in behaviour, Granovetter [14] suggests a threshold model to quantify and predict the eventual behaviour of people in groups. This model was first applied to information security behaviour by Snyman and Kruger [15]. In this sub-section, the model is only briefly described in concept.

For a detailed report on the underlying sociological and mathematical mechanisms, refer to the work of Granovetter [14] and Growney [16]. The behavioural threshold model is applicable to situations where actors (individuals) have a choice of participating in two diverging alternatives of behaviour, i.e. the decision to conform to the behaviour of the group, or not. The principle states that, given a group situation, the decision of whether to conform to the group is no longer only determined by the individual, but also by the example that is set by the other members in group. Each person has an innate threshold for when group example will override their own decision-making faculties. This threshold is expressed as the proportion of other people in a group that will have to exhibit a certain behaviour before the current actor will participate in the behaviour. The concept can be simplified by saying, *if the number of group members that do something is big enough, an individual will be inclined to also join in the behaviour.*

Thus, when a group is actively engaging in a certain behaviour, the number of participating people in the behaviour should theoretically increase, given the group members' thresholds for participation. The instigators (i.e. the first group members to perform an action) have a very low to non-existent threshold and will therefore exhibit behaviour without the example of others. Their participation will encourage the following wave of participants with slightly higher thresholds. This pattern continues until there are no more individuals whose thresholds for participation are being satisfied by the current number of actors and the increase in participation stops. The increase may also continue until all group members participate in the behaviour.

The model states that each individual has a measurable threshold that can be explicitly stated. The eventual level of participation, i.e. how many participants will eventually join in the behaviour, becomes a function of the cumulative aggregation of all the members in the group's thresholds. When graphed, an equilibrium (or point where the number of participating actors stabilises) is reached when the cumulative frequencies for the members' thresholds, equals a uniform distribution of frequencies.

When applied to information security, this model can be implemented to determine the number of people in an organisation that will exhibit insecure behaviour, given specific information security focus areas. An example in this context can be expressed as, *how many group members will have to open unsolicited email attachments, before an actor will also open unsolicited email attachments?* By analysing the underlying thresholds for all the organisation members, a glimpse into the current state of information security of the organisation may be obtained. Based on the observation, the organisation can make informed changes to their information security landscape.

The following section describes how this behavioural threshold model was implemented in a decision support system and how the analysis can inform management decision-making.

3 Description of the System

The system in question is a web-based implementation of a behavioural threshold model as presented by Granovetter [14] and threshold analysis as presented by Growney [16]. The platforms and environments that the system is based on include: Laravel PHP framework, JavaScript in Node.js (with NPM) and Vue.js, including HTML and CSS. Support for multiple devices and operating systems is provided through their native browsers.

The following steps (A) are completed <u>before</u> the system is put to use by management:

A1. Based on an evaluation of the unique requirements of an organisation by management, relevant information security focus areas are identified. Applicable questions about information security behaviour, relating to the focus areas, are then compiled; and

A2. An information security behavioural threshold analysis measurement instrument (online questionnaire) is constructed. The instrument is ensured to adhere to the methodological and practical considerations as prescribed by Snyman and Kruger [10].

After the initial evaluation, the management of the organisation (hereafter referred to as the user) then proceed with the following step (B):

B1. The questionnaire is distributed to members of the organisation through an online platform like Google Forms and anonymous responses are uploaded to the online system;

The system completes the next set of steps (C):

C1. The responses are automatically pre-processed into the correct format and care is taken to ensure the integrity of the data;

C2. The system extracts the information security focus areas which were determined for the organisation, as well as organisational groupings (i.e. departments or job level) that were reported by the individual respondents;

C3. From the responses and the extracted information, the system performs behavioural threshold calculations and completes the threshold analysis. A dashboard is then displayed from which the user can gain insight into the current state of information security behaviour for the organisation and departments under review.

The advantage of this step is that users do not have to understand the aforementioned analysis themselves and perform the required calculations. It is therein that the novelty and value of the system lies. The application of the behavioural model, that will help in supporting management decisions, is automated and the results are simplified and displayed on an interactive dashboard (C4), even a layperson is able to gain insight into the information security challenges and how members of an organisation behave.

C4. The system dashboard, that displays the results from C.3., is divided into three main areas, i.e. a *security heatmap*, an *analysis and reporting area*, and a *what–if analysis area*. These three areas are discussed individually below in terms of their functionality:

Heatmap – The heatmap (pictured in Fig. 1) is the main point of departure for the system. It entails a matrix that shows the information security focus areas, relative to each organisational grouping. The number at each matrix intersection describes the percentage of participants that will eventually participate in unwanted behaviour for the specific information security focus area.

The different levels of participation are color-coded to provide another dimension to the representation that assists the user in detecting problem-areas. A total row shows a summary of the organisation as a whole, and the average levels of participation in unwanted behaviour for the different organisational groupings are indicated by an average column to the right of the matrix.

For an illustrative example, the heatmap in Fig. 1 displays information security behaviour in five information security focus areas for 52 university students of different academic levels (analogous to the organisational departments), that live together in a

Heatmap

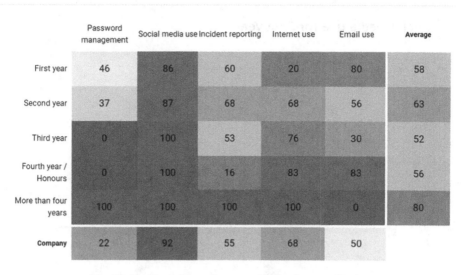

	Password management	Social media use	Incident reporting	Internet use	Email use	Average
First year	46	86	60	20	80	58
Second year	37	87	68	68	56	63
Third year	0	100	53	76	30	52
Fourth year / Honours	0	100	16	83	83	56
More than four years	100	100	100	100	0	80
Company	22	92	55	68	50	

Fig. 1. Dashboard area: heatmap (Color figure online)

single university residence (as the organisational environment). This is based on preliminary real-world data from another, ongoing research project on the security behaviour of individuals living together in close quarters and is used here in order to illustrate the working of the system.

In reference to the row/column intersection of "First years" and "Social media use" that is highlighted in Fig. 1, the high level of participation (denoted by the number 86, i.e. the percentage of members of the organisational group that will exhibit the behaviour), accompanied by the reddish shading of the cell indicate a problematic focus area/department combination. This indicates an immediate risk-area which management of the organisation should pay specific attention to by implementing an intervention of sorts. In contrast, the low participation score and green colour for "Fourth years/Honours" and "Incident reporting" indicate that the outlook for the combination is currently favourable and may be regarded as low-risk at this point in time with no immediate intervention required.

Each row/column intersection on the matrix, as well as the total row, is clickable to allow the user to drill down into the specific behaviour for the specific grouping to see more detailed information in the *Analysis and Reporting area.*

Analysis and Reporting – Firstly, after selecting a focus area and grouping from the heatmap, the reporting area shows a cumulative frequency graph for the behavioural thresholds which were reported by the respondents. This view provides insight into the manner in which the behavioural threshold analysis model was used to determine the level of participation for the specific information security behaviour and is depicted in Fig. 2. The graph, and more specifically the intersection of the graph with the equilibrium

Analysis and Reporting

Social media use for First year

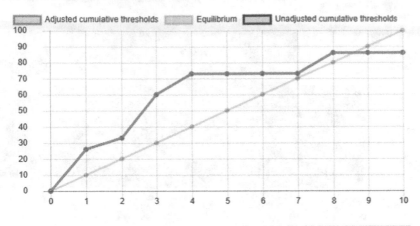

Heatmap report

Overview

The current outlook for the participation in unsafe information security behaviour for **first year** members, with regards to **social media use** is **high**. The percentage of first year members that will act in a contraindicated manner, is currently **86%**. This requires **immediate attention** as unwanted social media use behaviour may put your organisation at risk.

The following common threats, among others, exist for social media use:
-- Exposure to online malware;
-- Exposure to social engineering attacks like phishing, identity theft;
-- Spamming due to publicly available email addresses; and
-- Improper disclosure of information which may lead to financial or reputational losses.

Suggestions

Employ **security awareness programs** that address the abovementioned threats. During training, it should be emphasised that:
-- Do not click on unknown links. They may lead to malware infections;
-- Keep sensitive information private. Do not disclose passwords or other details to any other person, in person or online;
-- Always restrict access to online profiles to only allow known persons;
-- Review organisational policies and guidelines relating to social media;
-- Do not post updates about operational or other sensitive organisational information; and
-- Review privacy policies of social media providers.

Fig. 2. Dashboard area: analysis and reporting

line, is used to determine the level of participation, based on the interpretation in Growney [16] and Granovetter [14]. For example, the intersection of the two lines on the graph in Fig. 2, indicate that the percentage of group members (Third years) that will participate in unwanted security behaviour, relating to the focus area (Incident reporting), will (based on the underlying model) rise until 53% of the group are participating in the unwanted behaviour. The model reaches an equilibrium and group participation should not grow and exceed this percentage but will also not decline on its own without an intervention.

Secondly, a textual report (seen in the bottom part of Fig. 2) is provided that highlights and explains the specifics of the behavioural threshold graph. The report helps the user interpret the meaning that the graph conveys by classifying and explicitly stating the magnitude of the possible security threats (classified as high-, medium-, or low-level threats) that the current level of participation in the information security behaviour might entail. The report also provides suggestions on interventions that may be made to improve upon the current state of information security behaviour.

The report shown in Fig. 2 is based on social media threats described in Hekkala, Väyrynen and Wiander [17], and Gardner and Thomas [18]. The functionality to download the report is also available which allows the user to distribute the Analysis and Reporting screen (Fig. 2) to other stakeholders without them requiring access to the system.

Generic reports and recommendations are provided beforehand when deciding on the information security focus areas that are relevant for the organisation (see A.1. above). Reports and recommendations that relate to high, medium, and low risk level evaluations of the security behaviour, are provided for each of the focus areas and are dynamically compiled, based on the results for the specific grouping. The resulting report that the system provides, is also dynamically updated with the relevant measurements, threat levels, and other information as the specific evaluation dictates.

What-if analysis – The final area on the dashboard is the what-if analysis area and is shown in Fig. 3. This area can be used by the user to see estimates on how changes in the information security behaviour of the members of the organisation will influence the overall outlook for the organisation. The effect of changing the participation levels will be highlighted by colour changes in all the affected areas. This allows the user to instantly see how a positive (e.g. a security awareness campaign) or negative (e.g. deteriorating information security behaviour) change will influence the organisation's levels of security and will help identify areas that require the most attention, e.g. by inclusion in security awareness programs.

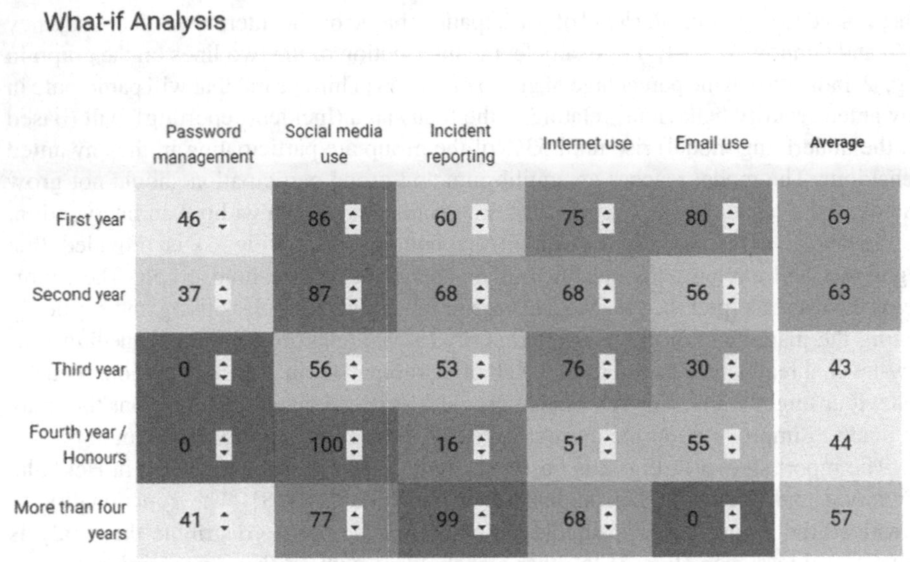

What-if Analysis

	Password management	Social media use	Incident reporting	Internet use	Email use	Average
First year	46 ⇕	86 ⇕	60 ⇕	75 ⇕	80 ⇕	69
Second year	37 ⇕	87 ⇕	68 ⇕	68 ⇕	56 ⇕	63
Third year	0 ⇕	56 ⇕	53 ⇕	76 ⇕	30 ⇕	43
Fourth year / Honours	0 ⇕	100 ⇕	16 ⇕	51 ⇕	55 ⇕	44
More than four years	41 ⇕	77 ⇕	99 ⇕	68 ⇕	0 ⇕	57

Fig. 3. Dashboard area: What-if analysis

4 Critical Reflection

In this section, a critical reflection of the system is presented in a twofold manner: (1) a reflection is provided on the contributions of the system and, by extension, the contributions of this paper; and (2) the limitations of the system are reflected upon.

4.1 Contributions of the System

Apart from a few earlier endeavours to quantify and analyse information security investment and technical controls using mathematical models [5, 8] as well as software artefacts to analyse the technical security of a specific system [7], the development of this system that takes into account human behaviour in information security by means of threshold analysis is, to the best of the authors' knowledge, the first of its kind. This kind of analysis of information security behaviour, by means of behavioural threshold analysis is a novel approach to decision support for management in an organisation.

Management (especially those with less comprehension of information security issues) may use the system to *gain insights into the security* proclivities of the members in their organisation. Once management is aware of the specific issues that may leave their organisation vulnerable, they are *empowered to address the shortcomings* and thus provide better levels of information security than the current status quo. The built-in reporting functions may help to provide concrete courses of action for management to investigate in order to address these issues.

Using the analysis that the system facilitates may provide insights into information security behaviour trends in the organisation. When a certain behaviour is identified that compromises the organisation's security, these behaviour trends may be addressed through the inclusion of *relevant topics in security awareness programs*. Similarly, when the analysis indicates that certain security behaviours are within acceptable limits, these behaviours might be left out from awareness programs as to *prevent security fatigue*. Security fatigue refers to the phenomenon where individuals forego good security practices because they are considered burdensome or the individual becomes desensitised to the possible dangers of their behaviour due to over-exposure to it through constant reminders thereof [12, 13].

By conducting behavioural threshold analysis exercises with the members of the organisation and including different information security focus areas in the exercise, the software may help *identify new risks* that were previously unknown or not overtly identifiable through traditional means of investigation.

Finally, the system may help in evaluating the success of intervention measures, e.g. in a situation where bad security behaviour was identified. After attempts to intervene and correct the behaviour have been implemented (i.e. through awareness programs or campaigns), a follow-up analysis of the organisation's security behaviour should indicate whether the interventions were successful or not. This would further help management to strategize and enhance their approaches to security behaviour improvement.

4.2 Limitations of the System

In its current form, the implementation does exhibit some limitations. While the system empowers management to make informed decisions about security behaviour, a certain level of expertise and evaluation of an organisation is still initially required to identify information security focus areas and construct the relevant measurement instrument. However, after this has been completed, the exercises may be repeated as many times as required without any further reliance on expertise.

The aforementioned system-based analysis of security behaviour is only as accurate as the data that the analysis is based on. Seeing as the behavioural threshold analysis is performed on data that are reported by humans, there is room for error. Occurrences of the social acceptability bias, also called social desirability, might influence the members of the organisation to misrepresent their security behaviour [19]. Basing the aggregation of behavioural thresholds on flawed data, may provide insights that are incorrect. The system, in combination with the measurement instrument (see Sect. 3), attempts to correct for such occurrences by adapting a member's behavioural thresholds if they are deemed untruthful in the reporting of their behaviour. The adapted aggregation, when present, is indicate by a blue line on the reporting graph in the *Analysis and Reporting* area (Fig. 3).

Finally, the system provides management with insight only into the behavioural aspects of information security. It makes no provision for the analysis of technical aspects of information security protection. This shortcoming may be addressed by combining the recommendations of this system with analyses similar to those suggested by other studies [5, 8, 20] to gain a more well-rounded insight into all the organisation's security aspects.

5 Conclusion and Future Work

This paper described the instantiation of information security behavioural threshold analysis in a web-based decision support system. The system allows for the evaluation of information security behaviour in an organisation. An in-depth knowledge of threshold analysis is not required by anyone who uses the system as the analysis is automatically performed by the system and insight is provided through representing the results on an online dashboard. Supplementary to the dashboard, textual reports provide suggestions on intervention measures that may help to address deviant security behaviour. This empowers decision-makers to make relevant organisational choices that may address the information security behaviour of organisation members.

The main contribution of this paper is that the system is the first of its kind to incorporate decision support for information security behaviour. Future work includes a possible evaluation of the system by a manager in an organisation. The evaluation may include different scenarios that the manager has to analyse (using the decision support system) and make organisational decisions based on members' security behaviour. Thereafter, a critical review on different success factors may be completed.

Acknowledgements. The authors would like to thank and acknowledge the contributions of Erik Jonker and Arno Strydom for their undertaking in programming the system based on the requirements as set out by the authors.

References

1. Alshaikh, M., Maynard, S.B., Ahmad, A., Chang, S.: An exploratory study of current information security training and awareness practices in organizations. In: 51st Hawaii International Conference on System Sciences, pp. 5085–5094 (2018)
2. Singh, A.N., Gupta, M.: Information security management practices: case studies from India. Glob. Bus. Rev. **20**, 253–271 (2019)
3. Werlinger, R., Hawkey, K., Beznosov, K.: An integrated view of human, organizational, and technological challenges of IT security management. Inf. Manag. Comput. Secur. **17**, 4–19 (2009)
4. Shao, X., Siponen, M., Pahnila, S.: To calculate or to follow others: how do information security managers make investment decisions? In: 52nd Hawaii International Conference on System Sciences, pp. 4885–4894 (2019)
5. Fielder, A., Panaousis, E., Malacaria, P., Hankin, C., Smeraldi, F.: Decision support approaches for cyber security investment. Decis. Support Syst. **86**, 13–23 (2016)
6. Kankanhalli, A., Teo, H.-H., Tan, B.C., Wei, K.-K.: An integrative study of information systems security effectiveness. Int. J. Inf. Manag. **23**, 139–154 (2003)
7. Shropshire, J., Warkentin, M., Sharma, S.: Personality, attitudes, and intentions: predicting initial adoption of information security behavior. Comput. Secur. **49**, 177–191 (2015)
8. Almeida, L., Respício, A.: Decision support for selecting information security controls. J. Decis. Syst. **27**, 173–180 (2018)
9. Furnell, S., Fischer, P., Finch, A.: Plugging the cyber-security skills gap. Comput. Fraud Secur. **2013**, 5–10 (2013)
10. Snyman, D.P., Kruger, H.A.: Behavioural threshold analysis: methodological and practical considerations for applications in information security. Behav. Inf. Technol. **38**, 1–19 (2019)

11. Bada, M., Sasse, A.M., Nurse, J.R.: Cyber security awareness campaigns: why do they fail to change behaviour? In: 1st International Conference on Cyber Security for Sustainable Society, pp. 118–131 (2019)
12. Furnell, S., Thomson, K.-L.: Recognising and addressing 'security fatigue'. Comput. Fraud Secur. **2009**, 7–11 (2009)
13. Stanton, B., Theofanos, M.F., Prettyman, S.S., Furman, S.: Security fatigue. IT Prof. **18**, 26–32 (2016)
14. Granovetter, M.: Threshold models of collective behavior. Am. J. Sociol. **83**, 1420–1443 (1978)
15. Snyman, D.P., Kruger, H.A.: Behavioural thresholds in the context of information security. In: 10th International Symposium on Human Aspects of Information Security & Assurance (HAISA 2016), pp. 22–32. Plymouth University (2016)
16. Growney, J.S.: I Will if You Will: Individual Thresholds and Group Behavior - Applications of Algebra to Group Behavior. COMAP Inc., Bedford (1983)
17. Hekkala, R., Väyrynen, K., Wiander, T.: Information security challenges of social media for companies. In: 20th European Conference on Information Systems, p. 56 (2012)
18. Gardner, B., Thomas, V.: Building an Information Security Awareness Program: Defending Against Social Engineering and Technical Threats. Elsevier, Amsterdam (2014)
19. Ashenden, D.: In their own words: employee attitudes towards information security. Inf. Comput. Secur. **26**, 327–337 (2018)
20. Pérez-González, C.J., Colebrook, M., Roda-García, J.L., Rosa-Remedios, C.B.: Developing a data analytics platform to support decision making in emergency and security management. Expert Syst. Appl. **120**, 167–184 (2019)

An Aviation Sector CSIRT for Sub-Saharan Africa

Faith Lekota[(✉)] and Marijke Coetzee[(✉)] [iD]

Academy of Computer Science and Software Engineering,
University of Johannesburg, Johannesburg, South Africa
nombulelol@atns.co.za, marijkec@uj.ac.za

Abstract. Computer Security Incident Response Teams (CSIRTs) provide information security incident response services to communities. The South African Cybersecurity Hub (SACH) acts as a national point of contact for the coordination of cybersecurity incidents in South Africa, but to date has only been successful in assisting with the establishment of a finance sector CSIRT. No mention of a transport or critical infrastructure sector CSIRT, under which an aviation CSIRT can report aviation sector cyber-attacks is made. The aviation community is mandated to sustain safety and security of operations and passengers in Southern Africa. Acknowledging the urgency and importance of protecting civil aviation's critical infrastructure, information and communication technology systems and data against cyber threats this research identifies that there is a need for a CSIRT framework for the Sub-Saharan aviation community. An aviation CSIRT should implement frameworks, programs and international information security standards, and aviation communities need to share cyber information with the CSIRT. To achieve such a framework, globally established CSIRTs are reviewed. Since the aviation sector is complex to manage, there is a need to establish an integrated CSIRT approach that include stakeholders within the ecosystem. A proposed aviation CSIRT requires the adoption of best practice cyber security incident response standards as a practical solution to manage aviation cyberattacks.

Keywords: Aviation · CSIRT · Cyber security · Critical infrastructure · ICT · Framework · CERT

1 Introduction

The growing threat to the safety and security of global aviation systems lie in cyberspace where malicious damage to ICT systems, theft of information, political motivations, and espionage can cause damage [1]. Cyberattacks are a becoming a major threat to the safety and reliability of the air transport industry. The European Aviation Safety Agency (EASA) reports in 2018 that there are 1,000 cyber-attacks on aviation systems each month. Aviation industry partners need to collaborate and share information as the industry is dependent on information and communication technology (ICT) to operate the global air transportation system. The goal is to improve overall performance, share situational awareness, refine their business processes and add value to real-time decision

© Springer Nature Switzerland AG 2020
H. Venter et al. (Eds.): ISSA 2019, CCIS 1166, pp. 28–42, 2020.
https://doi.org/10.1007/978-3-030-43276-8_3

making, operational efficiency, and information flow [2]. While it is essential for aviation stakeholders to share information efficiently and in a coordinated manner, the challenge lies in the management and security of aviation ICT systems.

Aviation ICT system architecture is complex and comprises of point-to-point, hardwired legacy and Internet Protocol (IP) communication systems that communicate within a limited wired boundary. Since legacy systems have limited connectivity, they are generally not protected with cyber security tools and can easily be compromised. Conversely, new systems are designed to interoperate with other systems using IP network connectivity [3]. IP networked systems are more resilient against cyber-attacks than legacy systems since they are protected with cyber security tools and controls.

Due to the complex nature of aviation ICT systems, there is a need to protect and mitigate the effects of a cyberattack on aviation critical infrastructure. Aviation stakeholders can adopt a formal cybersecurity incident response approach to be able to set goals and strengthen resilience against attacks. Currently, no such approach is formally applied by the aviation sector in the Sub-Saharan Africa region. In this regard, the purpose of this paper is to identify the need for and to provide recommendations for incident response management approach for aviation participants in a rapidly changing national and international landscape.

To identify recommendations for a Sub-Saharan Africa aviation cybersecurity incident response approach this paper first describes interconnected aviation ICT systems in Sect. 2. Next, aviation ICT system cyber-attacks are described in Sect. 3. Section 4 describes internationally implemented cyber security response frameworks as well as implemented Cyber Security Incident Response Teams (CSIRTs). Cyber security incident response approach is discussed in Sect. 5. From the discussions incident response approaches and frameworks, the importance of CSIRTs are identified and recommendations are made in Sect. 6 for an aviation sector CSIRT. The proposed Sub-Saharan aviation cyber security incident response management approach is discussed in Sect. 7. Finally, the paper is concluded.

2 Aviation ICT Systems

As a global industry aviation comprises of interconnected systems to ensure the safety and security harmonisation of air traffic flow. A performance-driven and technology enhanced aviation ICT systems architecture is regarded as critical for achieving greater connectivity and ensuring sustainability of the aviation ICT sector [4].

In the aviation sector, traditional ICT systems such as radar technology are connected to sophisticated industrial controls systems, namely, baggage handling, weather and temperature, airline, and airport systems. Together these systems support safe operation of aircrafts, development and maintenance of airport facilities, check-in, screening of passengers and various activities [5]. For that reason, stakeholders of the air transport system like airlines, airports and air traffic control are more and more interlinked and, thus, depend on secure means of data exchange [6]. Figure 1 depicts aviation ecosystem stakeholders and interconnected ICT systems.

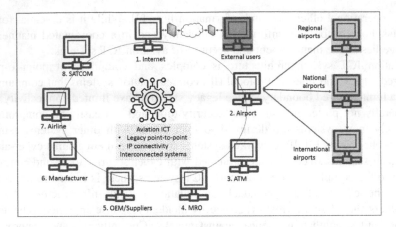

Fig. 1. Aviation Stakeholders and ICT systems

Several stakeholders in the aviation ecosystem collaborate and exchange information through system interfaces as follows:

- *Internet:* Wi-Fi network used by ground towers or airports and external users or passengers.
- *Airport:* Airport Management systems used by Service providers for cargo, catering, and customs ICT systems provide data used by other stakeholders such as baggage information, catering and passengers' personal identity cleaning, catering, and de-icing. Airport Management systems are also connected to regional, national and international airports ICT systems.
- *Air Traffic Management (ATM):* Used by aircraft operators for navigation and airport operations.
- *Aircraft maintenance, repair and overhaul (MRO):* Aircraft maintenance for airworthiness to safely transport passengers and cargo.
- *Original equipment manufacturer (OEM) and Suppliers:* Suppliers of aviation equipment.
- *Manufacturer:* Manufacturers of aircraft and ATM systems.
- *Airlines:* Air transport enterprise and related services.
- *Satellite Communication (SATCOM):* Transmit aircraft communications addressing and reporting system (ACARS) messages.

From the list of interconnected aviation ICT systems identified, it is evident that aviation stakeholders can commit to support and ensure efficient air traffic management operations. The main challenges are the sharing of critical information, security risks, cyber security, and passenger and cargo security screening. Augustin de Romanet, President ACI Europe, argues that to overcome aviation security challenges, there is a need to increase and coordinate use of data, intelligence sharing and international cooperation within industry players and states [7]. When connected devices share data, there is a high possibility of creating a vulnerable environment for cybercrime, and a threat to aviation business continuity [8]. Through ICT system collaboration, there is increased complexity, connectivity, and integration of air traffic management (ATM), airport and aircraft systems.

Aviation ICT environment contain legacy systems or applications with less secure communication mechanisms. These systems remain unprotected, unencrypted and unsecured, increasing the potential risk for security breaches to occur [5]. Thus, some of aviation ICT systems therefore lack basic security controls. The 2015 ICAO (International Civil Aviation Organization) report [9] states that the variety of aviation ICT systems and exchange models makes it challenging to devise security frameworks across systems and stakeholders. Reliance on potentially insecure legacy applications and platforms that support core aircraft operational activity is challenging to aviation stakeholders [10].

Currently, the global aviation sector is a major target for those who want to cause substantial loss to life or inflict major reputational damage. The increasing risk in aviation ICT systems demands that cyberattacks cannot be ignored [11]. Luftfahrt [6] conducted a comprehensive study to determine specific attack vectors from internal or external aggressors. For example, the incorrect representation of an airspace during a transatlantic, or near airport positioning of an aircraft caused by incorrect reading could lead to loss of data integrity. The spoofed data link between air transport stakeholders could result in the entire air transport system being compromised [6]. Both scenarios, indicate the complexity and interconnectedness of aviation ICT systems. If a cyber-attack occurs on a vulnerable system, it could result in loss of life especially where data is compromised.

Due to the fact that aviation security is such a wide topic, the following are outside the scope considered here namely airspace security that manages any aircraft hi-jacks, airport security that maintains the integrity of the airport perimeter, and aircraft security that ensures the security of the actual aircraft while on the ground and in the air.

From this discussion, it is clear that the aviation sector is vast and complex. The next section describes aviation ICT system cyber-attacks that have occurred.

3   Cyber-Attacks on Aviation ICT Systems

Cyber-attacks are perceived as global risks to critical infrastructure including aviation ICT systems. Several security incidents have allegedly been attributed to cyber-attacks, demonstrating that vulnerabilities in the civil aviation system certainly exist and need to be urgently addressed. As illustration, a number of attacks attributed to cyber security incidents are identified in Table 1 below. Note that these attacks are a small representation of all such attacks.

Table 1. Aviation cyber attacks

Affected systems	Types of cyber-attacks			
	Malware	Hacking/Phishing	Denial of service	Human error
ATC systems	(2006) [12]	(2011) [11]		
Aircraft central computer system	(2008) [12]	(2016) [13]	(2015) [14]	(2017) [15]
Airport Management systems		(2013) [12, 16]		
Corporate computer systems	(2009) [12] (2017) [17]			
Passport control system	(2013) [12] (2013) [18]	(2013) [12]		
Customer Information Management System	(2013) [19]			
Flight information screens and sound systems		(2017) [20]		
Booking system	(2016) [15]	(2016) [15]		

In Table 1, the vertical column to the left represents aviation ICT systems. The horizontal columns are types of cyber-attacks, where each attack is identified by the year and the reference [n] to the attack. Next, each of the cyber-attack and the affected system is described.

Malware: Malware is malicious code such as viruses or worms that can destruct files or systems and can replicate themselves once a system is compromised [21, 22]. In 2006 the US Federal Aviation Administration (FAA) was forced to shut down some of its air traffic control (ATC) systems in Alaska due to an attack on the Internet. In February 2009 hackers obtained access to personal information of 48,000 past and present FAA employees; July 2013 saw a cyber-attack at the departure terminals at Istanbul Atatürk and Sabiha Gökçen airports that led to the shutdown of the passport control systems causing many flights to be delayed [12]. In September 2013, Japan Airlines suffered a cyber-attack on its Customer Information Management System. The attack was ascribed to a Trojan horse virus which attacked computer terminals in the airline's network. Due to the interconnected ICT systems between alliances and airlines, the hackers were able to steal up to 750,000 frequent-flier program members' personal information [19]. In 2016, two US airlines experienced system failures that led to major disruption to the booking programmes and even flight cancellations. In March 2018, Boeing corporate systems were compromised by the WannaCry virus due to a flaw in the Windows operating system. The defect enabled the virus to gain access to the network [17].

It is therefore evident malware attacks have been intensifying and various aviation ICT systems have been adversely compromised making it vital to protect systems and data of aviation stakeholders.

Hacking/Phishing: Hacking and phishing attacks either access aviation ICT systems through unauthorised access and/or using social engineering attacks to access data. In 2011, radio hackers broke into frequencies used by British air traffic controllers and gave false instructions to pilots or broadcast fake distress calls [11]. 75 USA airports were affected by malicious hacking and phishing attacks in 2013 [12]. In the same year 2013, the Aviation Information Sharing and Analysis Center (A-ISAC) partner identified an Advanced Persistent Threat (APT) attack campaign targeting airports across the United States. The attack was allegedly caused by a user on the airport network who clicked on a link in a phishing email which downloaded a malicious executable files [16]. Hacking incidents caused delays, and loss of information, at US, Turkey, Sweden, Spain, and Poland airports [13]. The incident occured after hackers attacked the airline ground computer systems used to issue flight plans. In July 2016, Vietnam's two largest airports experienced loss of data and sound from the flight information systems. The attack was attributed to hacking and phishing attacks [20]. Screens displaying flight information and the public address system were hacked with derogatory messages against Vietnam and the Philippines in their territorial row against China in the South China Sea [23]. It is once again evident that hacking and phishing attacks have intensified over time.

Denial of Service (DoS): In a DoS attack, critical infrastructure, components and supporting systems are affected causing denial of service for intended users of targeted in aviation ICT systems. In June 21 2015, State-owned LOT Polish Airlines experienced a DoS attack against the airline's flight-plan systems at the airport [14]. As a result, 10 airplanes were grounded, and 1400 airline passengers were stranded after a hacking incident. LOT's computer system was unable to send flight plans to the aircraft. A flight plan contains the important data such as, airplane details, route, weather and other important information. Without this information it is not possible for an airplane to takeoff.

Human Error: In cyber security, human error can be defined as intentional or unintentional behavior that can cause vulnerabilities in ICT systems resulting in information security breaches. These errors could be caused as a result of lack of computer knowledge, technical errors or simply through carelessness by the users. It has been reported that human errors contribute to more than 80% of the accidents in venues, ranging from air transport operations to nuclear power plants [26]. In May of 2017, the computer systems of the British flag-carrier airline failed, apparently due to human error. The result caused 75,000 passengers stranded and huge financial implications. The parent company explained that the cost of the incident was £80 m and experienced reputational damage [15].

To be able to maintain the safety and security of operations and passengers in Sub-Saharan Africa, all members of the aviation community should implement cybersecurity response frameworks and programs. The next section describes locally and internationally established cyber security incident response frameworks.

4   Current and International Cyber Response Frameworks

To be able to maintain safety and security of operations and passengers in South Africa, all members of the aviation community should implement cybersecurity response frameworks and programs. When a cyberattack occurs at any aviation facility, it is vital that other such facilities, both locally and globally, are speedily informed of the cyberattack to mitigate the effect of such an attack both nationally and globally. International standards should be followed and a concerted approach on information sharing should be followed. This can be achieved if aviation sector CSIRTs are established.

The Forum for Incident Response and Security Teams (FIRST) (www.first.org) provide guidelines for the creation of CIRSTs. FIRST is a community that has been created by Computer Emergency Response Teams (CERTs) and Cyber Security Incident Response Teams (CSIRTs). The focus of FIRST is not to share operational information, but rather to enable incident response teams to better respond to security incidents by providing best practices, identifying quality tools, and by understanding how to facilitate communication with member teams [28]. For more than ten years ENISA has been supporting Member States and CSIRT communities to build and advance their CSIRT capabilities. Individual teams represent different sectors and businesses as well as existing CSIRT communities in ensuring indispensable elements of shared responsibility and activities [29].

4.1   Globally Established CERTs

According to FIRST statistics, there are 471 Teams in 91 different countries. Figure 2 outlines a schematic view of globally established CERTs and CSIRTs. Examples of countries where such teams are established are shown in Fig. 2. Figure 2 is adapted from FIRST and ENISA globally established CERTs and CSIRTs respectively. The established organisations are by far well established and member states are affiliated to the organisations to provide best practice standards and defined shared responsibility standards [28, 29].

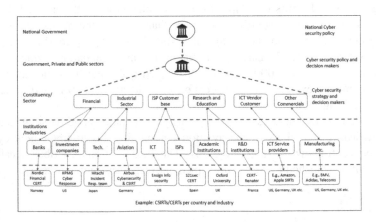

Fig. 2. Overview of globally established CERTs/CSIRTs

There can be more than one CSIRT in a country serving the interest of various parties such as academic, banking, commercial, critical infrastructure, governmental/national sector, military, energy sector, and financial sector and within organisations. The five core groups identified in Fig. 2 deal with the main cyber security incident response structures identified globally. The structures are identified as follows:

– *National Government*: A higher authority of government responsible for establishing national cyber security policies.
– *Government, public and private sector*: A high decision-making authority, a cabinet body as well as other structures in both public and private sector whose mandate is to develop cyber security policies at institutional and sector level.
– *Constituency or Sector*: A constituency or sector is identified by the decision-making authority and is clustered according to different industries. In other instances, constituencies or sectors are identified as critical infrastructures. As a result, national cyber security policies are developed to protect identified critical infrastructures against cyber security threats,
– *Institutions/Industries*: Institutions and industries are clustered according to constituencies and sectors. For example, aviation as an industry is grouped under the Industrial Sector constituency.
– *Established CERTs/CSIRTs*: Examples of established CERTs and CSIRTs are identified per country and industry at the bottom of Fig. 2 [28, 29].

The implementation of international aviation CERTs/CSIRT and related structures is best highlighted by recent approaches followed in Europe, described next.

4.2   European Aviation Security

As cyber-attacks easily propagate or replicate across international borders, it is recognized in Europe that member States and operators are becoming more dependent on each other for their security. If information about recent cyber-attacks is not immediately shared, neighbours cannot protect themselves and the industry cannot accurately assess the probability of a future attack [41]. A number of initiatives have been initiated to protect the European skyline.

The European Aviation Safety Agency (EASA) collaborates with the Computer Emergency Response Team of the European Union Institutions (CERT-EU) since 2017 to assist the European aviation industry. From this collaboration the European Centre for Cyber Security in Aviation (ECCSA) is established, of which the first phase from 2017 to 2018 is the creation of a web site that reports security news and initiatives [40].

In March 2017, CERT-EU signed a service level agreement to improve cyber security with EUROCONTROL. EUROCONTROL is an intergovernmental aviation organisation with 41 Member and 2 Comprehensive Agreement States. It provides general aviation services to all member states [42]. From this, the European Air Traffic Management Computer Emergency Response Team (EATM-CERT) was created that provide services of common interest to the air traffic management stakeholders of

EUROCONTROL members. CERT-EU makes available information and cyber-security tools to EATM-CERT as well as experiences, expertise, advice and procedures on how to operate a CERT efficiently.

EATM-CERT provides services that are made possible through collaboration with national and international stakeholders, manufacturers, sectorial and national CERT's and CSIRT's, European Aviation Safety Agency (EASA)/European Center for Cyber Security in Aviation (ECCSA), among others. Services that are provided are proactive cyber-security services such as penetration testing, vulnerability assessment, and best practices reviews, the collection, generation and distribution of relevant cyber intelligence to all stakeholders and coordination with national CERTs as required [42].

It is thus clear that the continent of Europe has recently started to actively create internationally collaborative cyber-attack response initiatives to protect themselves better. The well-established CERT-EU supports the aviation sector in more than one initiative, where specifically aviation is addressed on a large scale.

4.3   Established CSIRTs in Sub-Saharan Africa

Sub-Saharan Africa countries such as Kenya, Tanzania, South Africa, to name a few have established some CSIRTs within organs of states. These CSIRTs are established mainly at National Government, private and public sectors. Cyber security policies have been developed at national level but not sector level. Figure 3 gives an overview of some of the established CSIRTs in Sub-Saharan countries and sector CSIRTs in South Africa in a similar manner to Fig. 2.

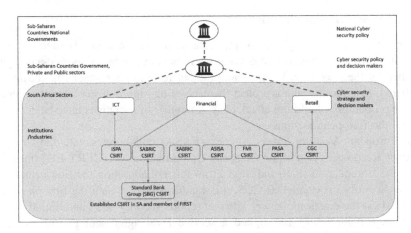

Fig. 3. Established CSIRTs in Sub-Saharan Countries

Within the South African context, the Electronic Communications Security ECS-CSIRT was established in 2015, and the National Cybersecurity policy framework (NCPF) was adopted as a national policy [30]. The ECS-CSIRT acts as a national point of contact for the coordination of cybersecurity incidents within SA. Established SA sector CSIRTs are recorded as follows:

Financial Sector:

• South African Banking Risk Information Centre (SABRIC)
• Association of Savings and Investments South Africa (ASISA)
• Payments Association of South Africa (PASA)
• South African Insurance Association (SAIA)
• Financial Markets Institutions (FMI)

Retail Sector:

• Consumer Goods Council (CGC)

ICT Sector:

• Internet Service Providers Association (ISPA)

The current state of established CSIRTs in Sub-Saharan countries do not address cyber security incident response management for aviation. There is no classification of critical infrastructures within the sector where CSIRTs have been established. The lack of classified critical infrastructures makes it difficult for organisations to put measures in place in protecting them against potential cyber-attacks. Critical Infrastructures (CIs) are defined as ICT systems that are essential for the operation of critical assets such as telecommunications, transport, health, water, banking and finance and so forth. The disruption or destruction to CIs could have a serious impact on the health, safety, security, or economic well- being of citizens, or on the effective functioning of government or the economy [31].

Aviation systems are declared critical infrastructures (CIs) that provide information resources to aviation stakeholders. These systems are used to monitor and control various aviation systems, such as baggage handling, heating, ventilation and air conditioning (HVAC) and airfield lighting. Baggage control systems (BCS), process control, supervisory control and data acquisition (SCADA) and industrial automation are all different categories of CIs [8]. Accordingly, the advent of new aviation technologies can bring about the emergence of new attacks or threats of attacks on CIs [32].

South Africa, and Sub-Saharan Africa need to consider international trends such as in Europe as a future direction to assist with improving critical infrastructure cybersecurity, where aviation is identified as a critical infrastructure within the industrial sector. The next section provides a review of incident response processes that can provide the aviation sector an outline of how to create a collaborative CSIRT within the Sub-Saharan countries.

5 Incidence Response

Incident response is defined as the protection of an organisation's information by developing and implementing an incident response process. Incident response processes support the management of security events and incidents which can be catastrophic to the organisations' critical infrastructure [33]. Incident response processes include plans, defined roles, training, communications, and management oversight. This is to enable organisations to discover cyber-attacks and effectively contain the damage, eradicate the attacker's presence, and restore the integrity of the network and systems [34]. The processes are underpinned by policies and procedures, defined roles and responsibilities, appropriate equipment, infrastructure, tools, and supporting materials ready, and qualified staff identified and trained to perform the work in a consistent, high-quality, and repeatable way [33, 35, 36].

As defined in the NIST cyber security framework, the cyber security incident Response phase supports the ability to contain the impact of a potential cybersecurity event. The Respond phase is defined to develop and implement the appropriate activities to act regarding a detected cybersecurity event. According to the framework, it consists out of Response Planning (RS.RP), Communications (RS.CO), Analysis (RS.AN), Mitigation (RS.MI) and Improvements (RS.IM) [35].

Given that the aviation ecosystem is a complex environment because of interrelated systems, a focused approach may be required to enable a global information sharing mechanism between governments and private sector. The approach can ensure effective reactions to cybersecurity incidents, and better protection against future attacks. If a new vulnerability is discovered, a CSIRT can inform others to ensure that all aviation sector members can prepare by taking preventive measures. Aviation stakeholders need to work together to put measures in place to protect their critical infrastructure against cyberattacks. The global chair of the Data, Privacy, and Cyber Security practice at White & Case LLP, alludes that a significant part of incident response involves communication [37]. Thus, there is a need for internal and external stakeholders to coordinate and share appropriate information.

The discussion relating to incident response and incident response frameworks indicates the importance of managing aviation cybersecurity incidences with due care by the establishment of aviation based CSIRTs, described next.

6   Sub-Saharan Aviation CSIRT – First Steps

Air transport is a global business managed similar civil aviation international standards. Since safety and security are important factors in the air transport industry, the need to respond to aviation cyber-attacks speedily cannot be ignored and overstated. Given the possible threats and attacks that have been explained in the previous section, there is a need to implement a collaborative CSIRT for the aviation community of specifically South Africa, including all countries in Sub-Saharan Africa.

An approach is now proposed to identify the way forward. An effective approach to cyber security is defined as management of complex processes, using technologies and appropriate techniques to manage potential cyber-attacks to Information and Communication Technologies (ICT) and critical infrastructures [38].

Figure 4 gives the proposed structure and components of the aviation CSIRT will be discussed.

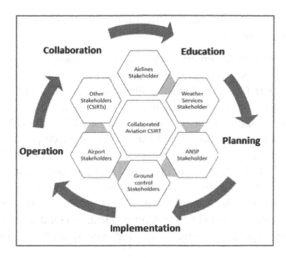

Fig. 4. Aviation sector CSIRT integrated model

The structure outlined in Fig. 4, indicates all possible role players in the aviation ecosystem. The composition thereof, is based on a premise that the aviation environment is complex, and therefore requires a collaborative approach for the implementation of a CSIRT. The collaborative approach requires integrated incident response policies, processes, and technologies to manage potential cyber-attacks on aviation critical infrastructure.

The main goals of such a national and/or regional CSIRT initiative can address [43]:

- Deciding on the national focal point within a country or region to coordinate incident handling activities.
- An analysis of how incident and vulnerability information is disseminated by well-established CSIRTs such as SABRIC.
- Providing channels for trusted communications between all stakeholders as there are multiple sectors to consider sharing information on widespread cyber-attacks, threats and vulnerabilities.

The creation of a national/regional aviation CSIRT should follow the general approach to establish a CSIRT [43] as shown in Fig. 4

- *Educating stakeholders about the development of a national team:* Aviation stakeholders are trained on CSIRT capabilities and goals.
- *Planning the CSIRT:* With the knowledge they have acquired, stakeholders are able to plan and design the requirements of the CSIRT including the establishment of aviation constituency as depicted in Fig. 2.
- *Implementing the CSIRT:* Input received from two steps enable the implementation of an aviation CSIRT. Funding and marketing of the CSIRT is required, and development of incident response policies and procedures.
- *Operating the CSIRT:* Aviation sector CSIRT provide incident response services, by developing incident response standards, reporting, and training.

- *Collaboration:* Trusted relationships with other stakeholders are built, to enhance aviation CSIRT communities.

Collaboration with supplementary sector CSIRTs is essential, as depicted in Fig. 4, especially in instances where data is shared amongst stakeholders. In matters regarding protection of passenger financial data, the financial sector CSIRT can play a pivotal role in managing such attacks. A coordinated body of aviation CSIRTs and other bodies can thus protect the aviation section locally, as well as globally. Internationally defined defensive measures against cyber threats can be made possible.

Information security best practise standards can be considered and incorporated in the aviation sector CSIRT approach to ensure adequate response and support recovery activities. Cyber security incident response communication capabilities should be planned across all stakeholder spheres with defined communication processes, functions, and communication networks [39]. Communication could also include voluntary information sharing, especially where critical data and systems are compromised.

7 Conclusion

It is evident that cyber attacks on aviation ICT systems are imminent and are gradually increasing. The complex nature of aviation ICT systems which comprise of legacy/old and IP connected ICT systems, make the environment more vulnerable to cyberattacks. Most systems are unprotected, unencrypted and unsecured, thus increasing the risk for security breaches. Examples of aviation cyber attack explained in the paper, is an indication that the aviation ICT system architecture is complex, integrated and information is shared between stakeholders.

Security management of an aviation ICT systems and cyber security incident response still remains a challenge in Sub-Saharan Africa. Established CSIRTs within the continent are established mainly at national government, private and public sectors, and a few established at sector level. A gap exists where established CSIRTs are currently not classified as critical to the broader economy.

There is a need to protect and mitigate the effects of a cyberattack on aviation critical infrastructure. The important feature of the cyber security incident response approach is the establishment of an integrate aviation sector-based CSIRT. The integrated approach will include all aviation stakeholders and other stakeholders external to the aviation ecosystem for information sharing and effective management of cyber attacks.

References

1. AIAA: A Framework for Aviation Cybersecurity. An AIAA Decision Paper, no. 8, pp. 1–16 (2013)
2. Khan, H.M.: Collaborative Decision Making in Aviation, Capgemini Consulting Outsourcing (2010). https://www.capgemini.com. Accessed 21 Apr 2019
3. GAO: FAA Needs to Address Weaknesses in Air Traffic Control Systems (2015)

4. SESAR: The roadmap for delivering high performing aviation for Europe: European ATM Master Plan (2015)
5. Murphy, R.J., Sukkarieh, M., Haass, J., Hriljac, P.: Report 140 Guidebook on Best Practices for Airport Cybersecurity, National Academy of Sciences (2015)
6. Luftfahrt, B.: Cyber resilience scenario analyses for the air transport system. https://www.bauhaus-luftfahrt.net/en/research/operations/cyber-resilience-scenario-analyses-for-the-air-transport-system/. Accessed 20 Apr 2019
7. De Romanet, A.: Welcome address. In: 27TH ACI European Annual Congress and Exhibition, Paris, pp. 1–5 (2017)
8. Willemsen, B., Cadee, M.: Extending the airport boundary: connecting physical security and cybersecurity. J. Airport Manag. 12(3), 236–247 (2018)
9. International Civil Aviation Organization (ICAO): Manual on System Wide Information Management (SWIM) Concept (2015)
10. PwC: Aviation Perspectives, Cybersecurity and the Airline Industry, vol. 4.3, pp. 1–8 (2016)
11. Iasiello, B.E.: Getting Ahead of the Threat: Aviation and Cyber Security, pp. 1–4. American Institute of Aeronautics and Astronautics, Inc. (2013)
12. Lim, B.: Aviation security. Emerging threats from cyber security in aviation – challenges and mitigations. J. Aviat. Manag. **2014**, 81–91 (2014)
13. Hoeven, E.: Cybersecurity: Information-sharing is Critical to Building Aviation System Resiliency. https://www.unitingaviation.com/strategic-objective/security-facilitation/cyberse curity-information-sharing-is-critical-to-building-aviation-system-resiliency/. Accessed 01 Jan 2019
14. Schwartz, M.: Airline 'Hack' Was Denial of Service, Bank Info Security. https://www.bankinfosecurity.com/airline-hack-was-denial-service-a-8342. Accessed 19 Apr 2019
15. Munger, H.: Cyber threats in aviation The sky's the limit? https://www.munichre.com/topics-online/en/digitalisation/cyber/cyber-threats-in-aviation.html. Accessed 19 Apr 2019
16. Francy, F.: The cybersecurity risk: what does it mean for airports? Airport Mag. **6** (2016)
17. ASERO: Cyber-attack against Boeing, pp. 1–3 (2018)
18. Urban, J.A.: Not your Grandaddy's aviation industry: the need to implement cybersecurity standards and best practices within the international aviation industry. Berkeley Law **62** (2017)
19. Fujikawa, M.: Japan airlines reports hacker attack. Wall Street J. https://www.wsj.com/articles/japan-airlines-reports-hacker-attack-1412053828. Accessed 17 Oct 2018
20. Guardian, T.: Flight information screens in two Vietnam airports hacked. https://www.theguardian.com/world/2016/jul/29/flight-information-screens-in-two-vietnam-airports-hacked. Accessed 19 Apr 2019
21. Tasril, V., Ginting, M.B., Putera, A., Siahaan, U.: Threats of computer system and its prevention. Researchgate **3**(6), 448–451 (2017)
22. Wanjala, M.Y., Jacob, N.M.: Review of viruses and antivirus patterns. Researchgate **17**(3), 6 (2017)
23. Stuff: Flight information screens at Vietnam's two major airports hacked. https://www.stuff.co.nz/travel/travel-troubles/82675571/flight-information-screens-at-vietnams-two-major-airports-hacked. Accessed 20 Apr 2019
24. Zager, R.: ODNI common cyber threat framework: a new model improves. Res. Transp. Econ. **10**(March), 18 (2018)
25. Abuzaid, A.M., Saudi, M.M., Taib, B.M., Abdullah, Z.H.: An efficient trojan horse classification (ETC). Int. J. Comput. Sci. **10**(2), 96–104 (2013)
26. Ahmed, M., Sharif, L., Kabir, M., Al-maimani, M.: Human errors in information security. Int. J. Adv. Trends Comput. Sci. Eng. **1**(2278), 82–87 (2012)

27. News Corp Australia: Air France Airbus 330 crash in Atlantic due to human error. https://www.news.com.au/travel/travel-updates/incidents/air-france-airbus-330-crash-in-atlantic-du e-to-human-error/news-story/32b32ea32461d976f6abf2368becc135. Accessed 20 Apr 2019
28. FIRST: FIRST Teams. https://www.first.org/members/teams/. Accessed 21 Apr 2019
29. ENISA: CSIRTs by Country. https://www.enisa.europa.eu/topics/csirts-in-europe/csirt-inve ntory/certs-by-country-interactive-map. Accessed 21 Apr 2019
30. CSH: Cybersecurity Briefing to the Portfolio Committee (2017)
31. OECD: Recommendation of the Council on the Protection of Critical Information Infrastructures (2018)
32. Njotini, M.N.: Protecting critical databases - towards a risk based assessment of critical information infrastructures (CIIS) in South Africa. Potchefstroom Electron. Law J. **16**(1), 450–481 (2013)
33. Killcrece, G.: Incident Management, Software Engineering Institute, pp. 1–23. Carnegie Mellon University (2005)
34. ENISA: Study on CSIRT landscape and IR capabilities in Europe 2025. ENISA, vol. 1.0, no. February, pp. 1–34 (2019)
35. NIST: Framework for Improving Critical Infrastructure Cybersecurity. National Institute of Standards and Technology, no. 1, pp. 1–39 (2014)
36. Haufe, K., Colomo-palacios, R., Stantchev, V.: A process framework for information security management. Int. J. Inf. Syst. Project Manag. **4**(4), 27–47 (2016)
37. Chabinsky, S.: Having Your Say in Cyber Response. https://www.securitymagazine.com/articles/87619-having-your-say-in-cyber-response. Accessed 12 May 2019
38. Catlett, C.: A Scientific Research and Development - Approach to Cyber Security, Department of Energy 30 (2008)
39. DHS: Recommended Practice: Developing an Industrial Control Systems Cybersecurity Incident Response Capability, no. 10, p. 49 (2009)
40. EASA: Initiates Aviation Cyber Security Program 2017. https://flightsafety.org/easa-initia tes-aviation-cyber-security-program/. Accessed 01 May 2019
41. Mana, P.: Overview of the EUROCONTROL's cybersecurity strategy and key initiatives. In: Integrated Communications Navigation and Surveillance (ICNS), pp. 1–19. IEEE (2016)
42. European Air Traffic Management Computer Emergency Response Team (EATM- CERT). https://www.eurocontrol.int/eatm-cert. Accessed 01 May 2019
43. Killcrece, G.: Steps for creating national CSIRTs, Software Engineering Institute, pp. 1–26. Carnegie Mellon University (2004)

PAUDIT: A Distributed Data Architecture for Fitness Data

Jaco du Toit[(⊠)] [iD]

University of Johannesburg, Johannesburg, South Africa
jacodt@uj.ac.za

Abstract. Centralized data architectures are the predominant architectures used by systems today. Decentralized data architectures, making use of data link networks, allow users to store private data in personal online data stores (POD). When fitness data is stored in a POD, the user has full control over the data and may modify fitness data. Medical aid providers that makes use of fitness data for benefit calculations cannot trust fitness data in existing POD architectures. PAUDIT is an architectural model that describes a decentralized data architecture that audits changes to access control lists on POD servers. The audit information allows medical aid providers to verify if users may have changed fitness data. PAUDIT describes an architecture that allows medical aid providers to verify the validity of fitness data.

Keywords: Privacy · Decentralized · Audit · Permissions · Fitness · Architecture

1 Introduction

Fitness tracking devices measure various exercise features. These features include the number of steps taken within a period, heartrate, speed and even weight. The exercise features are normally transferred from the fitness device using an application to a smart phone or computer and sent to a remote server. The fitness application, running on the smart phone or computer, allows the user to get information regarding their fitness or activity levels and may even provide certain gamification features to entice users to exercise more [1].

Several insurance companies provide incentive programs to customers that share their fitness data with the company. The incentive program has been adopted in the medical aid industry where it was proven that medical aid members that is physically more active has lower medical aid costs [2].

It is important for the medical aid providers that the data collected from their customers was not modified and represents a fair reflection of the customer's activity and fitness levels [3]. Unfortunately, this also provides an incentive to the customer to try and manipulate the data. If the data can be changed to indicate a higher level of fitness level, then the customer can directly benefit from the data modification.

Another aspect of fitness data is that it is undeniably personal information. Regulations, such as defined by the European Union General Data Protection Regulation (GDPR), require organizations that work with private data to ensure several controls

© Springer Nature Switzerland AG 2020
H. Venter et al. (Eds.): ISSA 2019, CCIS 1166, pp. 43–56, 2020.
https://doi.org/10.1007/978-3-030-43276-8_4

[4]. Companies that store personal information require an investment in GDPR-based controls.

One data architecture that reduces the required GDPR-based controls is a distributed data architecture as implemented by the Solid project [5, 6]. The Solid project proposes the use of personal online data stores (PODS). Each user stores their personal information in a POD. The user has full control over the POD. When the user uses an application, the data never leaves the POD, instead it is only linked to by the application.

The problem that may arise when fitness data is stored inside a POD is that the owner of the POD has, by default, full permissions to modify the data in the POD. The owner of the POD can also modify access control of data, assigning and removing permissions to the data. The ability to modify the access control is referred to as control in this paper. The control property in a POD is a problem for medical aid providers that require data integrity of fitness data.

An abstracted version of the problem statement can be formulated as: *In a distributed data architecture, the control property belongs to the POD owner. Certain types of personal information may require oversight from a third party, to ensure that the owner do not modify data when it is stored in a distributed data architecture*. In this paper the abstracted problem statement is quantified to apply specifically in cases of fitness data inside a specifically implemented distributed data architecture.

This paper proposes an architectural model, called PAUDIT. PAUDIT describes an architectural model that allows data generated by fitness trackers to be stored in a POD. PAUDIT further describes the ability of a medial aid provider to read the fitness data in a POD and monitor audit logs which keeps track of changes to access control lists. PAUDIT provides information to a medical aid provider that can be used to determine if the user modified fitness data. The audit component of PAUDIT has been implemented as a prototype and the prototype design and testing is discussed in this paper. PAUDIT applies existing theory, mechanisms, and aspects to a unique problem domain that does not see adoption from industry. It may be argued that the problem described in this study may act as a deterrent for industry adoption of distributed data architectures.

This paper is organized as follow. Section 2 discusses the methodology followed during the study. Section 3 provides background information on distributed data architectures, specifically the implementation proposed by the Solid project. Section 4 describes the PAUDIT architectural model that allows fitness data to be stored on a POD, but still establishing a level of trust using audit logs. Section 5 describes the prototype implementation and testing of the audit component of the PAUDIT model. Section 6 discusses some of the lessons learned and future research resulting from the research conducted for this paper.

2   Research Methodology

The research presented in this study follows the design science research paradigm. Design science concerns itself with the creation of "purposeful artifact for a specified problem domain" [7]. The artifact created in this study is a model and is called

PAUDIT. The problem domain in which PAUDIT plays a role is a distributed data architecture designed to facilitate the storage of personal information in a POD.

The research presented in this study follows six activities defined by Peffers et al. [8]. Each of the six activities is discussed below, as well as a where these activities are applied in this paper [8]:

1. **Problem identification and motivation.** Section 1 described the problem with fitness data that may be stored in a distributed data architecture. The problem as, specified in Sect. 1 is that private information stored in a POD, may require oversight from a third party, to ensure that any modification of the personal information is audited.
2. **Objectives of the solution.** The solution has as set objective. The objective is to create a model, based on requirements defined in both Sects. 1, 4 and 5. The requirements that are generated to specifically address the problem defined in Sect. 1.
3. **Design and development.** The artifact created in this study must be designed and developed. Sections 4 and 5 discusses the creation of the PAUDIT model, as well as the specific audit module.
4. **Demonstration.** To ensure the model solves the problem a prototype of the audit module was developed and implemented on an existing distributed data architecture framework. Section 3 discusses the background of distributed data architectures with the prototype implementation discussed in Sect. 5.
5. **Evaluation.** The audit module goes through a testing phase in Sect. 5.3. The testing is performed on the prototype implementation of the PAUDIT model, with the focus on the integrity aspect of the personal information.
6. **Communication.** The last activity in design science is the communication of the problem. The communication activity concerns itself with communicating the study to a relevant audience. Communication may occur when presented as a paper or at conferences [8].

3 Background

From an application's perspective, a user's personal information is usually stored in a centralized database (a in Fig. 1). Another architectural design is where the data is decentralized from the applications perspective (b in Fig. 1). The decentralized approach can also be called the sovereign approach. In the sovereign approach, each user has sovereign power of his\her personal data. The approach introduces the aspect of a personal online data store (POD). This section describes the existing standards and technologies that enables a decentralized data architecture.

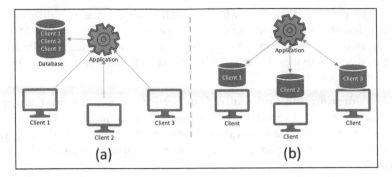

Fig. 1. Data storage architectures in (a) a typical centralized data architecture and (b) decentralized data architecture (By author).

The decentralized data architecture makes use of standards and concepts originally defined by the semantic web [9, 10]. The semantic web proposes a "web of data" instead of the existing "web of documents". The "web of data" can be applied to personal information, that is stored on the Internet and only linked to by applications. Solid proposes a POD to store personal information on the Internet.

The scenario depicted in Fig. 2 is used to describe the various components in a data linked network. A hypothetical data linked application that makes use of the sovereign approach is described in Fig. 2. The developers of the application host the application on a server on the Internet. The user opens a web page and navigates to the web site of the application. The application may be a JavaScript-based application, which are (a in Fig. 2) executed by the user's Internet browser. When the application executes the user is required to login. The login credentials, provide by the user, consist of a WebID [11], which helps locate the user's POD. The application sends an authentication request to the user's POD (b in Fig. 2). The application uses the address of the WebID (i in Fig. 2) to get the URL of the POD. After a successful authentication, the application retrieves other components from the POD. The components may include various workspaces (ii in Fig. 2) and application specific resources (iii in Fig. 2).

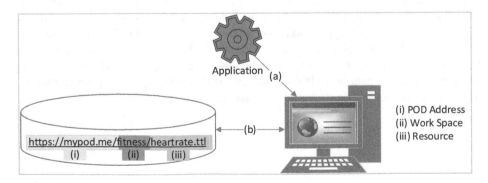

Fig. 2. A data linked application (By author).

A WebID is a standard way in which entities are identified. A WebID may have the following syntax: https://mypod.me/card#me. The #me references the entity inside a document, which, in the example, is the user. At this point in time, authentication of a WebID is supported using either a username and password, or a client-side X.509 certificate-based authentication mechanism, called WebID-TLS.

Access to resources and workspaces in the POD is controlled by the POD server using WebAccessControl [12] and Cross-Origin Resource Sharing (CORS) [13]. After successful authentication, the application may access the resources in the POD through CORS.

WebAccessControl define four modes of access. The modes are Read, Write, Append and Control. The modes are defined in access control lists and may be implemented as .acl – files. Read, write, and append allow the specified subjects to read, write or append resources. The control mode specifies the subjects that can set access control lists. This implies that the control permission allows a subject to modify access control lists.

By default, the WebID of the POD owner has read, write, append, and control authorisation to any resources in the POD. It is possible to remove the default permissions on a resource and only allow a specific subject access to a resource. It may even be possible for the WebID of the owner of a POD to remove itself from the control of a resource, effectively loosing control over a resource stored inside the POD.

Fitness data, such as heart rate, is personal information and should be stored in a POD in a decentralized data architecture. A medical aid provider may require access to the fitness data to measure the user's fitness and exercise activities to offer cheaper medical aid rates, or other loyalty program advantages. The next section provides and overview of the PAUDIT model that uses a POD for fitness data and allow a medical aid provider access to the data.

4 Overview of Architectural Model

When a medical aid provider uses fitness data for benefit calculations, the provider needs a high level of assurance that the data has not been modified. One of the challenges in a distributed data architecture is the sovereign property of data. This implies that a user has full control over all the data stored inside a POD.

To help define an architecture that solves the above problem a list of requirements is defined. The requirements are:

1. The user of the data should stay in control of the fitness data and should not give away control to a third party.
2. The user should not have permissions to modify the fitness data after it has been created.
3. The medical aid provider should have read permissions to the fitness data.
4. The medical aid provider should have the ability to verify any access control changes that might have occurred over time on the fitness data. Changes in access control may highlight potential changes in permission that might have allowed the user to modify the fitness data.

The WebAccessControl standard supports the above requirements except for requirement four. An implementation of the WebAccessControl in an access control list is displayed in Fig. 3. The access control list depicted in Fig. 3 is applied on a Fitness folder inside the user's POD. Fitness data is stored inside the Fitness folder on the user's POD.

The access control list consists of three sections. (a) in Fig. 3 show that the user has Read and Append permissions on the resource. The read permission allows the user to read the resources in the Fitness folder. The append permission allows the user to append data to the existing set of resources, but it does not allow the user to change any of the existing data. (b) in Fig. 3 shows a medical aid provider's WebID having Read permissions. The Read permissions allow the medical aid provider the ability to read the fitness data in the folder. (c) in Fig. 3 enable the user to stay in Control of the access control list. The Control permission allows the user to modify the access control list.

```
@prefix : <#>.
@prefix n0: <http://www.w3.org/ns/auth/acl#>.
@prefix A: <./>.
@prefix c: </profile/card#>.
@prefix c0: <https://medicalaid.me/profile/card#>.
```

```
:AppendRead
    n0:accessTo A:;          (a) Append and read permissions
    n0:agent c:me;
    n0:defaultForNew A:;     assigned to the user
    n0:mode n0:Append, n0:Read.
:Read
    n0:accessTo A:;          (b) Read permissions assigned to MAP
    n0:agent c0:me;
    n0:defaultForNew A:;
    n0:mode n0:Read.
:Control
    n0:accessTo A:;          (c) Control permissions assigned to the
    n0:agent c:me;
    n0:defaultForNew A:;     user
    n0:mode n0:Control.
```

Fig. 3. Access control list for fitness data (By author).

The WebAccessControl settings described in Fig. 3 fulfils requirements, one, two and three, but not requirement four. The fourth requirement states that medical aid provider should have the ability see changes to the access control list over time. This implies that if the user should change the access control list and potentially modify the fitness data, the medical aid provider should have the ability to see that the access control list has changed in such a way.

PAUDIT is a model that describes how fitness data is generated on a fitness tracking device, gets uploaded to a POD and allows a medical aid provider to read the fitness data. It also allows the medical aid provider to track changes to access control lists on the POD.

Figure 4 describes the architectural model called PAUDIT. The model consists of six major components. The interaction between the components describe the flow of data from a fitness device into a POD. It further clarifies how the user stays in control of the fitness data while a medical aid provider can verify modification of access control lists which may indicate data tampering.

The six components of the PAUDIT model is described in Fig. 4 and is the following:

(a) The user makes use of a fitness tracking device. Fitness devices can track various biometric features of the user. This include fitness activities such as heart rate, exercise location tracking, and even sleep patterns and blood glucose levels [14]. Once the device has collected the relevant data the fitness device may interact with a relevant app on a smartphone or computer. Data is usually uploaded from the fitness device to the smartphone using protocols such as Bluetooth [3].

(b) The app on the smartphone is written to make use of a distributed data architecture. The user is identified on the app using the user's WebID. The app uploads the fitness data into a fitness specific folder on the user's POD. Even though Fig. 4 does not indicate this, the fitness device may also have an app installed that directly uploads the data to the POD, instead of first going through an app installed on a smartphone.

(c) The POD has been configured with a Fitness folder. The Fitness folder contains several other folders and resources. The sub-folders describe data sorted according to year, month, and day. The fitness data reside inside resource descriptive framework (RDF) files.

(d) The Medical Aid Provider receives the WebID of the user, when the user registers for the provider's special fitness related program. During the registration process, the Medical Aid Provider request read access to the Fitness folder on the POD.

(e) The Medical Aid Provider also requests the user to change the permissions on the Fitness folder so that the user only has Read, Append and Control permissions. If the user is denied Write permissions to the Fitness folder, then the Medical Aid Provider is assured that the user cannot modify the existing data.

(f) One each POD server, a special audit module runs that keeps track of changes in access control lists. Whenever an update to an access control list is made the audit module takes the requested change and records the change in an audit log file.

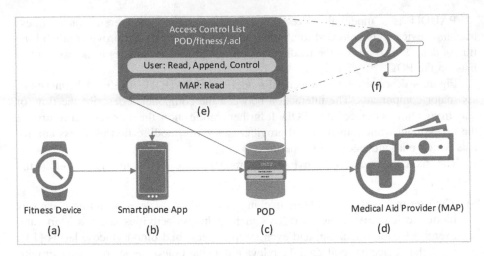

Fig. 4. PAUDIT fitness application architecture (By author).

The PAUDIT model allows a user to use a fitness device and still stay in control of the fitness data generated. What makes the model unique is the audit module that keeps track of changes in access control lists. The change tracking functionality provided by the audit module is not a standard or an accepted feature in existing implementations of a decentralized data architecture.

The next section describes how the audit module works and provide results from a prototype implementation of the audit module.

5   Auditing Module

The audit module creates audit log files and stores them in the same folder as the relevant access control lists. The Solid project provides existing POD server software that can be used for testing or production purposes. The existing POD server implementations are available on GitHub as part of a node-solid-server repository[1] in the solid organization[2]. No audit feature currently exists in Solid server implementations. A proof of concept audit module was written for testing purposes. The POD servers are referred to as Solid servers from this point onwards, to indicate that the testing was conducted using source from the node-solid-server GitHub repository.

This section describes the design, implementation and testing of the audit module in the following corresponding sections.

---

[1] https://github.com/solid/node-solid-server.

[2] https://github.com/solid.

5.1   Audit Module Design

The design of the audit module defines several design requirements, the content available in the log files and the integration of the audit module into the existing components of the solid server.

The following requirements were defined for the audit module:

1. For each access control list file, a corresponding audit log should exist.
2. Audit logs should have the same filename as the relevant access control list file, but with an .adt file extension.
3. Audit logs should be appended to instead of overwritten.
4. Audit log files should be searchable, and the data in the log should have the capacity to be filtered and ordered.

The content of the audit log should provide enough information so that changes to access control lists can be tracked. The specific information provide by the audit log files are the following:

- **Timestamp.** The timestamp records the date and time on the server when an action occurs.
- **UserId.** The userId field is the WebID of the user that initiates the change in the access control file.
- **Action.** The action field describes the specific node-solid-server handler that fulfils the request. There are two distinct handlers that can modify an access control list. The two handlers are: put and patch.
- **Detail.** The detail field is the data that gets applied by the handler. Depending on the handler, the data is either a just an update to the existing access control file, or the file gets re-written with new content.

5.2   Audit Module Implementation

The Solid server uses handlers to modify resources stored in the user's repository. The two handlers that handle changes to existing resources in the POD repository is the put and patch handler.

The put handler overwrites the existing resource with new content. It effectively deletes the existing resource and creates a new resource with new content. Testing have shown that the put handler is used in most cases when access control changes occur.

The patch handler creates, update or delete data in existing resources. It corresponds with typical SQL insert and delete commands, except it affects data in existing RDF resources. The language used to update the resources is called SPARQL. In the tests performed the node-solid-server user interface does not make use of the patch handler to update access control lists, but the handler may be called indirectly by users using operating system commands such as curl [12, 15].

The audit module is implemented as a JavaScript module that gets called by both the put and patch handlers. The put and patch handlers are modified to call the audit module only when the resource in question is an access control list. The audit module receives an object from the calling module describing various properties of the system at the time of calling.

The audit module extracts the properties of the system and creates a relevant .adt file if it is not already created. The timestamp, user, action, and details of the change is appended to the .adt file. The .adt file is a json data file describing the different fields, so that it can easily be interrogated by an external application.

Figure 5 is an extract of the prototype audit log that was created after a change was initiated on an .acl file. Figure 5 highlights the four components created for each log entry. The "timestamp" field was the time in universal time coordinate on the server when the specific action occurred. The "userId" field shows the userId of the subject that initiated the change. "action" highlights the solid server handler that handled the change to the .acl file. The last field, "detail" shows the content of the newly created .acl file in this example.

The logfile displayed in Fig. 5 was created as a uniform resource identifier (URI) with the following path: https://user.localhost/public/fitness/.adt. The /.adt file-name given to the audit log filename corresponds to the /.acl file which is the corresponding access control list. The relationship between the two files can be used by the Medical Aid Provider to track the changes to the access control file as it occurs over time.

```
{
    "logentries": [
    {
        "timestamp" : "2019-04-22T09:47:19Z",
        "userId" : "https://user.localhost/profile/card#me",
        "action" : "put",
        "detail" : "@prefix : <#>.
                    @prefix n0: <http://www.w3.org/ns/auth/acl#>.
                    @prefix A: <./>.
                    @prefix c: </profile/card#>.
                    :ReadWriteControl
                        n0:accessTo A:;
                        n0:agent c:me;
                        n0:defaultForNew A:;
                        n0:mode n0:Read, n0:Write, n0:Control."
    }
    ]
}
```

Fig. 5. Audit log for a specific.acl file (By author).

Section 5.1 listed four requirements for the audit module. The four requirements together with a comment on the implementation of each requirement is summarized in Table 1. The implementation of the prototype audit module fulfilled each of the original requirements.

Table 1. Design requirement tracking.

Number	Requirement	Implemented? (Yes\No)	Comments
1	For each access control list file, a corresponding audit log should exist	Yes	When an .acl file is created or modified an .adt file is created
2	Audit logs should have the same filename as the relevant access control list file, but with an.adt file extension	Yes	The name of the .acl file is used to create the filename of the .adt file
3	Audit logs should be appended to instead of overwritten	Yes	.adt files are appended to by default
4	Audit log files should be searchable, and the data in the log should have the capacity to be filtered and ordered	Yes	The .adt files are in json format, which can be imported into external tools

The audit module was implemented to create and update audit log files for corresponding access control files. The next section describes the tests performed on the audit module to verify if the audit module is functional and fulfils requirement four of the PAUDIT model.

5.3   Audit Module Testing

The implemented audit module wat implemented in a testing environment. Requirement four of the PAUDIT model states that the medical aid provider should have the ability to verify any access control changes over time on the fitness resources. The following tests were performed on the audit module to see if there were specific cases which did not generate a log entry.

1. Verify existence of .adt files of default .acl files.
2. Verify existence of .adt files after default .acl files were modified.
3. Verify the existence of an .adt file after a new .acl is created.
4. Verify log entries are recorded for changes to an .acl file.

The results of the four tests are discussed in each of the following sub-sections.

Audit Log Files Are Created for the Default Access Control Files

When a new user registers on a POD server, a standard template with various folders are created for the user. The default folders are the root folder, profile, inbox, public and private. Each of these folders contain a nameless .acl file.

Each .acl file is a template that gets assigned to each new user. Since there is no put or patch activities on these access control files, not audit files are created automatically.

Result: Initially no audit log files are created for default access control files.

Audit Log Files Are Created When Default Access Control Files Are Modified
To verify that an audit log file is generated when a default access control list is modified, the following steps were performed:

1. Select the private folder.
2. Allow Everyone viewer authorisation on the private folder.
3. Use the browser to access /private/.adt file and confirm that it contains the details of the changed access control list.

The relevant .adt file was created and contained a full record of the new .acl file as it was created. The audit file also contained the timestamp, the user and put action that caused the change.

Result: Changes to default access control files are audited.

Newly Created Access Control Files Have a Corresponding Audit Log File
The following steps were performed to confirm if an audit log file is created when a new access control list is created.

1. Select the private folder.
2. Create a sub-folder called, fitness.
3. Change the option on the fitness folder to "Set specific sharing for this folder".
4. Use the browser to access /private/fitness/.adt file and confirm that it contains the details of the new access control list.

The .adt file was created and it also contained the timestamp, user, handler, and detail of the access control list as it was created.

Result: Newly created access control lists also generates a corresponding audit log file.

Changes to Existing Access Control Lists Are Appended to Existing Audit Log Files
The following steps were performed to confirm if changes to existing access control files appends an entry to the audit log file.

1. Select the /private/fitness folder.
2. Allow Everyone submitter permissions on the fitness folder.
3. Use the browser to access /private/fitness/.adt and confirm if it contains two entries. The first entry should correspond to the initial creation of the .acl file. The second entry must have the latest timestamp and should reflect that Everyone has submission authorisation.

The relevant .adt file contained two entries. The entries were the correct information and reflected the changes as it occurred in the access control list file associated with the fitness folder.

Result: Changes to existing access control lists are appended to audit log files.

All the tests performed on the prototype were successful, except that there were no initial audit log files created for the initial default access control lists. The creation of the initial audit log files may not be problematic, except that it may generate unusual circumstances that may require special handling by third-parties when looking for audit log files and not finding any.

The next section evaluates the PAUDIT model and states if the audit module as implemented for the prototype solved the problem stated in Sect. 1.

6 Conclusion

A distributed data architecture allows users of systems, to stay in control of their personal information. A distributed data architecture introduces the concept of a personal online data store (POD) that stores personal information. A user has full control over all data stored inside their POD and can authorize other users access to the data.

Medical aid providers (MAP) may use fitness data to provide more benefits to its members. The benefits may include lower monthly premiums, but it may also include other benefits, such as cheaper gym memberships, airplane tickets etc. A MAP that uses fitness data to determine benefits needs assurance that the user cannot manipulate fitness data after it has been generated by a fitness device.

The PAUDIT model describes a model which takes data generated from a fitness device and either directly or indirectly appends the data to a fitness folder on the user's POD. The PAUDIT model describes the access control required to ensure that the user stays in control of the data, while allowing the user to append fitness data to the existing folder. PAUDIT also describes the access control required on the fitness folder to ensure that the MAP can read the data.

PAUDIT contributes to the existing Solid server implementation, by describing an audit module. The audit module creates audit log files when access control files are modified. The audit log files describe the changes to access control. The MAP can use the information in the log file to determine if a user changed permissions and potentially modified the data, thereby making the data untrustworthy. Untrustworthy data cannot be used by the MAP to calculate benefits.

The audit module was implemented in a testing environment and passed all the tests described in this paper. It should be noted that tests involving operating system commands such as curl, to manipulate access control files, were not completed. Manipulation of resources on POD servers using curl, requires WebID-TLS integration, which is currently an obstacle in the test environment. It is also the author's view that before the audit module can be accepted as a trustworthy component that tests using curl should be performed. A feature request on the node-solid-server GitHub repository is also currently being investigated to test the audit module further.

Another aspect that may require future research is the adoption of digital signatures on health data. Digital signatures on health data may negate the requirement for an audit module, since digital signatures can provide non-repudiation of health data. This will allow a MAP to verify the author of health data stored in a user's POD but may have negative consequences on the battery life of fitness tracking devices.

PAUDIT fall under the exaptation quadrant of knowledge contribution as defined by Gregor and Hevner [16]. Exaptation is defined as presenting known solutions extended to new problems. The problem domain and architecture discussed in this study is a domain that has not been observed in real-world implementations. This, however, does not detract from the validity of the problem, as the problem may become reality and act as detractor before adoption. The PAUDIT model does not define or describe any new components that does not exist in other environments. The novelty lies in the use of the existing theory, components, and mechanisms in a new problem domain.

References

1. Cotton, V., Patel, M.S.: Gamification use and design in popular health and fitness mobile applications. Am. J. Health Promot. **33**, 448–451 (2019)
2. Patel, D., et al.: Participation in fitness-related activities of an incentive-based health promotion program and hospital costs: a retrospective longitudinal study. Am. J. Health Promot. **25**, 341–348 (2011)
3. Fereidooni, H., Frassetto, T., Miettinen, M., Sadeghi, A., Conti, M.: Fitness trackers: fit for health but unfit for security and privacy. In: 2017 IEEE/ACM International Conference on Connected Health: Applications, Systems and Engineering Technologies (CHASE), pp. 19–24 (2017)
4. Gines, K.: Getting up to speed with GDPR. Success. Meet. **67**, 72–78 (2018)
5. Mansour, E., et al.: A demonstration of the solid platform for social web applications. In: Proceedings of the 25th International Conference Companion on World Wide Web, pp. 223–226. International World Wide Web Conferences Steering Committee, Republic and Canton of Geneva (2016)
6. The Solid Project: Solid (2017). https://solid.mit.edu. Accessed 19 Jan 2018
7. Hevner, A., March, S.T., Park, J., Ram, S.: Design science research in information systems. MIS Q. **28**, 75–105 (2004)
8. Pfeffers, K., et al.: The design science research process: a model for producing and presenting information systems research. In: Proceedings of the First International Conference on Design Science Research in Information Systems and Technology (DESRIST 2006), Claremont, CA, USA, pp. 83–106 (2006)
9. Mohn, E.: Semantic Web. Salem Press Encyclopedia of Science (2017)
10. W3C: Semantic Web - W3C (2015). https://www.w3.org/standards/semanticweb/. Accessed 18 Apr 2019
11. W3C: WebID - W3C Wiki (2018). https://www.w3.org/wiki/WebID. Accessed 19 Apr 2019
12. W3C: WebAccessControl - W3C Wiki (2018). https://www.w3.org/wiki/WebAccessControl. Accessed 19 Apr 2019
13. W3C: Cross-origin resource sharing (2014). https://www.w3.org/TR/cors/. Accessed 19 Apr 2019
14. Kellogg, S.: Every breath you take: data privacy and your wearable fitness device. J. Mo. Bar **72**, 76–82 (2016)
15. Stenberg, D.: Curl - how to user. https://curl.haxx.se/docs/manpage.html. Accessed 22 Apr 2019
16. Gregor, S., Hevner, A.R.: Positioning and presenting design science research for maximum impact. MIS Q. **37**, 337–355 (2013)

Threats and Vulnerabilities Affecting Fitness Wearables: Security and Privacy Theoretical Analysis

Sophia Moganedi[1](✉) and Dalenca Pottas[2](✉)

[1] CSIR, Pretoria, South Africa
smoganedi@csir.co.za
[2] School of Information and Communication Technology,
Nelson Mandela University, Port Elizabeth, South Africa
Dalenca.Pottas@mandela.ac.za

Abstract. The introduction of fitness wearables has encouraged users to take control of their health and fitness habits. These wearables are capable of collecting real-time data through the sensors embedded within the devices. The collection of real-time data about the users is a concern, as exactly what data is collected by these wearables is not clear to the users. Security threats and vulnerabilities in the fitness wearable domain continue to increase due to the increasing use of these wearables. This study aims to investigate and analyse security vulnerabilities and threats that affect fitness wearables from a security and privacy perspective. The execution of this study involves two phases of methodology. The first phase employs a systematic literature review and qualitative content analysis to identify the threats and vulnerabilities affecting fitness wearables. The second phase employs the Microsoft STRIDE framework and CIA triad to conduct an analysis of the threats and vulnerabilities. The output of this study indicates that security is still a great concern, as these fitness wearables are exposed to various security threats. Furthermore, these security threats increase due to the many components that are part of the fitness wearable architecture creating multiple entry points for attackers.

Keywords: Internet of Things (IoT) · Fitness wearables · Security · Vulnerability · Privacy · Threats

1 Introduction

The introduction of electronic wearables with sensor features has enormous value in various fields such as but not limited to, healthcare, military, sport and entertainment [1]. These wearables are part of the Internet of Things (IoT) domain and have the capability to collect and exchange data with little or no interference from the users [2]. Fitness wearables are known to be the most popular wearables due to the increasing interest in self-tracking, where users are able to track and monitor their daily fitness and health-related activities, i.e. walking, physical workout, and vital signs [3, 4].

© Springer Nature Switzerland AG 2020
H. Venter et al. (Eds.): ISSA 2019, CCIS 1166, pp. 57–68, 2020.
https://doi.org/10.1007/978-3-030-43276-8_5

These wearables can be broadly defined as a form of small hardware or mobile electronic devices with an application for tracking and monitoring fitness metrics that can be un-obtrusively embedded in the user's outfit as part of clothing or as an accessory [5–7]. Furthermore, they perform day-to-day acquisition and analysis [8].

There are various fitness wearables that are publicly available on the market, including, but not limited to, Fitbit, Jawbone UP, Withings Pulse, and Nike+ FuelBand, which can monitor health-related conditions such as sleep, calories burned, heart rate, and distance travelled on a real-time basis [1, 9, 10]. These fitness wearables come in different style forms, including wristbands, clip-ons, patches, and smart clothing fabric [11–14]. Most of the wearables in the IoT domain are connected to the Cloud through smartphones using wireless connections [8, 15]. In all existing wireless connectivity solutions, Bluetooth Low Energy (BLE) has been considered the common communication interface of wearables [16].

The remainder of this paper is set out as follows: Sect. 2 provides a discussion on the methodology used in this study, which is divided into two phases. Section 3 presents the results and findings of the two phases of the approach discussed in Sect. 2. Section 4 presents the theoretical analysis. Section 5 makes recommendations regarding future research directions in fitness wearable security.

2   Methodology

The purpose of this section is to discuss the methodology used in this study. The execution of the study follows a two-phased approach. In Phase 1, the study employs a literature review and qualitative content analysis. The purpose of Phase 1 is to identify the threats and vulnerabilities affecting fitness wearables. Phase 2 employs the Microsoft STRIDE framework and CIA triad together with the Authentication and Non-Repudiation. The purpose of Phase 2 is to map the identified threats to the identified vulnerabilities. The discussion and presentation of these phases can be found in Sub-sects. 2.1, 2.2, and 2.3. The purpose of executing this study in two phases is to utilize the output from Phase 1 as in input in Phase 2, as shown in Fig. 1.

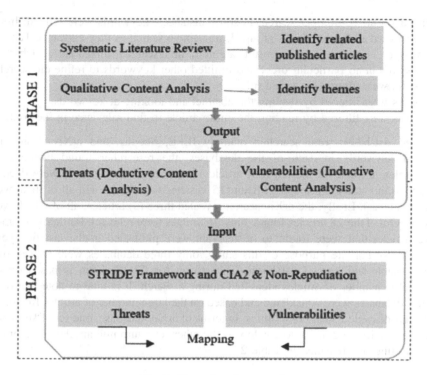

Fig. 1. Tow-phased approach

2.1   Systematic Literature Review (Phase 1)

To identify the threats and vulnerabilities that affect fitness wearables from a security and privacy perspective, the researcher performed a structured literature review as described by [17].

The purpose of performing a systematic literature review was to identify information related to fitness wearables security and privacy concerns that affect these wearables. Database searches were done using related keywords shown in Table 1.

Table 1. Search keywords

keywords	*Fitness wearables, Security, Vulnerability, Privacy, threat*

The purpose of using these keywords was to identify the articles that discuss threats and vulnerabilities that affect fitness wearables from a security and privacy perspective. The results from the search using the identified keywords were filtered in the following manner:

- Based on the results per search, in some instances, keywords were refined. Initial search used all keywords (as grouped) in a single search as they appear in Table 2. However, in instances where results are null, the researcher mixed and matched the keywords in no particular order and omitted other keywords to refine the search.
- Results were filtered by article title.
- Results were filtered by reading the abstract and looking at keywords.
- Results were filtered by reading the entire article to find relevance in the content.

Three databases were searched, namely IEEE, Scopus, and arXiv. Using the specified keywords in each of the databases, the researcher found twenty-eight (28) articles in total. Of the ten (10) articles found in IEEE, eight (8) were deemed relevant to this study. In Scopus, fifteen (15) articles were found and all of them were deemed relevant. Lastly, the arXiv search revealed three (3) articles, all of which were relevant. Out of the 28 articles found, only 26 articles were relevant. Furthermore, most of the articles that were found to be relevant were published in the last five years (2014–2018). For the purpose of this study, only three databases were chosen over other possible and known databases. The reason for this decision is based on the manageable number of articles identified during a search. It is vital to note that other existing databases were considered and based on the large number of articles found, the researcher discarded such possibilities. In terms of arXiv database, one set of keywords were used as depicted in Table 2 below as the other set return null articles. A summary of the findings is presented in Table 2.

Table 2. Summary of search keywords article findings

Databases/sources searched	Keywords used for search	No of papers identified
IEEE	Fitness wearable, vulnerability, security	6 (6 relevant)
	Fitness wearable, threats, privacy	4 (2 relevant)
Scopus	Fitness wearable, vulnerability, security	10 (10 relevant)
	Fitness wearable, threats, privacy	5 (5 relevant)
arXiv	Fitness wearables, vulnerability, security	3 (3 relevant)
	Fitness wearable, threat, privacy	0

2.2   Qualitative Content Analysis (Phase 2)

According to [1], "content analysis is a method that may be used with either qualitative or quantitative data; furthermore, it may be used in an inductive or deductive way". This involves replicable and valid methods for making an inference from observed communication of the context, with the purpose of providing knowledge, new insight, a representation of facts, and a practical guide to action [2]. Content analysis allows the researcher to test a theoretical issue to enhance understanding of the data [1]. Content analysis may be used in either quantitative or qualitative approach, where a quantitative approach provides numerical outcomes and a qualitative approach is more concerned with meaning [1, 3].

In the context of this study, the nature of the analysis will be qualitative, because the findings will be presented in words, and the interpretation thereof will be drawn solely from the words [4]. Qualitative content analysis is a qualitative method that is used to analyze data and interpret its meaning, with an objective to systematically transform a large amount of text into a highly organized and concise summary of key results or themes [5, 6]. The analysis and the interpretation of the content will be conducted using the data found in the literature and will organize the content into a summary of key results.

Through qualitative content analysis, the study followed two approaches. An inductive content analysis approach was used to derive themes. During the content analysis, the researcher used this approach to look for similarities and differences in the content [7]. A deductive content analysis was the second approach followed. This approach was followed in a manner that allowed the researcher to use existing theory to formulate categories or themes [7]. These two approaches were used to identify threats and vulnerabilities affecting fitness wearables.

The inductive content analysis was used in the following manner:

The researcher formulated the following question that needed to be answered: *What vulnerabilities affect fitness wearables from a security and privacy perspective?*

The purpose of this question was to identify vulnerabilities that affect fitness wearables and identify themes in the content. The researcher did not use any existing theory for guidance to derive themes. However, themes were identified and highlighted during the reading of the existing and published literature articles. After all the articles had been read, all the themes highlighted were categorized and recorded in an Excel spreadsheet. In each category, the researcher specified the number of articles that discussed that particular theme.

The deductive content analysis was used in the following manner:

The researcher used an existing theory, the STRIDE framework, as a guide to find the threats that affect fitness wearables. While the researcher read through the articles from published literature, relevant themes that matched the framework were highlighted, categorized, and recorded in an Excel spreadsheet. The total number of articles that addressed a certain theme was also recorded. Furthermore, while the researcher read articles to identify vulnerabilities, threats were also identified concurrently.

All findings were recorded in an Excel spreadsheet for interpretation and analysis. Each article that was found to be relevant was recorded and categorized based on its content.

2.3 Theoretical Frameworks (Phase 2)

The study will employ the Microsoft STRIDE theoretical framework and CIA triad model to construct an analysis of the identified vulnerabilities. STRIDE is an acronym for Spoofing, Tampering, Repudiation, Information Disclosure, Denial of Service, and Elevation of Privileges [8]. CIA is an acronym for Confidentiality, Integrity, and Availability.

By employing the STRIDE framework and CIA triad model, the researcher will be able to identify and understand the potential threats that may affect the components, or rather exploit the vulnerabilities, of fitness wearables. STRIDE speaks to the threats that can exploit vulnerabilities found in fitness wearables, while the CIA model speaks to the security objectives that can be violated by STRIDE components. Although the CIA model is a useful guideline for developing security objectives and requirements, it has limitations, as it does not underline other security objectives such as Authentication and Non-Repudiation [9, 10]. A more concise collection of security objectives would include the CIA triad with the addition of Authentication and Non-Repudiation [9]. The CIA triad together with Authentication and Non-Repudiation are known to be the five pillar of information security [11]. For the purpose of this study, these five pillar will be referred to as CIA2 and Non-Repudiation Model.

3 Results and Presentation

This section aims to present the outcome of the implementation of the qualitative content analysis methodology and the analysis framework discussed in the previous section.

The fitness wearable architecture shown in Fig. 2 is provided to assist in the discussion of the results.

Fig. 2. Fitness wearable high-level architecture

Figure 2 presents the high-level architecture of fitness wearables and the various components involved in assisting fitness wearables in functioning to their full capability. The architecture indicates various components involved in passing collected data from one phase to another, as well as the different surfaces where attacks can occur as data is relayed from one component to another [12]. Fitness and health-related data is collected by the sensors embedded in the fitness wearable (labeled "**A**"). The collected data is transmitted to the pairing smartphone device (labeled "**B**") using the Bluetooth communication protocol. Thereafter, the data is transmitted to the cloud server (labeled "**C**") for long-term storage using the Wi-Fi communication protocol. Furthermore, the data can be transmitted from the cloud server back to the smartphone whenever the user requests to view the stored data in the form of fitness activity records.

Table 3 presents the vulnerabilities found to be affecting fitness wearables from a security and privacy perspective. Each vulnerability is discussed below in terms of its impact on each component of the architecture in Fig. 2.

Table 3. Vulnerabilities affecting fitness wearables

Vulnerabilities	No of article that discussed the vulnerability
Lack of authentication	6
Lack of encryption	8
Insecure communication	5
Insecure cloud server storage	4
Lack of physical security	2

Lack of Authentication: Most fitness wearables generally do not offer an authentication functionality. In cases where a fitness wearable offers a built-in authentication scheme, it is not convenient and as a result, users are hesitant to use it [13]. The lack of authentication in any of the components shown in Fig. 2 is a vulnerability and can provide hackers with an opportunity to steal fitness and health-related information.

Lack of Encryption: The study in [14] investigated the state of security in Fitbit One, and the result of the investigation showed that all traffic between the base station and vendor's website was unencrypted. Thus, the data stored on the cloud server of the wearable manufacturer or service provider is highly vulnerable as a result of the lack of encryption by the service providers [15]. The lack of encryption at any point, whether the data is being stored or transmitted, is a vulnerability.

Insecure Communication: According to [16], the most common security vulnerabilities that can be found in fitness wearables from the attack surfaces are factors such as the insecure transmission of data using Bluetooth Low Energy (BLE) for local device storage. This is because BLE and fitness wearables are becoming widely used, and the private information that leaks through the BLE communication has remained largely unexplored [17]. The lack of security consideration means that these wearables and their communications are more likely to be attacked or have data stolen [18]. With the lightweight security mechanism that is employed, sensitive information is readily accessible to attackers and can be used for malicious activities such as identity theft [19].

Insecure Cloud Server Storage: Fitness wearables transmit the gathered data to smartphone or computer and eventually transmit the data to cloud server for long-term storage [20]. However, the cloud storage lacks associated physical space or control. Therefore, cloud storage can be vulnerable to data breaches by hackers [21].

Lack of Physical Security: The potential loss of the fitness wearable itself, which due to its size it is likely to be misplaced, is a vulnerability [16, 22].

Table 4 presents the threats that are affecting fitness wearables from a security and privacy perspective.

Table 4. Threats affecting fitness wearables

Threat	No of articles that discussed the threat
Spoofing	6
Tampering	3
Repudiation	1
Information disclosure	4
Denial of Service	4
Elevation of Privileges	Not applicable

Spoofing: Spoofing occurs when an attacker tries to masquerade as someone else by falsifying data and gaining legitimate access [23]. Most fitness wearables do not offer an authentication functionality. Even if the wearable offers an authentication scheme, it is not convenient and as a result, users are hesitant to use it [24]. This type of threat focuses on authentication [12].

Tampering: Tampering occurs when the attacker modifies the original state of the data during transmission or when the data is stored [25]. A team of researchers from the University of Edinburgh conducted a study to explore this threat in two fitness wearables by intercepting and extracting personal data from them. As a result, the researchers were able to modify the data and create falsified activities [26, 27]. According to [28], most fitness wearables have no data integrity checks.

Repudiation: Repudiation occurs when the attacker performs actions that cannot be traced back to them [29]. The IoT domain, to which fitness wearables belong, faces various sophisticated attacks, such as eavesdropping, modification, and repudiation, where the attacker can escape the crime due to a lack of efficient tracking mechanisms [30].

Information Disclosure: Information disclosure occurs when the attacker or malicious user is able to access confidential information [31]. The users are not made aware of the sensitive nature of the information that is gathered by these wearables, which exposes them to potential long-term misuse of their gathered information [32, 33]. Users can be identified by their wearables [34]. Wearables can be used to learn about the activities of the user (i.e. stress level, habits, sleeping patterns, exercise, physical activities, or movements). This information can then be shared with third parties, thus compromising the privacy of the individual user [33, 35].

Denial of Service (DoS): DoS occurs when the attacker floods the network with a request that renders the service unavailable [36]. This threat category violates the availability security objective.

Elevation of Privileges: Elevation of privileges occurs when a malicious attacker gains access to user privileges. The "Elevation of Privileges" threat is irrelevant in the context of fitness wearables. This particular element is applicable to systems that contain many users and the factors that can be used to exploit this environment [12].

4 Vulnerability and Threat Analysis Findings

The purpose of this section is to present the analysis of the vulnerabilities found in fitness wearables that may affect the users of these wearables. In order to construct the analysis, a theoretical STRIDE framework together with the five pillars of information security were employed. The researcher in this study chose to use two theoretical analysis frameworks, the Microsoft STRIDE framework and the CIA2 and Non-Repudiation Model to strategically analyze the fitness wearables and their associated components while considering possible attack surfaces that may affect the system [11, 37]. This theoretical analysis was conducted using data findings from the existing literature with a focus on vulnerabilities of and threats to fitness wearables from a security and privacy perspective. Furthermore, the analysis was conducted using theoretical analyzing frameworks.

The components involved in the fitness wearables' architecture were analyzed because security threats (as categorized using STRIDE) and vulnerabilities may exist that do not affect the fitness wearables directly. However, they may affect other components within the architecture and thereby still be the cause of user data privacy challenges as data moves from one component to another.

Table 5 presents the analysis summary for fitness wearables with regard to the STRIDE framework and CIA2 and Non-Repudiation. Column 1 ("**Threats**") presents the threats, as defined by the STRIDE framework, that formed the basis of the analysis. Column 2 ("**Vulnerabilities**") presents the vulnerabilities that can be exploited by the threats. Column 3 ("**Security Objectives**") presents the security objectives that can be violated by the threats identified in Column 1. Column 4 ("**Target Components**") presents the components in the architecture, as presented in Fig. 2, that can potentially be targeted by the threats identified.

Table 5. Analysis summary for fitness wearables

Threats	Vulnerabilities	Security objectives	Target components
Spoofing	Lack of authentication	Authentication	Fitness wearables
Tampering	Lack of encryption	Integrity (and Authentication)	Fitness wearables, mobile fitness apps, cloud server storage
Repudiation	Lack of encryption, authentication	Non-Repudiation (and Integrity)	Cloud server storage
Information disclosure	Lack of encryption, authentication, insecure communication, lack of physical security	Confidentiality (and Authentication)	Cloud server storage, mobile fitness apps, fitness wearables
Denial of Service (DoS)	Insecure communication, cloud server storage	Availability	Cloud server storage, mobile fitness apps

The purpose of Table 5 is mainly to illustrate the correlation between the identified threats and vulnerabilities. Through the analysis and with the support of literature, the study discovered that the relationship between the identified threats and vulnerabilities is a many-to-many relationship. This means that one threat can exploit one or multiple vulnerabilities, and multiple threats can exploit a single vulnerability.

Furthermore, the violation of one security objective by the exploited vulnerability can have an impact on another security objective, as illustrated in Table 5 with the security objectives in brackets. For instance, should an attacker be able to eavesdrop on the communication at any phase of data transmission shown in Fig. 2. The attacker could modify the original state of the data as it moves from one component to the other, thereby violating the integrity of the data. As data flows from one component to the other, it is susceptible to potential threats. Each component of the architecture presented in Fig. 2 acts as a potential threat entry point, as an attacker can access user data by compromising any component.

5 Future Research

The use of fitness wearables will continue to grow as users discover the benefits of tracking and monitoring their fitness and health-related activities. However, the security and privacy concerns surrounding this domain outweigh these benefits. Therefore, extensive research into proper security measures that will ensure that these vulnerabilities are minimized is still required. Furthermore, the IoT domain as a whole is a competitive field and as a result, manufacturers are always eager to release their products. Many of the products released to the market have little or no security. Those that have security have it as an add-on feature that cannot withstand security threats from attackers. Future research should focus on how to integrate security into the initial development phases of these wearables.

6 Conclusion

Fitness wearables are the greatest emerging market within the IoT domain. Through the combination of a systematic literature review and qualitative content analysis, the researcher was able to identify threats and vulnerabilities that affect fitness wearables from a security and privacy perspective. Furthermore, through the combination of the Microsoft STRIDE framework and CIA2 and Non-Repudiation, an analysis was conducted to show the correlation between the identified threats and the vulnerabilities. Five (5) threats and five (5) vulnerabilities were identified. Four out of five threats were found to be relevant in the context of the fitness wearables and as a result, only four threats were mapped to five vulnerabilities.

References

1. Elo, S., Kyngas, H.: The qualitative content analysis process. J. Adv. Nurs. **62**(1), 107–115 (2007)
2. Krippendorff, K.: Content Analysis an Introduction to its Methodology, vol. 31, no. 6, 2 edn. Sage Publications, Inc., Thousand Oaks (1980)
3. O'Connor, H., Gibson, N.: A step-by-step guide to qualitative data analysis. Pimatiziwin: A J. Aborig. Indig. Community Health **1**(1), 63–90 (2017)
4. Bengtsson, M.: NursingPlus open how to plan and perform a qualitative study using content analysis. NursingPlus Open **2**, 8–14 (2016)
5. Erlingsson, C., Brysiewicz, P.: A hands-on guide to doing content analysis. Afr. J. Emerg. Med. **7**(3), 93–99 (2017)
6. Schreier, M.: Qualitative Content Analysis. SAGE, Thousand Oaks (2012)
7. Graneheim, U.H., Lindgren, B.M., Lundman, B.: Methodological challenges in qualitative content analysis: a discussion paper. Nurse Educ. Today **56**, 29–34 (2017)
8. Shostack, A.: Threat Modeling: Designing Security. Wiley, Hoboken (2014)
9. Savol, R.M., Abie, H.: Development of measurable security for a distributed messaging system. Int. J. Adv. Secur. **2**(4), 358–380 (2009)
10. Savola, R.M.: A security metrics taxonomization model for software-intensive systems. J. Inf. Process. Syst. **5**(4), 197–206 (2009)
11. Koul, A.: What's the 5 pillars of information security? (2017). https://www.quora.com/Whats-the-5-pillars-of-information-security. Accessed 10 July 2019
12. Mnjama, J., Foster, G., Irwin, B.: A privacy and security threat assessment framework for consumer health wearables. In: Information Security for South Africa (ISSA) 2017 (2017)
13. Rahman, M., Carbunar, B., Topkara, U.: Concise paper: SensCrypt: a secure protocol for managing low power fitness trackers. In: IEEE 22nd International Conference on Network Protocol 2014, pp. 191–196 (2014)
14. Rahman, M., Carbunar, B., Banik, M.: Fit and vulnerable: attacks and defenses for a health monitoring device. In: 34th IEEE Symposium on Security and Privacy (2013)
15. Carlson, H.: Potential security threats to wearable technology (2017). https://axiomcyber.com/cybersecurity/potential-security-threats-to-wearable-technology/. Accessed 20 July 2018
16. Ching, K.W., Singh, M.M.: Wearable technology devices security and privacy vulnerability analysis. Int. J. Netw. Secur. Appl. **8**(3), 19–30 (2016)
17. Das, A.K., Pathak, P.H., Chuah, C., Mohapatra, P.: Uncovering privacy leakage in BLE network traffic of wearable fitness trackers. In: HotMobile 2016 Proceedings of the 17th International Workshop on Mobile Computing Systems and Applications 2016, pp. 99–104 (2016)
18. Walter, C., Riley, I., He, X., Robards, E., Gamble, R.F.: Toward predicting secure environments for wearable devices. In: Proceedings of the 50th Hawaii International Conference on System Sciences 2017, pp. 1402–1410 (2017)
19. Siboni, S., Shabtai, A., Tippenhauer, N.O., Lee, J., Elovici, Y.: Advanced security TestBed framework for wearable IoT devices. J. ACM Trans. Internet Technol. Spec. Issue Internet Things Smart Secur. Serv. Deliv. **16**(4), 1–25 (2016)
20. de Arriba-Pérez, F., Caeiro-Rodríguez, M., Santos-Gago, J.M.: Collection and processing of data from wrist wearable devices in heterogeneous and multiple-user scenarios. Sensors **19**(9), 1538 (2016)
21. Banerjee, S.S., Hemphill, T., Longstreet, P.: Wearable devices and healthcare: data sharing and privacy. Inf. Soc. Int. J. **34**(1), 49–57 (2018)

22. Mahinderjit, M.S., Ching, K.W., Manaf, A.A.: A novel out-of-band biometrics authentication scheme for wearable devices. Int. J. Comput. Appl. 1–13 (2018)
23. Määttä, J., Hadid, A., Pietikäinen, M.: Face spoofing detection from single images using texture and local shape analysis. In: International Joint Conference on Biometrics 2012, p. 3 (2012)
24. Shrestha, P., Saxena, N.: An offensive and defensive exposition of wearable. J. ACM Comput. Surv. **50**(6), 1–39 (2017)
25. Yang, Z., Zhang, Z.: The study on resolutions of STRIDE threat model. In: Proceedings of the 2007 1st International Symposium on Information Technologies and Applications in Education, ISITAE 2007, pp. 271–273 (2007)
26. McGoogan, C.: Fitness devices can be hacked, research shows (2017). https://www.telegraph.co.uk/technology/2017/09/14/fitbit-devices-can-hacked-research-shows/. Accessed 27 Sept 2018
27. Sandle, T.: New cybersecurity vulnerability with fitness monitors. Digit. J. (2017). http://www.digitaljournal.com/tech-and-science/technology/new-cybersecruity-vulnerability-with-fitness-monitors/article/504514. Accessed 10 Mar 2019
28. Fereidooni, H., Frassetto, T., Miettinen, M., Sadeghi, A.R., Conti, M.: Fitness trackers: fit for health but unfit for security and privacy. In: Proceedings - 2017 IEEE 2nd International Conference on Connected Health: Applications, Systems and Engineering Technologies, CHASE 2017, pp. 19–24 (2017)
29. Islam, M., Lautenbach, A., Sandberg, C., Olovsson, T.: A risk assessment framework for automotive embedded systems. In: Proceedings of the 2nd ACM International Workshop on Cyber-Physical System Security 2016, pp. 3–14 (2016)
30. Zhou, J., Cao, Z., Dong, X., Vasilakos, A.V.: Security and privacy for cloud-based IoT: challenges, countermeasures, and future directions. IEEE Commun. Mag. **55**, 26–33 (2017)
31. Khan, S.A.: Fuzzy preferences based STRIDE threat model for network intrusion detection. Int. J. Comput. Netw. Technol. **5**(3), 107–111 (2017)
32. Hallam, C., Zanella, G.: Wearable device data and privacy: a study of perception and behavior. World J. Manag. **7**(1), 82–91 (2016)
33. Lowens, B., Motti, V.G., Caine, K.: Wearable privacy: skeletons in the data closet. In: Proceedings - 2017 IEEE International Conference on Healthcare Informatics, ICHI 2017, pp. 295–304 (2017)
34. Do, Q., Martini, B., Choo, K.R.: Is the data on your wearable device secure ? An android wear smartwatch case study. Softw. Pract. Exp. **47**, 391–403 (2017)
35. Banerjee, S., Hemphill, T., Longstreet, P.: Is IOT a threat to consumer consent? The perils of wearable devices' health data exposure (2017)
36. Saikiran, P., SureshBabu, E., Padmini, D., SriLalitha, V., Krishnnand, V.: Security issues and countermeasures of three tier architecture of IoT - a survey. Int. J. Pure Appl. Math. **115**(6), 49–57 (2017)
37. UcedaVelez, T., Morana, M.M.: Risk Centric Threat Modeling: Process for Attack Simulation and Threat Analysis, 1st edn. Wiley, New Jersey (2015)

A Conceptual Model for Consent Management in South African e-Health Systems for Privacy Preservation

Lelethu Zazaza[1,2]([✉]) [iD], H. S. Venter[1] [iD], and George Sibiya[2] [iD]

[1] University of Pretoria, Pretoria, South Africa
hventer@up.ac.za
[2] Council for Scientific and Industrial Research, Pretoria, South Africa
{lzazaza,gsibiya}@csir.co.za

Abstract. Consent management is a significant function in electronic healthcare. Given the rise of personal data stored on electronic devices, there is a need to ensure that personal data of individuals is protected — in particular, healthcare user information stored on health information systems. In addition to the basic protection of healthcare user information, healthcare users should also be informed how and by whom their personal information may be used. Through the adoption of transparency by the healthcare service provider, healthcare users are placed in a position to control access to their health information and to reduce the risks for reputational and personal harm. This paper presents a conceptual model for consent management in e-healthcare. The application of the model in e-healthcare will ensure that the following four main requirements are satisfied for the healthcare user: informativity, modifiability, controllability and end-to-end security.

Keywords: e-Consent · e-Health · Privacy · Information security

1 Introduction

The introduction of Health Information Systems (HISs) in healthcare has enabled healthcare staff (such as clerks, surgeons, general practitioners, radiologists and pharmacists) to have easier access to healthcare users' information as had previously been allowed by traditional paper-based approaches [3]. However, this ease of accessibility introduced the risk that healthcare information may be accessed by unauthorised personnel and not for the purposes originally intended by the healthcare user [3]. The inappropriate disclosure of his/her personal information such as demographic details, HIV/AIDS status, previous abortions, substance abuse, psychiatric illnesses and genetic predisposition to diseases [6,8,20] may influence decisions to grant him/her access to education, employment and insurance; additionally, it may expose the healthcare user to reputational or personal harm [8,22]. This paper presents a conceptual model

© Springer Nature Switzerland AG 2020
H. Venter et al. (Eds.): ISSA 2019, CCIS 1166, pp. 69–82, 2020.
https://doi.org/10.1007/978-3-030-43276-8_6

for consent management in South African e-health systems in order to facilitate privacy preservation in healthcare.

This remainder of this paper is structured as follows. Section 2 provides background on e-consent and information security in the healthcare context. Section 3 discusses the requirements for e-consent management in healthcare. Section 4 presents the conceptual model for e-consent management in e-health and Sect. 5 presents the architectural design for the e-consent management system. Section 6 provides a discussion of the model and architectural design. The paper is concluded in Sect. 7.

2   Background

This section provides some background on South African legislation, e-consent and information security in the healthcare context. This background will service the model development process for e-consent management.

2.1   South African Legislature on Privacy

The South African constitution is based on legislation that protects healthcare users as the rightful owners of their own data. Statutory bodies such as the Health Professions Council of South Africa (HPCSA) (established in terms of the Health Professions Act) aim to protect the public and guide the healthcare professionals in their conscientious use and protection of user's personal data [12]. In healthcare, the implications for practitioners who do not pay proper regard to the privacy of healthcare users may result in sanctions from the HPCSA, breach-of-privacy lawsuits, monetary penalties or even imprisonment [2]. Examples of privacy violations in healthcare include student nurses who capture and share pictures of healthcare users, and health practitioners who may mistakenly disclose healthcare user information without the consent of the healthcare user [18]. Acts such as the Health Professions Act exist to protect healthcare users and ensure that healthcare staff conduct themselves in accordance with the law [12].

The South African Protection of Personal Information Act (PoPIA) exists to protect the processing of information by public and private bodies and to prevent the abuse of personal information either by individuals or corporations [2]. The PoPIA was only partially enacted in 2013, owing to delays in appointing an Information Regulator and fully enabling its mandate and powers [25]. Thus, it is yet to fully commence and take effect. Seeing that it is an integral function of healthcare to obtain healthcare user information, it is not illegal—provided that healthcare user confidentiality is maintained, and healthcare user information is protected [2]. In accordance with PoPIA, examples of illegal healthcare user information processing include the following [2]:

- using a mobile device to take a photograph of a patient's body without his/her consent;
- using a mobile device to take a photograph of a patient's hospital record and not ensuring that the image is securely stored;

- storing patient information on a data-storage device without restricted access;
- accessing patient information on a public computer and leaving it open so that passers-by can see it;
- storing patient information for longer than five years without requesting an extension for historical, statistical or research reasons from the respective authority.

The PoPIA is based on the eight privacy guidelines of the Organisation for Economic Co-operation and Development (OECD) which provides practical ways to facilitate privacy [15]. These eight guidelines are incorporated into PoPIA as its principles, namely accountability; processing limitation; purpose specification; further processing limitation; information quality; security safeguards; openness and data subject participation [2].

The next section discusses consent in the context of e-health given that there is a requirement that a healthcare user should give his/her consent—whether it is for medical treatments, research participation, advance care directives or the use and disclosure of personal information.

2.2   e-Consent

Consent is the mechanism that allows healthcare users to exercise the directives related to their medical treatment and personal health information. Consent is considered informed when the healthcare user is provided with enough information on the relevant processes, when adequate opportunity is given to the healthcare user to consider alternative options and when all the healthcare user's questions, with respect to the relevant processes, are answered [14]. Once the healthcare user has been sufficiently informed, he/she may sign a document to confirm that he/she has entered into the agreement of his/her free will and with enough knowledge about the relevant processes to make a decision.

E-consent is thus the facilitation of the process described above through the use of electronic media. The benefit of an electronic approach as opposed to a paper-based one is that paper and printing costs are expensive [26]; physical documents make healthcare user information difficult to store, search and retrieve [14]; it is difficult to enforce access control for physical documents [6] (however, digitising information may make it susceptible to hacking); and forms filled in by hand are often incomplete, inaccurate or illegible [24].

Whilst consent may be given for medical treatments, participation in research or advance care directives (e.g. Do-Not-Resuscitate orders) [11], the focus of this paper is with respect to information privacy preservation and the e-consent directive that deals with the electronic collection, access, use and disclosure of information. The e-consent directive should specify the subject of care, the grantee, the purpose and the time period covered by the consent [11].

The next section provides an overview of information security in the e-health context and discusses specific fundamental security services such as identification and authentication; access control; confidentiality; integrity; non-repudiation; availability and auditing.

2.3   Information Security Services

Information security is the practice of defending information against unauthorised access, use, examination, disclosure, modification, copying, moving or destruction [16]. Information security is achieved through the application of fundamental security services as are defined in the list below.

Identification and Authentication. Identification and Authentication refers to the process where a known individual is identified on a system and verified that he/she is really who he/she claims to be [19]. Once the individual has been successfully identified and authenticated, he/she may be given access to the system. Common identification and authentication mechanisms include, but are not limited to, usernames and passwords, logon tickets, one-time passwords and passwords.

Access Control. Access control (also known as authorisation) is a security service that limits access to healthcare user information, based on restrictions enforced by the Health Information System (HIS) [27]. Healthcare user information in a HIS may include confidential information such as: laboratory results, daily drug administration and physician notes [23]. Using access control, HIS users are only allowed to access healthcare user information necessary for them to do their jobs; as such, doctors will have access to clinical data while secretaries will not [23].

Confidentiality. Confidentiality is the protection of personal information shared with an individual (such as a physician, therapist or attorney) that cannot be disclosed to third parties without the consent of the client. Confidentiality can be accomplished through the implementation of the encryption mechanism.

Integrity. Integrity refers to information that is "precise, accurate, unmodified, modified only in acceptable ways, modified only by authorised people, modified only by authorised processes, consistent, internally consistent, meaningful and usable" [19]. When a system can provide integrity as a security service, it means that all of its information and communication remain in the condition intended by the originator.

Non-repudiation. Non-repudiation refers to the ability of a system to confirm that a sender can not convincingly deny having sent something [19]. Non-repudiation provides proof of the origin and integrity of the data and so makes the successful denial of who/where a message came from or its authenticity difficult [4]. A common security mechanism that can be used to facilitate non-repudiation is a digital signature. Digital signatures are based on asymmetric cryptography where the individual who creates the digital signature uses his/her private key to encrypt the information and only the paired public key can be used to decrypt the information.

Availability. Availability refers to the guarantee that authorised persons, processes and programs can get reliable access to information or a service [16]. Availability is compromised if the system's hardware fails or its operating system environment is jeopardised. Security mechanisms that can facilitate availability include (but are not limited to) the following [10]: backups and over-provisioning; early detection and quick reaction to availability attacks; fail-safes and scalability.

Auditing. Unlike the information security services discussed in the previous sections, auditing does not pro-actively defend information from unauthorised access. Instead it helps keep track of actions as they happen on a system. One of the mechanisms that are used to facilitate auditing are audit logs, as they detail who accessed the HIS, when and for what reason [7]. Audit trails assist in resolving disputes [9] concerning the abuse of permissions, illegal access attempts and improper disclosure of healthcare user data [7].

The next section discusses the functions that an e-consent management system should perform.

3   Requirements for e-Consent Management in e-Health

This section presents the requirements that an e-consent management system should satisfy. The PoPIA is based on the eight privacy guidelines of the OECD. The OECD privacy guidelines provide practical ways for privacy to be facilitated [15]. Given that the PoPIA is based on the best features of international privacy legislation and the OECD guidelines for the protection of privacy [2], the requirements listed below have been aligned with the PoPIA and OECD guidelines in mind. These requirements exist in four broad categories: informativity [14,21]; modifiability [5,17,21]; controllability [5,13,17,21] and end-to-end security [5,13,17].

Informativity
1. Provide a healthcare user with relevant and qualitative information so that he/she can give informed consent. *PoPIA principles: purpose specification & openness.*
2. Provide a healthcare user with an avenue to easily ask questions that relate to his/her consent directive. *PoPIA principles: openness & data subject participation.*
3. Provide a healthcare user with a report that details requests that were made using his/her consent directives. *PoPIA principle: data subject participation.*
4. Provide a healthcare user with the option to receive communication in his/her home language or preferred language in order to receive qualitative responses. *PoPIA principle: information quality.*

5. Notify the healthcare user about any changes requested for his/her consent directives by the service provider. *PoPIA principle: further processing limitation.*

Modifiability

6. Allow the healthcare user to easily modify his/her consent directives. *PoPIA principles: data subject participation & processing limitation.*

Controllability

7. Allow the healthcare user to easily revoke the consent he/she gave to a service provider. *PoPIA principles: data subject participation & processing limitation.*

End-to-End Security

8. Log all requests made using the healthcare user's consent directives for auditing purposes and to facilitate accountability. *PoPIA principles: accountability & security safeguards.*

9. Enforce the consent directives of the healthcare user at all times. *PoPIA principle: security safeguards.*

The next section discusses how the requirements listed above can be incorporated into a model for e-consent management in e-health.

4 Conceptual Model for e-Consent Management in e-Health

Section 2 provided the background for information security services, namely identification and authentication; access control; confidentiality; integrity; non-repudiation; availability and auditing. These security services can now be used to enforce the privacy principles mentioned in the PoPIA (see Fig. 1), namely accountability; processing limitation; purpose specification; further processing limitation; information quality; security safeguards; openness and data subject participation. Once the security and privacy dimensions have been established, the consent dimension (which offers the informed consent management system functionality) is facilitated by offering informativity, controllability and modifiability.

This conceptual model satisfies all the requirements mentioned in Sect. 3 at a high-level, whereas Fig. 2 illustrates a taxonomy that satisfies all the requirements in Sect. 3 at a more granular level than Fig. 1. Figure 2 shows the security and privacy dimensions as illustrated in Fig. 1. Additionally, more detailed attributes are represented for the informativity, controllability and modifiability requirements. The taxonomy illustrates that an e-consent management system should securely store informed consent directives that can easily be accessed and reviewed by healthcare users and service providers.

The following section applies the requirements from Sect. 3 and the conceptual model developed in Sect. 4 to illustrate the architectural design of an e-consent management system.

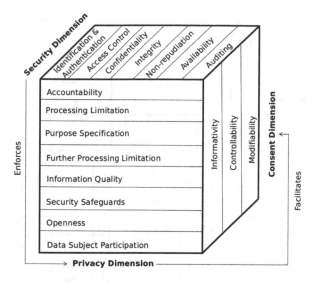

Fig. 1. The relationship between the security, privacy and consent dimensions

5 Architectural Design of an e-Consent Management System

This section presents the architectural design of the proposed e-consent management system. Section 5.1 presents the system components and Sect. 5.2 describes the main processes that exist.

5.1 e-Consent Management System Components

Figure 3 illustrates a UML class diagram that gives an overview of the components of the e-consent management system and how they interact with one other. The Consent Directive Manager is responsible for authenticating the requester (service provider), notifying the beneficiary (healthcare user) about pending requests and approving or rejecting requests. The figure also shows the Auditor class which logs the activities of the e-consent management system. The final component is the HL7Formator, which is responsible for standardising the beneficiary consent directives. Health Level-7 (HL7) International is an accredited body that sets up standards for the transfer of clinical and administrative data between healthcare software applications [11]. Given that the HL7 mission is to develop standards that enable global health data interoperability, it plays a significant role as far as the exchange of communication is concerned. The HL7 standard defines the structure for a consent directive so that HISs can expect a specific structure of the input. The HL7 standard is used to facilitate communication between e-health systems and the e-consent management system.

In the next section, the processes that exist in a e-consent management system are discussed and the interactions among components are described.

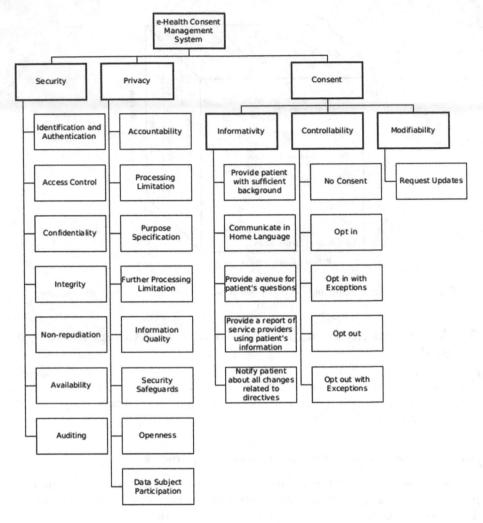

Fig. 2. Taxonomy of an e-Consent management system

5.2   e-Consent Management System Processes

The functions of the e-consent management system include providing the healthcare user with sufficient information to make informed decisions regarding
his/her personal health information; generating the necessary consent directives;
evaluating all requests made against healthcare user consent directives; and managing consent directives issued by the healthcare user. This section presents the
main process of the e-consent management system and discusses the interactions
between the requester and consent directive manager. It also considers the interactions between the beneficiary and the consent directive manager. To conclude,

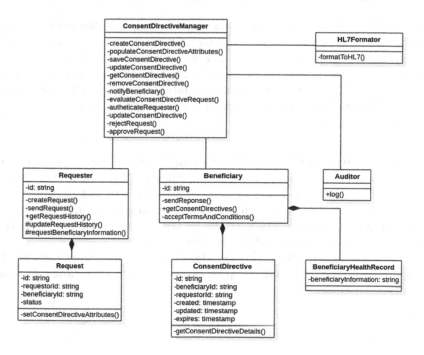

Fig. 3. Class diagram for an e-consent management system

the behaviour of the system is illustrated when the requester wishes to access beneficiary information.

Interactions Between the Requester and Consent Directive Manager.
Figure 4 illustrates the behaviour of the system when the requester interacts with the consent directive manager to create, update, retrieve or remove a healthcare user's consent directive.

Consider a scenario where a doctor named Jacob Fischer, who works at the Center for Endocrinology, makes a request for the update of a consent directive for his patient named Jane Smith. Dr. Fischer requires the consent directive to be updated so that Jane Smith can give permission to Dr. Maria Roberts, who works at the oncology department, to access Jane Smith's electronic health record as he suspects she may have endocrine cancer and he wishes to refer Jane to Dr. Roberts. The consent directive manager will begin by identifying and authenticating Dr. Fischer and the Center for Endocrinology to ensure that they are valid stakeholders. The outcome of the authentication process is logged and the work flow for consent directive creation begins. The consent directive manager then checks if Jane is registered on the HIS and whether she has a health record. When both these conditions are met, the consent directive is updated with its appropriate attributes, i.e. the grantee (Dr. Roberts); the purpose (access to electronic health record of patient for specialised opinion); and the time period

(1 month). The request is saved, and this action is logged. Following the successful update of the consent, the consent directive manager updates the Center for Endocrinology's request history and Dr. Fischer is notified that the request was successful. Next, Jane is notified that a decision is required for a new consent directive request. The following section illustrates and describes the interactions between the beneficiary and the consent directive manager once the beneficiary responds to a request.

Interactions Between the Beneficiary and Consent Directive Manager.
Figure 5 illustrates the behaviour of the system when the beneficiary interacts with the consent directive manager to give a decision to opt in, opt in with exceptions, opt out or opt out with exceptions regarding his/her consent directives. In this section, we continue with the scenario in the previous section which introduced Dr. Fischer, Jane and Dr. Roberts.

Consider a scenario where Jane decides to give her informed consent. The consent directive manager begins by presenting Jane with terms and conditions,

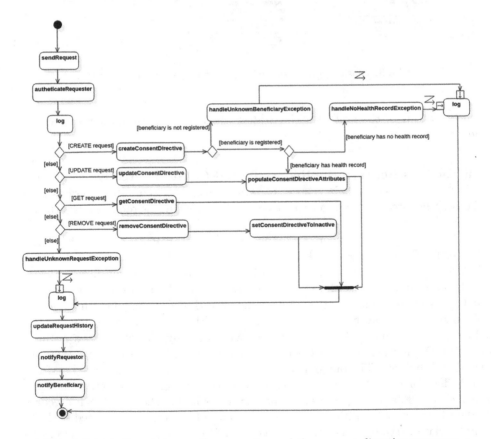

Fig. 4. Interactions between the requester and the consent directive manager

which may be supported with videos or other types of media to provide her with enough information to make an informed decision. Once Jane accepts the terms and conditions, she makes a further decision to opt in on the conditions specified by Dr. Fischer. The consent directive is then populated with the Jane's decision and the consent directive is formatted according to the HL7 standard and saved in the database. Next, the action is logged.

In the next section, we describe the process when Dr. Roberts requests information from Jane's electronic health record.

Requesting Beneficiary Information. Figure 6 illustrates the behaviour of the system when the requester interacts with the consent directive manager to request beneficiary information. It also shows how the consent directive manager either approves or rejects the request. The consent directive manager begins by checking if Jane exists on the HIS, and whether or not she has a consent directive as well as an electronic health record. When all three conditions are fulfilled, the consent directive manager proceeds to retrieve the consent directive and evaluates the request against the conditions stipulated in the consent directive. Based on the evaluation result, the request is either approved or rejected. The trans-

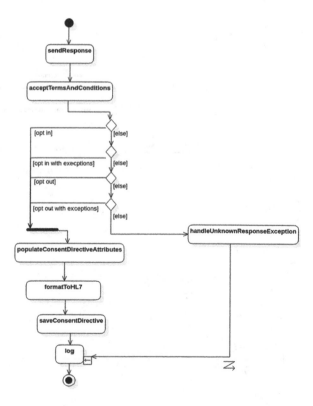

Fig. 5. Interactions between the beneficiary and the consent directive manager

action is then logged, and the process terminates. The next section presents a discussion of the e-consent management model and architectural design presented in this paper.

6 Discussion

The e-consent management model and architectural design satisfy the requirements listed in Sect. 3 namely, informativity, controllability, modifiability and end-to-end security. Transparency from the service provider is facilitated and the health user's privacy is protected through the implementation of the OECD guidelines. Furthermore, a healthcare user is benefited with the ability to be in control and aware of the individuals who are accessing his/her information and the reasons why the personal information is being accessed—thus, allowing the user to give his/her informed consent. The practice of providing reports that lists all service providers that are currently utilising a patient's personal information and notifying patients about all amendments related to his/her consent directives allows for improved trust and transparency. One of the ways to ensure that

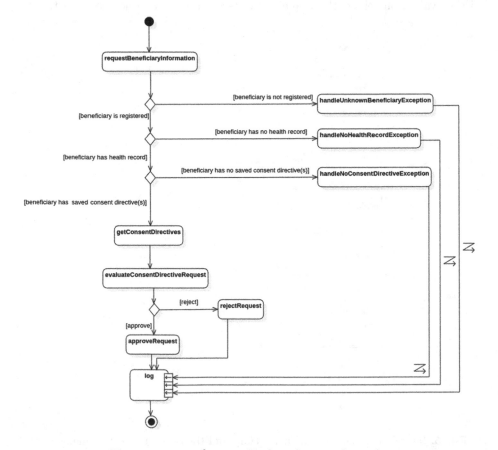

Fig. 6. Process of requesting beneficiary information

a patient is sufficiently informed about the processes in which he/she is needed to participate, is to provide sufficient background in his/her home language. South Africa has 11 official languages where only 8.4% of the population speaks English in their homes and 17.6% of the population speaks English outside the household [1]. Subsequently, automatically delivering formal communication in English is not ideal as the patients are unlikely to understand the correspondence fully. Providing patients with an avenue for patients to ask questions ensures that they can easily contact professionals to seek clarity surrounding their consent directives. The following section concludes this paper.

7   Conclusion

This paper presented a conceptual model for e-consent management system as well as its architectural design. For the architectural design, the components for the e-consent management system were described and the interactions between them were illustrated. The model illustrated the relationship between the security, privacy and consent dimensions where requirements were aligned with the OECD and PoPIA privacy guidelines. The requirements were categorised in four categories namely, end-to-end security, informativity, modifiability and controllability. The security services in the security dimension are used to enforce the privacy principles in the privacy dimension, and once the security and privacy dimensions are satisfied, the consent dimension can be facilitated. Future work includes developing the e-consent management system prototype and applying the model and architectural design.

References

1. Statistics South Africa: General household survey. https://www.oecd.org/internet/ieconomy/privacy-guidelines.htm. Accessed 21 May 2019
2. Buys, M.: Protecting personal information: implications of the Protection of Personal Information (PoPI) act for healthcare professionals. SAMJ: South Afr. Med. J. **107**(11), 954–956 (2017)
3. Coiera, E., Clarke, R.: e-consent: the design and implementation of consumer consent mechanisms in an electronic environment. J. Am. Med. Inform. Assoc. **11**(2), 129–140 (2004)
4. Cryptomathic: What is non-repudiation? https://www.cryptomathic.com/products/authentication-signing-digital-signatures-faqs/what-is-non-repudiation. Accessed 13 Nov 2018
5. Dankar, F.K., Gergely, M., Dankar, S.: Informed consent in biomedical research. Comput. Struct. Biotechnol. J. **17**, 463–474 (2019)
6. Eskeland, S., Oleshchuk, V.A.: EPR access authorization of medical teams based on patient consent. In: ECEH, pp. 11–22 (2007)
7. Fernández-Alemán, J.L., Señor, I.C., Lozoya, P.Á.O., Toval, A.: Security and privacy in electronic health records: a systematic literature review. J. Biomed. Inform. **46**(3), 541–562 (2013)
8. Gaba, A., Havinga, Y., Meijer, H.J., Jan, E.: Privacy and security for analytics on healthcare data (2014)

9. Ghazvini, A., Shukur, Z.: Security challenges and success factors of electronic healthcare system. Procedia Technol. **11**, 212–219 (2013)
10. Hastings, N., Peralta, R., Popoveniuc, S., Regenscheid, A.: Security considerations for remote electronic UOCAVA voting. National Institute of Standards and Technology (NIST), US Department of Commerce, NISTIR 7770 (2011)
11. HL7: FHIR release 3 (STU). http://www.hl7.org/fhir/consent.html. Accessed 27 Sept 2018
12. HPCSA: About HPCSA. http://www.hpcsa.co.za/About. Accessed 14 Nov 2018
13. Lo, N.W., Wu, C.Y., Chuang, Y.H.: An authentication and authorization mechanism for long-term electronic health records management. Procedia Comput. Sci. **111**, 145–153 (2017)
14. Madathil, K.C., et al.: An investigation of the efficacy of electronic consenting interfaces of research permissions management system in a hospital setting. Int. J. Med. Inform. **82**(9), 854–863 (2013)
15. OECD: OCED privacy guidelines. https://www.oecd.org/internet/ieconomy/privacy-guidelines.htm. Accessed 05 June 2019
16. OpenText: Information security and privacy. https://www.opentext.com/products-and-solutions/business-needs/information-governance/ensure-compliance/information-security-and-privacy. Accessed 13 Nov 2018
17. O'Connor, Y., Rowan, W., Lynch, L., Heavin, C.: Privacy by design: informed consent and Internet of Things for smart health. Procedia Comput. Sci. **113**, 653–658 (2017)
18. Park, E.H., Kim, J., Park, Y.S.: The role of information security learning and individual factors in disclosing patients' health information. Comput. Secur. **65**, 64–76 (2017)
19. Pfleeger, C.P., Pfleeger, S.L.: Analyzing Computer Security: A Threat/Vulnerability/Countermeasure Approach. Prentice Hall Professional, Upper Saddle River (2012)
20. Rindfleisch, T.C.: Privacy, information technology, and health care. Commun. ACM **40**(8), 92–100 (1997)
21. Rowan, W., O'Connor, Y., Lynch, L., Heavin, C.: Exploring user behaviours when providing electronic consent on health social networks: A 'just tick agree' approach. Procedia Comput. Sci. **121**, 968–975 (2017)
22. Russello, G., Dong, C., Dulay, N.: Consent-based workflows for healthcare management. In: IEEE Workshop on Policies for Distributed Systems and Networks 2008, POLICY 2008, pp. 153–161. IEEE (2008)
23. Smith, E., Eloff, J.H.: Security in health-care information systems-current trends. Int. J. Med. Inform. **54**(1), 39–54 (1999)
24. St John, E., Scott, A., Irvine, T., Pakzad, F., Leff, D., Layer, G.: Completion of hand-written surgical consent forms is frequently suboptimal and could be improved by using electronically generated, procedure-specific forms. Surgeon **15**(4), 190–195 (2017)
25. Treadaway, A.: Getting GDPR-ready was painful, but PoPI compliance is yet to follow. https://memeburn.com/2018/06/gdpr-south-africa-popi-businesses/. Accessed 13 Dec 2018
26. Yu, B., Wijesekera, D., Costa, P.C.G.: Informed consent in electronic medical record systems. In: Healthcare Ethics and Training: Concepts, Methodologies, Tools, and Applications, pp. 1029–1049. IGI Global (2017)
27. Yüksel, B., Küpçü, A., Özkasap, Ö.: Research issues for privacy and security of electronic health services. Future Gener. Comput. Syst. **68**, 1–13 (2017)

Federation of Services from Autonomous Domains with Heterogeneous Access Control Models

Abdramane Bah[1,2], Pascal André[1], Christian Attiogbé[1(✉)],
and Jacqueline Konate[2]

[1] LS2N CNRS UMR 6004, University of Nantes, Nantes, France
{abdramane.bah,pascal.andre,christian.attiogbe}@univ-nantes.fr
[2] FST-USTTB, University of Science and Technology of Bamako, Bamako, Mali
jacqueline.konate@gmail.com

Abstract. Service-oriented architectures implemented by web services technologies provide standardized protocols for communicating and sharing information across organizational boundaries. The access control of shared services becomes an essential requirement for a secure federation of services. The identity federation provides part of the response by allowing users to authenticate once in an organization and to access the services of others with its authorization information or attributes. However, in a federation, the organizations may have different access control models and authorization attributes with different or even incompatible semantics. Interoperability between the access control models becomes crucial to the federation of services. Existing federated access control solutions are based on the single sign-on with common authorization attributes or the identity mapping that is not scalable in a service-oriented environment. In this paper, we propose a cross-organizational access control method for the federation of services protected by heterogeneous access control models. Our method is based on a new federation architecture that responds to the heterogeneity of authorization attributes via independent attributes introduced at the federation level.

Keywords: SOA · Service composition · Federation · Access control · Attribute mapping · Federated single sign-on

1 Introduction

Service Oriented Architecture (SOA) implemented through web service technologies provides standardized protocols to utilize distributed services under the control of independent security domains [1]. A *security domain* or domain is an autonomous security administration unit that includes services, users, and security policies to manage user access to services [2,3]. In SOA, the resources of a domain are service-oriented. The federation of domains compliant with SOA makes it possible to leverage independent domain business services as part of a

© Springer Nature Switzerland AG 2020
H. Venter et al. (Eds.): ISSA 2019, CCIS 1166, pp. 83–98, 2020.
https://doi.org/10.1007/978-3-030-43276-8_7

composite application called *federation of services*, in order to quickly achieve common goals (for example, improve productivity, create new business value) [4]. A *federated service* is a service shared by a federated domain and accessible to authorized users of the federation.

The access control are based on authorization models such as Attribute-Based Access Control (ABAC) model, Role-Based Access Control (RBAC) model [5]. ABAC defines access permissions with a set of boolean rules specified in terms of the attributes assigned to the subjects (e.g. user, application, service) and objects (e.g. service) and environment conditions [6]. All the access control models can be transformed into ABAC [5]. In the case of RBAC, the role is considered as an attribute. The subject attributes that can be considered in the access decisions such as user's role are here called *authorization attributes*. A consistent definition of the subject attributes allows a domain B to grant access to the subjects of a domain C without requiring prior registration of their identities in B [7]. The authentication and authorization of users can be performed and administered in separate domains, while maintaining the appropriate levels of security. The identity federation enables users to authenticate once in their domain (home) and to access the services from other domains (target) based on their authorization attributes obtained in the (home) domain [8]. However, the federated domains can have different authorization attributes with different or even incompatible semantics. This can lead to unauthorized access to the shared services. It becomes crucial to overcome the heterogeneity of domain authorization attributes for a secure federation of services.

Current federation solutions such as Shibboleth, WS-Federation [9] utilize two main approaches to address the heterogeneity of domain authorization attributes: (1) the standardization of authorization attributes; (2) the mapping of domain authorization attributes. In the first approach, the federation imposes to the domains its authorization attributes called here the *federated attributes* (e.g. the shibboleth eduPerson LDAP schema, Renater's SupAnn schema) based on which the access control policies of the domains are specified. Although the domains retain control over the security of their services, their security policies become tightly coupled with the standards of the federation. In the second approach, domains negotiate mappings between their authorization attributes. In spite of its point-to-point nature and the inconsistency of domain authorization attributes (e.g. different role concepts), this approach requires the disclosure of information about security policies, such as business roles, information on the security infrastructure considered in [10] as information leakage of security policies.

In this paper, we propose a federated access control method based on a new federation architecture that allows loose coupling between the domains and the federation in terms of access control. Our method is based on the mapping technique using the federated attributes to address information leakage of security policies. The benefits of service-oriented architectures such as agility are achieved through the composition of services. The heterogeneity of the authorization attributes of service providers is a major obstacle to the secure composition of federated services. Our method supports access control of the service composition.

The rest of the paper is organized as follows: the Sect. 2 introduces the basic concepts of the federation of services, as well as the challenges and limitations of existing federated access control solutions. The Sect. 3 describes in detail our access control method. The implementation of the proposed method is described in the Sect. 4. The Sect. 5 presents the evaluation of our method applied to a case study. Related works are presented in Sect. 6. We end with the conclusion in Sect. 7.

2   Federation of Services

SOA is an approach to organize distributed resources as autonomous and remotely accessible units of functionalities called services [11]. Services are discoverable and accessible to end-user applications or other distributed services via standard message interfaces and protocols. The main SOA principle is: the *service provider* hosts and executes the service on the behalf of the *service consumer* which discovered the service description in the *service registry*. *Web services* provide a standard-based implementation of SOA accessible through internet protocols such as HTTP. A web service is a self-describing, self-contained software component that can perform actions on behalf of a user or application [12]. Web services rely on standard protocols such as SOAP and WSDL for the description of the service interface and communication messages. Web Services enable the creation of distributed applications that can be dynamically assembled by composing existing services as needed.

Each service is located in a (security) *domain*, including security authorities and governed by a security policy. A common way to achieve interoperability between domains is to federate them. A *federation* is a set of autonomous domains that adhere to common rules and governance policies to control interactions between them [13]. The federation creates a trusted environment for the secure sharing of services between domains. Access control is a security mechanism to ensure that only authorized users have access to resources (considered as services here). Access control starts with the authentication of users and then checks their authorizations. The federation allows users of one domain to access the services from other domains where each domain is assumed to be independent meaning it has its own access control model. To facilitate the management of identity and authentication of users, which can be numerous, identity federation allows users to authenticate only once in the domain they belong to and access the services of others using a single identity. The domain that provides the identity is called the *identity provider* (IdP) and the domain that use this identity to provide the services is called service provider or *relaying party* (RP). The users authenticate with IdPs who create and transmit the proof of authentication to the RPs as a security token. A *security token* represents a set of *claims* that are declarations made by a third party about the user's identity attributes, such as his name, and his authorization attributes such as his role. Access control in domains (service provider) is based on these authorization attributes.

The exchange of security tokens between IdP and RP allows the *federated single sign-on* (FSSO) between the domains. The security tokens are described using the *Security Assertion Markup Language* (SAML) to ensure interoperability between domains. A domain can ensure both the role of IdP (service consumer) and the RP. The federation of services allows to create distributed applications using the services provided by the domains of a federation. Given the decentralized access control at the domains levels, the federation of services remains a major challenge [14,15].

The access control consists of two essential steps: (i) identification and authentication of users; (ii)authorization of users. The authentication of users is delegated to IdPs through identity federation. The authorization of users remain under the control of RPs. However, the latter depends on federation architectures, the main ones being Shibboleth, Liberty Alliance, and WS-Federation [9,16].

With Shibboleth, IdP and RP agree to use common authorization attributes whose semantics are defined through LDAP schema such as the *eduPerson* schema. The access control policies of the RPs are defined on these attributes. Shibboleth also allows to IdPs and RPs to map their own authorization attributes on those of the standard schema. But, these attribute mappings are managed by each IdP and are therefore unreliable. For example, when the attribute teacher does not have the same meaning for two different universities, one of which (IdP) considers a PhD student as a teacher and the other (RP) as a student. This may result in unauthorized access. With Liberty Alliance, the user has distinct identities with different IdPs and RPs that are connected for authorization.

WS-Federation supports Shibboleth and Liberty Alliance access control techniques through specialized services such as *authorization service, attribute service* and *pseudo-nym service*. WS-Federation also provides identity mapping solutions that consists of converting an identity of one domain into an identity in another domain by a trusted third party [2]. However, these identity mappings solutions are not flexible enough because they require point-to-point negotiations between each pair of domain. The access control of service composition requires authorization negotiations going beyond two domains. The federated services access control requires a federation architecture that supports authorization negotiations for service composition.

The federation of services faces major challenges: (i) Heterogeneity of domain authorization models. Each domain specifies its access control policies on its own authorization attributes such as role. When domains use authorization attributes with different or incompatible semantics, access to services is either hindered or granted to unauthorized users. (ii) Autonomy of domains. One domain may belong to different federations or collaborate in pairwise way. In any case, the context must not interfere with the local security policy. (iii) Composition of federated services. The composition of federated services must take into account the access control of each service and therefore the heterogeneity of domain authorization attributes. The secure federation of services from independent domains must meet the following requirements:

- *Federated single sign-on.* A user must be able to authenticate once to the federation and then use the services for which he has a valid authorization.
- *Decentralized authorization.* Users must acquire authorizations from their domains and access the services on the basis of these authorizations.
- *Autonomy of domains.* Each domain controls the access to its services.
- *Dynamic adaptation to the federation growth.* The domain's access control mechanisms should not require significant maintenance efforts during authorization changes in the federation.
- *Confidentiality of internal security informations.* The authorization attributes are sensitive informations and should not be disclosed beyond the domain boundaries.

In the next section, we propose an access control method that addresses these needs.

3   A Method for Federated Access Control

Our method is based on a specific federation architecture adapted from current practices to support the attribute mappings.

Federation Architecture. The domains are federated by considering that the services in one domain are accessible to other domains based on the trust relationships and access control policies. Cross-domain access control requires that the authorization attributes of a domain be understandable in other domains. The access control policies of domains are specified on their authorization attributes. Domains map their authorization attributes to prevent their access control policies from being dependent on the attributes of other domains. The attribute mappings serve as a means of granting permissions to users outside the domain using only the domain authorization attributes. In order to establish flexible mappings between domain authorization attributes while avoiding information leakage of security policies, we introduce an independent entity called *Global Access Control Mediator (GACM)* at the level of the federation. The GACM serves as a trusted third party between domains. The domains no longer need to negotiate access authorizations with each other (plain arrows in Fig. 1), they only need to negotiate access authorizations once with GACM (dashed arrow in Fig. 1) and then access domain services directly with these authorizations as shown in the Fig. 1. The main interests of GACM are on the one hand to ensure the secure granting of authorizations to users outside the domains and on the other hand to facilitate the management of trust between domains. The readers can access a detailed introduction in our reserach report [17].

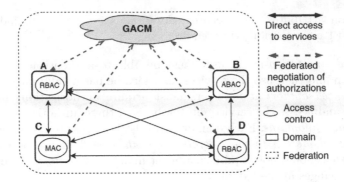

Fig. 1. The proposed federation architecture

Attribute Mapping Through the GACM. GACM does not define domain access control policies or grant access permissions to users. It represents the federation authority serving as a bridge between the domains. The primary purpose of attribute mapping for domains is to understand the authorization attributes of each others in order to determine the local access permissions for the external authorization attributes. However, the federation evolves; new domains join it with new authorization attributes and others leave. Attribute mapping must dynamically adapt to the evolution of federation and authorization attributes changes in domains. To achieve these objectives and avoid leakage of security informations, the GACM defines the authorization attributes of the federation, the *federated attributes*, independently of those of the domains. Federated attributes are public and understandable by all domains.

We define mappings between federated attributes and domain authorization attributes at two levels as shown in Fig. 2:

- At the GACM level: the domains negotiate once with the GACM, the mappings between their authorization attributes and the federated attributes. This first mapping, called the *federated mapping* is registered with the GACM and a copy is registered in the domains;
- At the domain level: each domain locally defines mappings between the federated attributes and its authorization attributes. This second mapping is called the *domain mapping*.

Interactions between domains are then performed using federated attributes. Using federated attributes, domains can grant access authorizations to all other domains of the federation without knowing their local authorization attributes. As a result, domains can access one another's services despite the heterogeneity of their authorization attributes. The advantage provided by our approach to the users is to obtain the access authorizations in other domains based on their original authorization attributes.

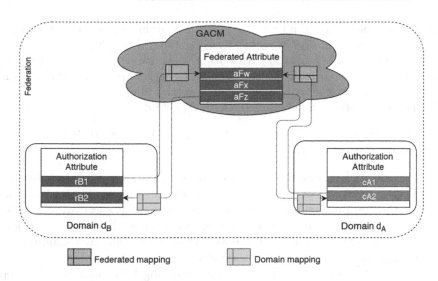

Fig. 2. Federated attribute for the mapping of domain authorization attributes

Now, the services of domains accessible in the federation are seen as federated services.

3.1   Access to Federated Services

We now present how to access the federated services.

Authentication and Trust Brokering. The access control of services relies on the authorization attributes of users asserted by a trusted third party. Each domain has its own authentication mechanism called *local token service* (LTS). The LTS authenticates users and issues a security token signed by the domain security certificate. The services of a domain are accessible only with a security token issued by the domain's LTS.

In order to establish trust between domains, we introduce in the GACM a specialized authentication mechanism called *federated token service* (FTS) for domain authentication. We identify the domains and the GACM with the public-key certificates. The security certificates of domains are forwarded to the GACM which in turn transmits its certificate to the domains. The domains authenticate to the GACM with the security tokens signed with their security certificates. In response, the FTS delivers the security tokens signed by the GACM's security certificate. Consequently, the domains of the federation trust each other through the *federated security tokens*.

As shown in Fig. 3, to access to a service (S_B) of domain B (d_B) from a domain A (d_A), the authentication of the user (U_A) is performed with the following steps :

1. the LTS of d_A authenticates U_A and delivers an security token (ST_A) signed with the d_A security certificate ((1.a) dashed arrow in Fig. 3);

2. d_A authenticates to the FTS using ST_A and obtains on behalf of U_A, a federated security token (ST_F) signed with the GACM certificate (1.b);
3. the service consumer use ST_F to obtain a security token (ST_B) from d_B signed with d_B security certificate. The ST_F signature proves that d_A and U_A belong to the federation and are trustworthy (1.c).
4. finally, S_B is called on behalf of U_A with ST_B (1.d).

The authorization attributes contained in the ST_B being specific to d_B, are used for the access control of S_B.

Authorization. The security token used to invoke a service must contain the authorization attributes of the domain providing this service. The user initially has the authorization attributes of his domain that must be successively mapped to the federated attributes and the target domain's authorization attributes during the authentication process. We assume that the federated mapping and domain mapping discussed in Sect. 3 are already established.

In the Fig. 3, we illustrate the attribute mapping by considering the steps presented in Sect. 3.1. To achieve the authorization of U_A, the authorization attribute of U_A (*cA1*) is used by the FTS to compute the federated attribute *aFx* corresponding to cA1. The aFx sent to d_B, allows the d_B's LTS to compute the authorization attribute *rB2* corresponding to aFx. This latter allows finally to access the service targetted by U_A.

3.2   Composition of Federated Services

Each composed service has its own authorization attributes requirements. The access control of the service composition is done at two levels: the composite service's access control and the composed services's access control. This creates two additional issues: (1) the specification of the composite service's access control

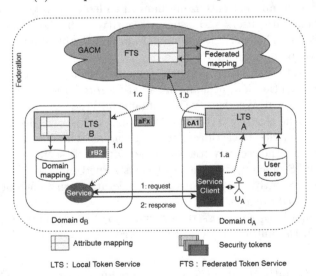

Fig. 3. Sequence of federated single sign-on and cross-domain authorization

requirements; (2) and the federated single sign-on between the composite service consumer (initial requester), the composite service and the composed services. We solve these issues by considering two scenarios: (i) we invoke the composed services on the behalf of composite service; (ii) we invoke composed services on the behalf of the intial requester.

In the first scenario, the access control of the composite service is performed like in any federated service. The access control requirements of the composite service are independent of those of the composed services. To invoke a composed service, the composite service follows the authentication steps described in the Sect. 3.1.

In the second scenario, the composite service's access control requirements depend on those of the composed services that may be different from one service to another. The composed services require a security token containing the authorization attributes of their domains. The composite service consumer must provide a security token that satisfies these requirements.

For this purpose, first, we introduce the *token store* at the composite service level to store the security token of the initial requester (ST_{init}). The composite service must convey the ST_{init} to invoke the composed services. But, the ST_{init} contains the authorization attributes of the domain that provides the composite service. Second we perform a new authentication process using the ST_{init} in order to have the authorization attributes of the composed service's domain corresponding to those contained in ST_{init}. Figure 4 illustrates the service composition with this scenario.

4   Implementation of Our Method

The goals are to develop the required software modules; to select and customize existing security services to support our access control method.

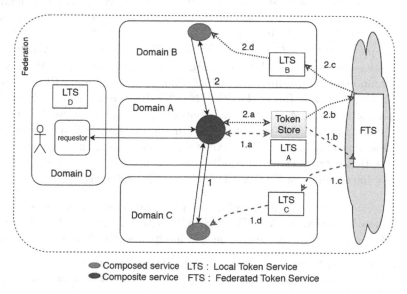

Fig. 4. Invocation of composed services on the behalf of the initial requester

WS-Trust, WS-SecurityPolicy and WS-Security provide the basic model of the federation of web services [18]. WS-Trust is implemented with *Security Token Service* (STS) that provides methods for issuing, validating, transforming, and renewing security tokens. The LTS of domains and the FTS of GACM are implemented with WS-Trust STS. We have three types of STS in our architecture: the STS in the services providers domains (named STS_{SP}), the STS in the services consumers domains (named STS_{SC}) and the STS of the GACM named STS_{GACM}. The implementation of our method involves four steps.

Step 1: *Definition of claim dialect of federated attributes.* The security requirements of federated web services must be specified using the federated attributes defined by the GACM. However, WS-SecurityPolicy does not define a claim dialect for the expression of claim requirements. We define a claim dialect (XML schema) to describe the federated attributes. Each web service specifies its authorization attributes requirements using this claim dialect.

Step 2: *Definition of federation-specific security requirements of STS_{SP} and STS_{GACM}.* First, the target web service requires a SAML[1] token issued by the STS_{SP} of its domain with specific claims. The STS_{SP} requires a SAML token issued by the STS_{GACM} which also requires a SAML token. The STS_{GACM} does not specify the token issuer because it trusts all STS_{SC} in the federation.

Step 3: *Implementation of attribute mapping of STS_{SP} and STS_{GACM}.* The STS_{SP} and the STS_{GACM} are customized in order to implement the attribute mapping. These STS must be able to retrieve authorization attribute (claims) contained in the SAML tokens and exchange them with the corresponding attributes stored in the *mapping module* that contains the pre-established attribute mapping. We implement the mapping module with a relational database to be queried in order to easily find the desired attributes.

Step 4: *Implementation of service's access control enforcement.* Web services access control is based on XACML[2] which has several logically distinct components, including the *Policy Enformcement Point* (PEP) and the *Policy Decision Point* (PDP). The PEP intercepts the SOAP request, extracts the authorization attributes contained in the SOAP message header and enforces access decision made by the PDP. We assume that domains already have access control policies defined on their local authorization attributes. As a result, the existing PDP are maintained. But, we implement the PEP with *Apache CXF[3] interceptors*.

Web services access control requires the composition of several security standards, namely WS-Security, WS-Trust, SAML, XACML and WS-Federation [19] [20]. SAML and XACML are implemented independently. But WS-Federation,

---

[1] Security Assertion Markup Language (SAML) OASIS Standard.

[2] eXtensible Access Control Markup Language (XACML) OASIS Standard.

[3] Apache CXF, https://cxf.apache.org.

WS-Trust, WS-Security are dependent. The deployment of WS-Federation depends on the those of WS-Trust which depends on WS-Security forming thus the layers of security protocols. This dependency is difficult to deal with because there are no solutions that deploy these layers together. The web service developers are constrained to deploy each of its layers separately. What is likely to generate configuration errors. The main web services development solutions providing the security layers are *Apache CXF*, *Axis2*[4], *Glassfish Metro*[5] for those that are compatible with *JAX-WS*[6] specification and *Microsoft's WCF*[7]. These solutions do not directly integrate the access control (XACML and SAML). Solutions that integrate access control such as *WSO2 Application Server*[8] are not customizable. Finally, the implementation of web services access control becomes quickly a real challenge.

5 Application and Evaluation

We present a case study on which we experiment the proposed method.

5.1 Case Study: Federation of Scholarship Services

The case is a federation of three institution systems involved in the payment of students scholarship. Initially, the scholarships were paid by the national treasury but three independant higher education institutions are responsible to grant the scholarship to students: the Center of University Studies (*CUS*), the Directorate of Higher Education (*DHE*) and Universities. The usual scholarship is allocated by CUS. An additional aid is allocated to disabled students by the DHE. Some universities grant on their budgets an aid to the non-scholarship students. The Treasury pays the scholarships and the various aids for the account of each institution that dispatches them to students. To this end, each institution establishes and submits to the treasury a scholarship payment card consisting of a set of attribution codes (*sc-code*) and their amount. Each sc-code represents a student's scholarship. In order to facilitate the payment of scholarships, the decision is taken that all payments should be now made by the accounting departments of universities. To put into practice, the CUS, DHE and universities decided to federate their systems to share securely the scholarships attribution codes. The CUS provides the sc-codes of the usual scholarship. DHE provides the sc-codes of disabled students aids. The Universities collect the sc-codes of their students at CUS and DHE to establish their payment cards. The scholarship of a disabled student is the sum of his sc-codes. The Table 1 describes the different domains that will participate in the federation.

---

[4] Axis2, http://axis.apache.org/axis2/java/core/.
[5] Metro web service stack, https://javaee.github.io/metro/.
[6] Java API for XML-Based Web Services, Sun Microsystems, Inc.
[7] Windows Communication Foundation.
[8] https://wso2.com/products/application-server.

Table 1. Description of the domains to be federate

Domain	A.C. model	Authorization attribute (role)	Web services
CUS	RBAC	Financial-officer, accounting-officer, chief-accountant	scholarshipService
DHE	ABAC	Cashier, accountant	disabled-grantService
UTS	RBAC	Administrator, financial, accounting-secretary	

As described in Table 1, the CUS and DHE are the service providers and the universities such as University of Technical Sciences (UTS) are the consumers of these services. Each domain has its access control model (A.C. model) with its authorization attributes that are the roles in the RBAC model. The role is considered in the ABAC model as an attribute. To create its scholarship payment card, the UTS accounting department must access the web services of the CUS and DHE. This requires establishing trust between their systems and the interoperability between their access control models.

5.2   Federation of Domains and Services

To federate the CUS, the DHE and the universities and their services, we follow the steps described in the Sect. 4.

Step 1 - Definition of Federated Attributes and the Claims Dialect. An autonomous department of DHE, the Department of Administrative Affairs (DAA) is designated to host the GACM. A security certificate is created for the DAA, CUS, DHE and all universities belonging to the federation. DAA registers the security certificates of the domains. The CUS, DHE and universities also register the DAA security certificate. The DAA and the domains of the federation can now trust each other. The DAA defines the federated attributes as shown in the Table 2 and creates the claim dialect to describe them. The DAA negotiates with the domains to establish the federated mapping. The CUS and the DHE establish their domain mapping. The DAA deploys the federated token service, the STSDAA. It is assumed that the domains already have their STS. Otherwise, the domains install their STS. The STS of the UTS is configured to support the claims dialect.

Table 2. The DAA federated attributes

	Authorization attribute (userAffiliation)
Finance	Finance-director, finance-assistant, finance-secretary, ...
Administration	Administration-director, administration-adjt, ...
Information technology	It-administrator, ...

Step 2 - Definition of STS Security Requirements. The CUS and DHE specify the access control requirements of their web services and their STS using the DAA claims dialect.

Step 3 - Implementation of Attribute Mapping. The DAA, CUS, and DHE create a database to store the federated mapping and the domain mapping respectively. Their STS implement the attribute mapping with a generic software component to query the mapping databases.

Step 4 - Web Services Access Control. The CUS and the DHE deploy SOAP message interceptors to extract the authorization attributes from the SAML assertions and enforce the services access decision.

After these steps, the UTS and other universities can then access the web services of the CUS and the DHE to collect the students sc-codes and create their scholarship payment card.

5.3   Evaluation

We evaluate our service federation architecture based on the following criteria:

- *Applicability*: the ease of implementation and integration into an existing security environment;
- *Scalability*: the adaptation to the evolution of the federation and changes of the authorization attributes in the domains;
- *Reliability and security*: The reliability of attribute mappings for granting access permissions to external users.
- *Extensibility*: the support of others access control models different from ABAC.

Applicability. For example, in Sect. 5.2, when an university—using an LDAP registry with OpenAM[9] as the authentication mechanism and RBAC as authorization model—participates in a federation built according to our method, the existing security mechanisms (LDAP, OpenAM and RBAC) are maintained. OpenAM is configured to support the dialect of the federation. Internal roles used for the authorizations are never disclosed to CUS and DHE. This reduces the dependencies between domains for the access control. The only change in CUS and DHE is the implementation of an STS in order to support the attribute mapping. Our architecture fits well with existing access control mechanisms of domains and its adoption requires minimal configuration efforts.

Scalability. The evolution of the federation has no effect on the access control of the CUS and DHE because of the stability induced by the incoming mapping of the domains. The domains (service providers) adapt themselves only to the evolution of the federated attributes.

Reliability and Security. The federated attributes of a user is asserted by the GACM through the federated mapping. This ensures the reliability of the authorizations granted by the service providers through their domain mapping.

---

[9] ForgeRock OpenAM, https://backstage.forgerock.com/docs/openam.

Extensibility. Our approach assumes different access control models in each domain of the federation. Since all access control models can be transformed into ABAC [5] and the mappings rely on the authorization attributes, our method supports other access control models.

However, our approach focuses more on the access control of external users to the domains. In the case where the federated service is also used within the domain, the access control of the service will always use the GACM. Internal use of the federated service requires a new service contract that does not employ the GACM.

6   Related Work

Jasiul et al. [21] present an analysis of authentication and authorization challenges for users and services in federated SOA environments. They identify SOA-specific requirements for federated access control and argue that only cross-domain, trust-based authentication and authorization can meet these requirements. They recommend the federated single sign-on (FSSO) mechanisms to avoid overloading security services and identity propagation to secure the service composition.

In a federation, users belong to different security domains. Two approaches are generally used to perform federated authentication: a central identity provider, a federation of local identity providers. The authors in [4] compare both approaches to illustrate the benefits of federated identity systems. For interoperability between heterogeneous access control models in the federation, Hafeez et al. [5] propose to transform the domain access control models into ABAC using XACML and apply the resulting policy to remote requests. In our approach, we assume that domain access control models are defined using XACML. Our challenge is rather the heterogeneity of domain authorization attributes.

Several solutions to the heterogeneity of authorization attributes have been proposed in the literature [6,14,15,22–24]. In [22], the mapping of attributes is proposed. It consists to transform the local attributes using derivation rules to federated attributes, which are attributes defined by the domains but recognized by the federation. The federated attributes in our approach are defined by the federation and are independent of those of the domains. A flexible architecture based on the ABAC model is proposed in [15] to ensure the heterogeneity of inter-domain access control. However, the authorisation decision to access a service is make in the service consumer side based on the collaboration contract as proposed in [10]. While this approach preserves the autonomy of the domains in terms of security, it is point-to-point and hardly supports the authorization changes. Preuveneers et al. [6] propose to align the authorization attributes of domains by declaratively defining equivalence relations between their names and their values. We use a similar approach, but we utilize intermediate attributes to define the equivalence relationships. Our goal for this is to minimize dependencies between domains and to avoid leakage of security informations.

7   Conclusion

We proposed a cross-domain access control method for service-oriented environments, based on a federation architecture where the domains stay responsible of the access control of their services. At the federation level, a third-party entity, the global access control mediator (GACM) handles trust, interoperability and service composition between the heterogeneous domain access control models. Federated attributes play the role of medium between domains with a double mapping mechanism between domain attributes (such as roles) and federated attributes to keep the domain independence. We proposed an implementation of our method for the access control of web services in which we detail the different steps of implementation, the necessary components and the difficulties encountered. Our method was applied to a case study in order to evaluate it according to feasibility, reliability, scalability and security criteria.

Short term perspectives involve the application of our method. We did not study the performance and scalability of our implementation. In particular, we plan to distribute GACM information into special areas of the domains to improve performance. We also plan to experiment the access control of service composition where composed services are invoked on the behalf on initial requester. Token store integration in the orchestration engines must be also implemented. We plan to extend attribute mapping with individual access permissions to allow fine-grained cross-domain access control. Further work is required to bring assistance in building the mappings when the models (both domain and federation) evolve. Ontologies may be helpful in this case. Since our approach is really modular, we are convinced that it fits to the case where a domain can belong to different federations and possibly to federations of federations.

References

1. OASIS: Reference Architecture Foundation for Service Oriented Architecture Version 1.0, 04 December 2012
2. OASIS: Web Services Federation Language (WS-Federation) Version 1.2. Standard, 22 May 2009
3. International Telecommunication Union: Baseline identity management terms and definitions, 04 April 2010
4. Fabian, B., Kunz, S., MüLler, S., GüNther, O.: Secure federation of semantic information services. Decis. Support Syst. 55(1), 385–398 (2013)
5. Hafeez, K., Rajpoot, Q., Shibli, A.: Interoperability among access control models. In: 2012 15th International Multitopic Conference (INMIC), 111–118, IEEE, Islamabad, December 2012
6. Preuveneers, D., Joosen, W., Ilie-Zudor, E.: Policy reconciliation for access control in dynamic cross-enterprise collaborations. Enterp. Inform. Syst. 12(3), 279–299 (2018)
7. Hu, V.C., et al.: Guide to attribute based access control (ABAC) definition and considerations. Technical report NIST SP 800–162, National Institute of Standards and Technology, January 2014

8. Beer Mohamed, M.I., Hassan, M.F., Safdar, S., Saleem, M.Q.: Adaptive security architectural model for protecting identity federation in service oriented computing. J. King Saud Univ. - Comput. Inf. Sci. (2019)
9. Kallela, J.: Federated identity management solutions. T-110.5190 Seminar on Internetworking (2008)
10. Menzel, M., Wolter, C., Meinel, C.: Access control for cross-organisational web service composition. J. Inf. Assur. Secur. **2**(3), 155–160 (2007)
11. Dikmans, L., Van Luttikhuizen, R.: SOA made simple discover the true meaning behind the buzzword that is "service oriented architecture". Packt Pub, Birmingham (2013). OCLC: 847034163
12. Papazoglou, M.P.: Web Services: Principles and Technology. Pearson/Prentice Hall, Harlow (2008). OCLC: 255863191
13. Duan, N.: Design principles of a federated service-oriented architecture model for net-centric data sharing. J. Defense Model. Simul.: Appl. Methodol. Technol. **6**(4), 165–176 (2009)
14. Decat, M., Van Landuyt, D., Lagaisse, B., Joosen, W.: On the need for federated authorization in cross-organizational e-health platforms. In: Proceedings of the 8the international conference on Health Informatics, vol. 8, pp. 540–546 (2015)
15. Haguouche, S., Jarir, Z.: Managing heterogeneous access control models crossorganization. In: Lopez, J., Ray, I., Crispo, B. (eds.) CRiSIS 2014. LNCS, vol. 8924, pp. 222–229. Springer, Cham (2015). https://doi.org/10.1007/978-3-319-17127-2_15
16. Fragoso-Rodriguez, U., Laurent-Maknavicius, M., Incera-Dieguez, J.: Federated identity architectures. In: Proceedings of 1st Mexican Conference on Informatics Security (MCIS 2006), p. 8 (2006)
17. BAH, A., André, P., Attiogbé, C., Konaté, J.: Federated access control in service oriented architecture. Research report, LS2N, Université de Nantes, April 2019
18. Bertino, E., Martino, L., Paci, F., Squicciarini, A.: Security for Web Services and Service-Oriented Architectures. Springer, Heidelberg (2010). https://doi.org/10.1007/978-3-540-87742-4
19. Aruna, S.: Security in web services- issues and challenges. Int. J. Eng. Res. **V5**(09) (2016). IJERTV5IS090245
20. Singhal, A., Winograd, T., Scarfone, K.A.: Guide to secure web services. Technical report NIST SP 800–95, National Institute of Standards and Technology, Gaithersburg, MD (2007)
21. Jasiul, B., Sliwa, J., Piotrowski, R., Goniacz, R., Amanowicz, M.: Authentication and authorization of users and services in federated SOA environments - challenges and opportunities, p. 13 (2010)
22. Rubio-Medrano, C.E., Zhao, Z., Doupe, A., Ahn, G.J.: Federated access management for collaborative network environments: framework and case study. In: Proceedings of the 20th ACM Symposium on Access Control Models and Technologies - SACMAT 2015, pp. 125–134. ACM Press, Vienna (2015)
23. Na, L., Yun-Wei, D., Tian-Wei, C., Chao, W., Yang, G., Yu-Chen, Z.: Cross-domain authorization management model for multi-levels hybrid cloud computing. Int. J. Secur. Appl. **9**(12), 357–366 (2015)
24. Diniz, T., Felippe, A.C.D., Medeiros, T., Silva, C.E.D., Araujo, R.: Managing access to service providers in federated identity environments: a case study in a cloud storage service. In: 2015 XXXIII Brazilian Symposium on Computer Networks and Distributed Systems, pp. 199–207. IEEE, Vitoria, May 2015

Security Aspects of an Empirical Study into the Impact of Digital Transformation via Unified Communication and Collaboration Technologies on the Productivity and Innovation of a Global Automotive Enterprise

Anthony Bolton[1] , Leila Goosen[2(✉)] , and Elmarie Kritzinger[1]

[1] University of South Africa, Johannesburg 1710, South Africa
49039210@mylife.unisa.ac.za
[2] University of South Africa, Pretoria 0003, South Africa
GooseL@unisa.ac.za

Abstract. The purpose of this paper is to focus on the security aspects of digital transformation through Unified Communication and Collaboration (UC&C) technologies impacting productivity and innovation within a global automotive enterprise. The rationale for the study came from a desire to address the challenge of integrating the complex technology landscape of the Internet of Things in the daily lives of people. This study explored the impact of digitization transformation on people in the context of the automotive industry. A framework for digital transformation via UC&C technologies was designed at a large automotive enterprise. Research leveraged qualitative and quantitative methods, following the implementation of the framework and digital transformation. Observational data combined with data from quantitative enterprise metrics to support analysis. Critical realist interpretation of results suggested that digitally transformed UC&C technologies are changing employees' work practices. The study concludes that digital transformation via UC&C technologies impact productivity and innovation within a global automotive enterprise.

Keywords: Digital transformation · Global automotive enterprise · Impact · Innovation · Productivity · Unified Communication & Collaboration technologies

1 Introduction

Against the background of the current state and future directions in terms of the *security* of the Internet of Things (IoT), automotive enterprises are characterised by the complex global nature of their enterprise operations, with the increasing technical complexity of the Internet of Things influencing manufacturing and vehicle systems [1]. Large automotive Original Equipment Manufacturers (OEM), such as General Motors (GM), face unique challenges in transforming their enterprises into the IoT and Industry 4.0 age, due to their scale and broad dependency on global supply chain and

© Springer Nature Switzerland AG 2020
H. Venter et al. (Eds.): ISSA 2019, CCIS 1166, pp. 99–113, 2020.
https://doi.org/10.1007/978-3-030-43276-8_8

product partnerships. Enterprises such as GM have a long history of industrial development (GM is a 109-year-old enterprise) and must contend with deeply rooted enterprise processes corporate culture. Shared challenges include transforming employee communication regarding increased efficiency, convenience and speed across a global workforce.

Multiple architectures, such as the Internet of Things Architecture (IoT-A) [2] and the Reference Model for Industrie 4.0 (RAMI4.0) [3], have emerged and developed in recent years. In their paper on the *security* and privacy of Internet of Things architectures and systems, however, Vasilomanolakis et al. [4] indicated that no ubiquitous industry standard, framework or reference architecture has been adopted. The lack of an industry-wide architecture increases the challenges associated with the broader horizontal digital transformation of the progressive enterprise. The absence of an industry standard framework for digital transformation can also lead to increased complexity and a lack of consistency in the experience of users. A robust transformation plan and deployment framework, tailored to an enterprise's specific business model, is required to avoid these issues. The requirement for structured planning, integrated into the business model of the target enterprise is increasingly essential where the digital transformation affects employee and customer communication. Digital communication is increasingly vital in Industry 4.0 and IoT enabled business models. Wolf [5] reminds us that digitalization has the propensity to transform industries and business models, rapidly affecting the entire enterprise involved. The transformation may be digital, but it is planned, led and executed by people.

In light of the afore-mentioned, the purpose of this paper is therefore to focus on the security aspects of digital transformation through UC&C technologies impacting productivity and innovation within a global automotive enterprise.

2   Enterprise Digital Transformation

2.1   Motivators for Enterprise Digital Transformation

In terms of motivators for enterprise digital transformation, and against the background of *security* for the digital world within an ethical framework, the Digital Enlightment Forum [6] pointed out the digital disruption is profoundly impacting industry and society. Enterprises that move ahead with digital transformation stand to disrupt industry, reaching new markets and customers almost immediately. Entry into expanded digital markets and customer bases in many cases can be achieved, while generating savings and optimizing gross profit margins [7]. Productivity impact can be introduced rapidly through combinatorial digital innovation. As the age of the fourth industrial revolution emerges, digital transformation will be a catalyst in defining and iterative redefining of the modern enterprise.

2.2   Challenges to Digital Transformation

Enterprise Challenges Relating to Model, Vision, Culture and Security: As enterprises transform to digital business models, they become more susceptible to the impact of *cybersecurity* attacks and infiltration. Data, intellectual property, business process structure, private customer information, financial reserves and reputation are increasingly at risk through exposure to digital attacks, malware and cyber-crime.

A robust digital and *cybersecurity* strategy is required to replace physical forms of *security*. A recent global survey of IT and *security* professionals engaged in digital transformation, sponsored by Dell [8], highlighted that 98% of the enterprises surveyed were facing challenges securing digital transformation technologies and only 11% were confident about their digital transformation *security* plan. Table 1 depicts the top *security* challenges outlined by the latter white paper [8].

Table 1. Digital transformation security challenges.

1	Need to secure technologies without additional resources
2	Increased risk of security breach
3	Finding a balance between security and employee productivity
4	Reduced control over system access and data
5	Finding the right expertise to support new technologies
6	Security tools not keeping up with changing needs
7	Increased vulnerabilities due to siloed security tools

3 Internet of Things

3.1 Origins of the Internet of Things

Advanced Research Projects Agency Network (ARPANET). Against the background of the implementation, management, and *security* related to cloud computing, Rittinghouse and Ransome [9] explained that in terms of the history of the Advanced Research Projects Agency Network (ARPANET), the decision was taken that the network would be entirely decentralized. No single master computer on the network would act as a central processing point responsible for the sorting and routing of data packets from source to destination. This design resulted in a more complex architecture. However, it also increased resilience over a centralized design. Advanced Research Projects Agency (ARPA) computer sites would be linked together and share the routing of packets [9]. This decision led to the establishment of modern routing and switching techniques for packet switching, forwarding and routing. The project team decided that a dedicated computer would manage routing and switching functions on each local network called an Interface Message Processor (IMP).

In December of 1968, Bolt, Beranek and Newman (BBN) was awarded the contract to build ARPANET's first IMPs, the first of which was delivered in only nine months and installed on August 30, 1969, in the Network Measurements Centre of the University of California at Los Angeles [10]. The second ARPANET node and IMP was installed and connected to an early hypertext system at Stanford Research Institute (SRI) [9]. The third ARPANET node, located at the University of California at Santa Barbara, and the fourth node at the University of Utah, were installed and connected by

December 1969 [11]. The node at the University of Santa Barbara connected to an IBM 360/75, while the node at the University of Utah connected using the Tenex operating system.

3.2   Evolution of IoT and Cognitive Internet

The Combinatorial Effects of Mobile, Transmission Control Protocol (TCP)/ Internet Protocol (IP) and Sensor Technologies. Especially in terms of data *security* and privacy in the Internet of Things environment, Internet connectivity is required, irrespective of fixed (wired) or mobile (wireless) use-cases [12]. The integration of mobile and sensor technology plays an increasingly prevalent role in IoT functional use-cases and solutions. Sensors that are a part of solutions, such as connected vehicles, personal devices, autonomous systems and drones, require fast, reliable and efficient methods of mobile communication [13]. The concept of sensors connecting to other sensors is expanding and providing opportunities to develop a plethora of fixed-to-mobile, fixed-to-fixed and mobile-to-mobile solutions [14].

Content and Information Centric Networking and Communication. Because of the demands of the IoT and mass generation of contextual data and information, Context Centric Networking (CCN), as it develops from concept to reality, is likely to further transform the Internet at an infrastructure level with the addition of new developments in routing, packet forwarding, cipher and *security* technologies [15]. Key differentiators of the CCN approach versus traditional Internet networking and data transfer are the proposed features relating to in-network caching, multi-party communication via smart replication and interaction models that decouple senders and receivers of data and information.

Building on the IoT paradigm, the next section of this paper will focus on reviewing some of the literature surrounding the emergence of Industry 4.0, considered to be the fourth industrial revolution, and Unified Communications and Collaboration technologies, which provides a pathway for cyber-physical integration in a digital world.

4   Industry 4.0

4.1   Challenges to Industry 4.0 Adoption

Challenges for adoption exist in a number of areas, including increased risk of *security*, counterfeiting, data analytics, machine to machine communication, cyber-physical integration and autonomous systems [16].

Security and Counterfeiting: The technology and process innovation that sits at the core of Industry 4.0 has the potential to act as a catalyst in the further enablement of counterfeiting of services and goods. With Industry 4.0 new processes, such as 3D printing and greater leverage of information, shared and contained in digital systems, can be both compromised and harnessed to rapidly duplicate services and products by illicit organisations. Highlights from the *Information Security* Solutions (Europe) 2015 conference, especially related to challenges in anti-counterfeiting, pointed out that protection measures, such as global trust infrastructure for the sharing of IoT data, approaches to robust authentication and verification methods will be required for industry 4.0 and manufacturing [17]. These countermeasures for the reliable transport of industrial data and information are likely, over time, to parallel the systems that are currently employed to protect critical financial transactions and information handled by the banking industry.

5   Research Design and Methodology

A sample group of 2,000 employees, chosen as representative across all GM business functions and regions, were invited to participate in the survey, while twenty-one employees agreed to participate in the interviews. The sample of interview participants again represented a broad mix of enterprise functions, with global and regional remit established within the scope of the study.

Table 2 represents data obtained regarding some of the questions posed to the interview participants, including each of their self-assessed technical proficiency, enterprise function at General Motors, type of function, tenure in role and years in industry. Participants ranged from novice users of technology through to highly experienced.

6   Empirical Research

6.1   Case Study Structure and Timeline

Scope and Timeline. Figure 1 provides a high-level timeline associated with the broader Enhanced Unified Communication and Collaboration (E-UC&C) technologies transformation deployment. Within the course of the GM case study, the limitations of a technology and user deployment strategy with an isolated focus on only UC&C core technology components were identified. In order to establish a fully integrated and scalable framework and technical architecture for UC&C technologies deployment, an enhanced framework, inclusive of dependent and adjacent technology systems (Network Transport, Quality of Service, Session Management, *Cybersecurity*, Telecom Expense Management & Operations), was developed.

6.2   Architectural Framework for Enhanced UC&C (E-UC&C)

Framework Primary Domain Modules (PDMs). The primary domain modules of the E-UC&C framework served as modular reference architectures for service governance, core technology services, service integration and service operation. These modules describe the sub-processes, stakeholders, interfaces and technologies, which were combined to deliver solutions aligned to the broader framework. Adherence to the framework facilitated high degrees of compatibility and re-use of common components, for example, Network Transport, Network Quality of Service, Voice and Video Session Management, Network and Voice *Security*, Video and Voice Transcoding, Change Management and Integrated Cross-Platform Monitoring.

Table 2. Interview participants' demographics.

Proficiency	Enterprise function	Function type	Years in role	Years in industry
Proficient	Facilities	Global	14 months	25
Fairly proficient/know enough	Design	Global	2	32
Proficient	Joint ventures	Regional	2	22
Highly proficient		Global	4	7
Know enough	Finance	Global	2	31
Expert	Manufacturing	Global	4	4
Expert	Sales & marketing	Global	3½	4
Highly proficient	Supply chain	Global	9 months	20
Expert	Real estate	Global	11	20
Highly proficient	Sales & marketing	Global	2	37
Proficient	Legal & HR	Global	3	28
Proficient	Finance & marketing	Global	3½	36
Proficient/know enough	Business operations	Global	1 month	13
Highly proficient	Share services IT	Global	2½	4
Proficient		Global	2	10
Highly proficient	Operations	Global	3 years and 9 months	3 and 9 months
Expert	Security	Global	2	4
Highly proficient	engineering & design	Global	2 weeks	4
Expert	Shared services IT	Global	3	4
Highly proficient	Human resources	Global	1 year 6 months	4
Know enough	Design/manufacturing	Regional	2 years 3 months	33½

6.3 Deployed Framework

Core Governance Domain. Please note that since the Core Governance Domain did not particularly relate to *security* issues, it is not discussed in any detail in this paper. Further details can, however, be accessed in Bolton, Goosen and Kritzinger [18].

Operational Management Domain. The Operational Management Domain aligns to the horizontal processes that facilitate system operation, delivered via four integrated modules. The four primary domains specified governance and processes that facilitated tactical delivery and coordination of individual initiatives and programs. Ever-green processes designed for driving end user adoption and *security* compliance and assurance, and supporting end user service and infrastructure operations, were also specified.

In the preliminary framework, design *security* was inferred within the **Integrated Feature Domain**, broadly aligned with the individually specified technology modules.

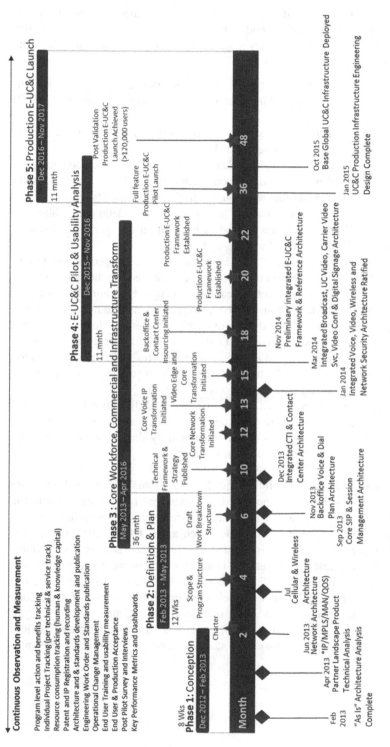

Fig. 1. High-level timeline and milestone summary – GM case study.

As the framework was deployed, the necessity for a dedicated module to provide focus on *security*, data loss protection and risk management were identified. The primary drivers for abstraction of the *security* requirements into a dedicated module in the final iteration of the production framework included:

- Enterprise drivers at a corporate level driving higher standards of policy specification and compliance associated with Data Retention and Loss Protection (DRLP) and *cybersecurity*.
- The need to bolster risk management, *cybersecurity* and data loss protection via defined *security* policy and auditable control processes.
- Identification of new sources of potential data loss risk and data retention strategies, because of the introduction of new digital communication services, such as Instant Messaging with integrated file and application sharing functionality.
- Identification that *security* and data risk and management definition within the Integrated Feature Domain modules tended to be focused on specific technology applications versus having a broad system-wide focus.
- The shift to a broader system-wide focused module within the production framework. The transformation of communication via a digital medium did not result in a 1:1 translation of old ways of communicating to a digital version. Messier [19] highlighted how the digitally transformed communication features of UC had increased the adoption of IP-based communication systems. Messier [19] also suggested that risk assessments were required to facilitate better decision making relating to technology selection and adoption. Architectures and solutions provided a broader integrated end state, which integrated chat with rich real-time video, file sharing, application sharing and voice communication. More data was stored electronically and digitally mediated. In Europe, Wong [20] argued that mandated *security* processes and policies were required to minimize data *security* breaches, as the level of electronically stored information created by the transition to digitally mediated technologies and communication increased.

Integrated Feature Domain. The Integrated Feature Domain contained the core technologies associated with features accessed and leveraged by end users within the scope of the communication solution. These features directly aligned with functionality that was embedded directly within technologies, such as the UC&C client (Skype for GM), video collaboration suites and integrated contact centre advisor applications. Technologies within the Integrated Feature Domain modules were specified at the application layer and applied in specific technologies for leverage by end users. For example, Instant Messaging and chat were delivered in multiple forms of standalone and embedded presentation to the end users, such as Contact Centre chat and Skype chat. However, these systems relied on shared services from the **Unified Services Domain** for integration and the provision of standard services, like routing, transport and *security* controls.

Figure 3 in [18] depicts a functional architecture proposed to articulate the primary technology service categories and specific technologies engaged in the delivery of a feature-rich, UC&C technologies digital transformation platform. This functional architecture built on the concepts and foundational UC&C technologies model proposed by Reimer and Taing [21], with the addition of modules and technologies associated with "security, service management and federated extensibility" [18, p. 6]. The enhanced functional architecture was leveraged as a basis for the core modules included in the GM framework. The framework was not restricted to the inclusion of specific technologies and had the flexibility to be adapted to expand or contract as the needs of the enterprise that it was applied to changed.

The adapted model also includes an expansion from the framework proposed by Rogers [22], through the inclusion of a module associated with data protection and *security* being added in consideration of recent Global Data Protection Regulation (GDPR) and *cybersecurity* priorities within industry.

Unified Services Domain. Specification and development of the Unified Services Domain structure were influenced by the distributed product realization environment [23] and eXtensible Distributed Product Realization framework proposed by Choi, Panchal, Allen, Rosen and Mistree [24]. Nakajima, Ishikawa and Tokunaga [25] highlighted the challenges of integrating complex enterprise networks and existing systems, such as corporate billing systems, with ubiquitous computing and communication systems. The challenges that Nakajima et al. [25] addressed in their proposed InterUbicomp framework showed significant parallels to the challenges encountered when developing an enterprise scale, digitally transformed, multi-modal and medium solution architecture. These challenges included heterogeneous service integration, context-aware embedded services, application specific networking, environmentally embedded devices, peer-to-peer communication, service survivability and *security*.

7 Results and Interpretation

The results from the current state assessment summarized in Fig. 2 were used as a reference asset for the development of the transformation architecture and resulting E-UC&C technologies framework reviewed in Sect. 6, as well as a transformation repository and architecture assessment process. Within each layer, the current state technical architectural components were summarized, along with pre-transformation limitations established from legacy baseline operational metrics and enterprise stakeholder feedback. Figure 2 presents the grid with the Instant Messaging and Textual Collaboration layer highlighted.

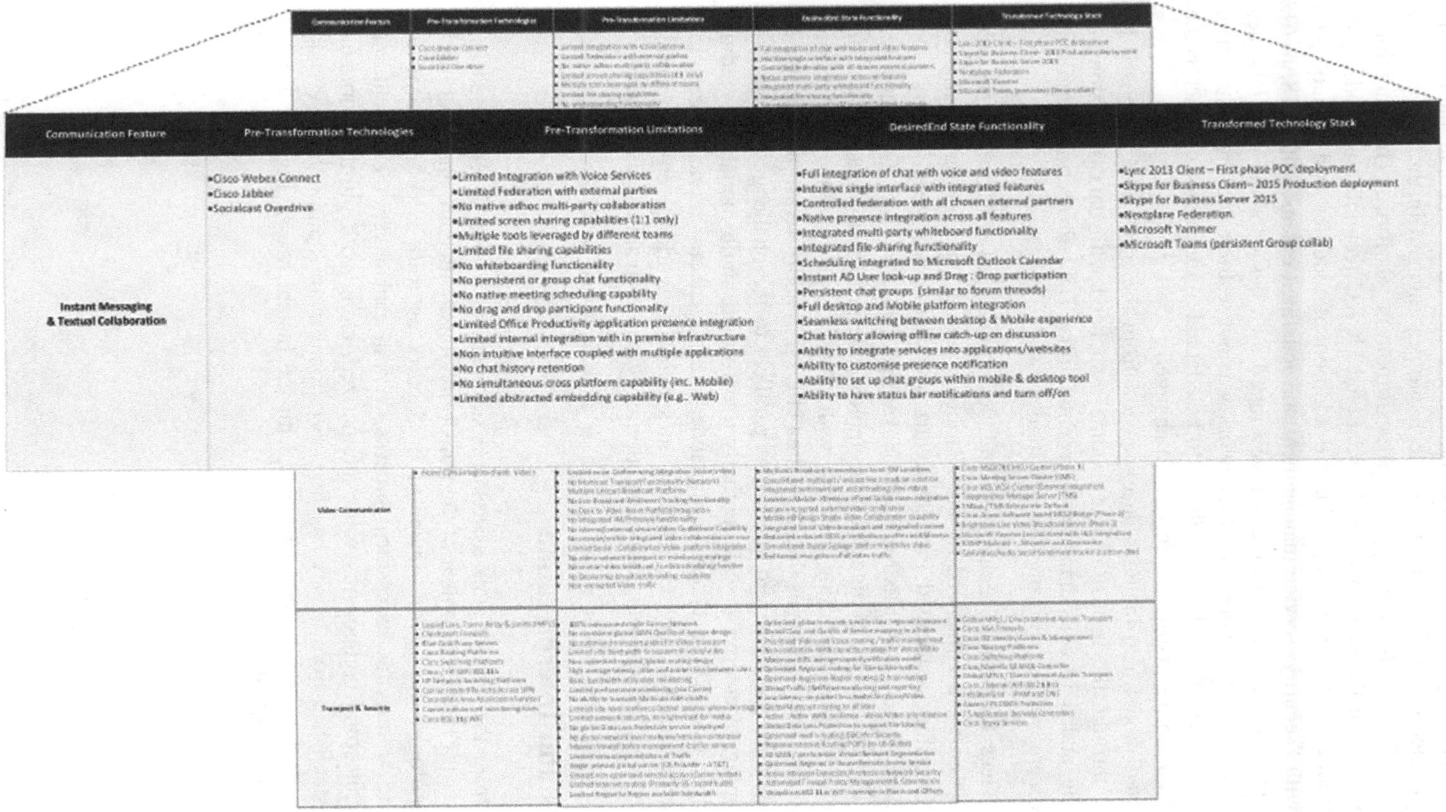

Fig. 2. Technology and service transformation grid.

7.1 Impact on Productivity

Digitally Transformed Multi-channel Persona Capabilities Facilitated Through a Consolidated Software Client Impact the Perception of Increased Productivity in Individuals. Findings from the research indicated that digitally transformation established via UC&C technologies and systems facilitated opportunities for users to establish and maintain changing work practices and relationships with colleagues and enterprise partners. Relationship building was enhanced and enabled through the facility of a virtual team and peer engagement. The research data showed that users perceived the ability to flexibly escalate communication through different levels and modes of communication to assist in the building of relationships through rich information sharing in a virtual workspace. Findings within the study also displayed that the consolidated features within the UC&C client, combined with the easy to use and adopt interface, resulted in many users establishing increased enterprise efficiency and changing work practices.

A small number of users reported having some difficulty in easily using and adopting or changing work practices to the UC&C technologies; however, they still reported these technologies as having the potential to impact their productivity. After being introduced to the digital technologies and UC&C features, most users preferred to keep their 'new' technologies, leading to legacy reduction and elimination. Users described the digital technologies as increasing the convenience and speed of their communication processes through the UC&C client, as a result of finding access to all of the features in one technology. The convenience and speed benefits of having one technology to access multiple channels for communication, both within the office and remotely, when travelling or at home, is likely to be associated with end users' perception of impact on productivity. The more convenience and speed are involved in doing something and/or executing a task, the more productive users are when executing the task.

Digitally Transformed Social Presence and Real-Time Status Indicators Positively Impact the Perception of Increased Productivity in Individual and Team Performance. Findings indicated that the virtual persona and presence established by the end users had a positive effect on personal productivity, as it increased the opportunity to engage in real-time collaboration when needed. Feedback from end users further showed that digital presence indicators were useful in identifying other users or groups, who may be available for immediate ad-hoc communication and engagement.

Also, it is likely that the custom presence indicators helped to set a baseline expectation for the requesting party in establishing the probable timeframe for response. For example, when a user is in an ad-hoc or scheduled meeting, that user's presence and status will be set to busy, indicating that the user is already engaged in collaboration or work of some form. When a user is presenting using their laptop or PC, the presence indicator is set to presenting, and blocks instant messaging pop-ups for the requested user, setting the expectation that an immediate response is unlikely to occur. It is likely that users reporting their experience of the UC&C technologies as having the effect of removing the sense of distance with their peers and partners was tied to the presence indicators, as they get real-time status views of their colleagues' location and engagement status. This status developed an arguable perception of virtual presence.

Users can additionally place commentary on what their current or planned daily activities are in the 'what's happening today' field of the UC&C client, further establishing the digital presence and persona.

7.2   Impact on Innovation

Digitally Transformed UC&C Technologies Can Impact Engagement in Innovation Generating Activities Across the Global Automotive Enterprise Value Chain. Four factors relating to innovation was identified within the study, which are related to changing work practices, collaboration, creativity and generating savings.

Users reported that the digitally transformed UC&C technologies led to changing work practices and impacted their ability to engage in collaboration. Users also found that multi-channel features facilitated richer virtual engagements and supported creative engagement, even when users were remote from each other. In their creativity processes, the ability to engage in an ad-hoc collaboration, as needed, helped users capitalize when they had ideas, or needed problems and questions quickly addressed. Engagement, which increased enterprise efficiency through the digitally transformed UC&C technologies, also increased speed-to-action creative thoughts or tasks. It is reasonable to assume that the convenience and speed of engagement offered by the UC&C technologies helped to maintain convenience and speed in creative collaboration, tied to innovation generation, such as sharing and working through new ideas, or rapidly developing plans and proof of concepts.

The factor related to convenience and speed of the UC&C technologies is likely to align with the changing work practices that the users reported. Users' changing work practices reflected the capabilities of the UC&C technologies and digitally transformed methods. Easy to use and adopt technologies, combined with positive results from convenient and speedy engagement, in a context of desired- versus restricted-schedule, lead users to positively associate these technologies with supporting their innovation and creativity processes. Many users identified generating savings associated with leveraging the digitally transformed UC&C technologies within their changing work practices and this is likely due to users seeing the generation of innovation as an asset to the enterprise. Innovation leads to new products, or product enhancement, and ultimately higher margins and revenue. If the users can engage and drive more innovation through digitally transformed technologies, or speed up innovation generation, the enterprise will benefit financially.

7.3   Impact via Digital Transformation Through UC&C Technologies

Digital transformation achieved through UC&C technologies results in increased inclusion and engagement of individuals and teams across the global automotive enterprise. Evaluation of the end user survey and interviews supported a view that communication delivered through the digital transformation of technologies enhanced the ability of people and groups towards engagement and collaboration. Findings from the research data show that users reported a positive experience aligned with leverage of the multi-channel communication features associated with UC&C technologies. Through the use of these features, users reported that it was easier to engage and collaborate efficiently with virtual teams. Users described the ability to engage in ad-hoc meetings with peers and virtual teams and obtaining answers to questions quickly.

These observations contrast with the reduction and elimination of legacy communication methods that required face-to-face communication to facilitate information exchange at any level beyond audio conference or basic slide sharing using external technologies. Users also described positive attitudes relating to the ability to engage personally with peers and partners when working in remote locations. The new digitally transformed capabilities made it easier to include other parties in media-rich virtual meetings and facilitate their direct participation. Tracking of feature-use across regions and room-to-room telepresence engagements supported the view of increased cross region and function engagement, inferring a high level of inclusion of people in virtual meetings outside of their local workplace locations.

8   Discussion and Conclusion

The purpose of this paper was to focus on the *security* aspects related to digital transformation, implemented through UC&C technologies, which impact productivity and innovation within a global automotive enterprise. Some of these included e.g. the *security* challenges to enterprise digital transformation, the *security* of the Internet of Things, and challenges to Industry 4.0 adoption, including increased risks related to *security* and counterfeiting. The research design and methodology incorporated e.g. a survey of IT and *security* professionals.

In terms of the structure, scope and timeline of the case study used in the empirical research, the enhanced framework was inclusive of dependent and adjacent technology systems, including e.g. *cybersecurity*. Adherence to the architectural framework for E-UC&C and PDMs facilitated high degrees of compatibility and re-use of common components, for example, Network and Voice *Security*. With regard to the Operational Management Domain in the deployed framework, ever-green processes designed for e.g. driving end user adoption and *security* compliance and assurance were specified. In the preliminary framework, design *security* was inferred within the Integrated Feature Domain, broadly aligned with the individually specified technology modules. Several systems relied on shared services from the Unified Services Domain for integration and the provision of standard services, like routing, transport and *security* controls.

Finally, the transformation grid presented as part of the results and interpretation section focused on four core layers, including Transport and *Security*.

A theory of enhancement through the lens of a UC&C technologies model and meta-framework for digital transformation have been analysed. The meta-framework and theoretical transformation model align to an enhanced UC&C technologies architecture. An empirical study focusing on the effects of the proposed E-UC&C technologies meta-framework and theoretical model for digital transformation was carried out – this involved a multi-year single subject case study of the General Motors global automotive enterprise. General Motors incorporated the E-UC&C meta-framework and theoretical model in their corporate strategy for Industry 4.0. E-UC&C technologies were adopted and applied to guide digital transformation for employees within that initiative. Analysis of the employee adoption rates, feature-use and experiential observation strongly suggest that digital transformation, delivered through a holistic framework for E-UC&C technologies, can have a positive impact on employee productivity.

If applied through a holistic framework including UC&C technologies, digital transformation can also impact an enterprise's opportunities towards generating savings and innovation, as well as increased enterprise efficiency, contributing positively to market differentiation. Further research is suggested to evaluate the application of the meta-framework and associated theories of digital transformation through UC&C technologies to other industries and enterprises experiencing business model digitization.

References

1. Dahabiyeh, L.: The security of internet of things: current state and future directions. In: Themistocleous, M., Morabito, V. (eds.) EMCIS 2017. LNBIP, vol. 299, pp. 414–420. Springer, Cham (2017). https://doi.org/10.1007/978-3-319-65930-5_33
2. Holler, J., Tsiatsis, V., Mulligan, C., Karnouskos, S., Boyle, D.: From Machine to Machine to the Internet of Things: Introduction to a New Age of Intelligence. Academic Press Inc, Orlando (2014)
3. Sendler, U.: The Internet of Things: Industrie 4.0 Unleashed. Springer, Heidelberg (2016). https://doi.org/10.1007/978-3-662-54904-9
4. Vasilomanolakis, E., Daubert, J., Luthra, M., Gazis, V., Wiesmaier, A., Kikras, P.: On the security and privacy of internet of things architectures and systems. In: International Workshop on Secure Internet of Things (SIoT) (2015)
5. Wolf, G.: New challenges of the digital transformation: the comeback of the vision-mission system. In: Klewes, J., Popp, D., Rost-Hein, M. (eds.) Out-thinking Organizational Communications. MP, pp. 113–128. Springer, Cham (2017). https://doi.org/10.1007/978-3-319-41845-2_9
6. Digital Enlightment Forum: Security for the Digital World Within an Ethical Framework. IOS Press, Amsterdam (2016)
7. Brush, K.: The Power of One: You're The Boss. CreateSpace Independent Publishing Platform, Scotts Valley (2012)
8. Dimensional Research, Digital Transformation - A Survey of IT and Security Professionals. https://software.dell.com/whitepaper/global-survey-digital-transformation-security-survey81 13164, last accessed 2016/10/21
9. Rittinghouse, J., Ransome, J.: Cloud Computing: Implementation, Management, and Security. CRC Press, Boca Raton (2016)
10. Poole, H., Lambert, L., Woodford, C., Moschovitis, C.: The Internet: a Historical Encyclopedia, vol. 1. ABC-Clio, Santa Barbara (2005)
11. Weber, S.: The Internet. Infobase Publishing, New York (2003)
12. Varadharajan, V., Bansal, S.: Data security and privacy in the internet of things (IoT) environment. In: Mahmood, Z. (ed.) Connectivity Frameworks for Smart Devices. CCN, pp. 261–281. Springer, Cham (2016). https://doi.org/10.1007/978-3-319-33124-9_11
13. Mavromoustakis, C., Mastorakis, G., Batalla, J.: Internet of Things (IoT) in 5G Mobile Technologies. Springer, New York (2016). https://doi.org/10.1007/978-3-319-30913-2
14. Slama, D., Puhlmann, F., Morrish, J., Bhatnagar, R.: Enterprise IoT: Strategies and Best Practices for Connected Products and Services. O'Reilly Media, Sebastopol (2015)

15. Guimaraes, P., et al.: Experimenting content-centric networks in the future internet testbed environment. In: IEEE International Conference on Communications Workshops (ICC), pp. 1383–1387 (2013)
16. Kagermann, H., Anderl, R., Gausemeier, J., Schuh, G., Wahlster, W.: Industrie 4.0 in a Global Context: Strategies for Cooperating with International Partners. Herbert Utz Verlag, Munich (2016)
17. Thiel, C.: Industry 4.0 - challenges in anti-counterfeiting. In: Reimer, H. (ed.) ISSE 2015: Highlights of the Information Security Solutions Europe 2015 Conference, pp. 111–119. Springer, New York (2015). https://doi.org/10.1007/978-3-658-10934-9_10
18. Bolton, A., Goosen, L., Kritzinger, E.: Enterprise digitization enablement through unified communication and collaboration. In: Proceedings of the Annual Conference of the South African Institute of Computer Scientists and Information Technologists, Johannesburg (2016)
19. Messier, R.: Collaboration with Cloud Computing: Security, Social Media and Unified Communication. Elsevier, London (2014)
20. Wong, R.: Data Security Breaches and Privacy in Europe. Springer, London (2013)
21. Reimer, K., Taing, S.: Unified communications. Bus. Inf. Syst. Eng. 1(4), 326–330 (2009)
22. Rogers, E.: Diffusion of Innovations, 4th edn. The Free Press, New York (2010)
23. Gerhard, J., Rosen, D., Allen, J., Mistree, F.: A distributed product realization environment for design and manufacturing. J. Comput. Inf. Sci. Eng. 1(3), 235–244 (2001)
24. Choi, H.-J., Panchal, J., Allen, J., Rosen, D., Mistree, F.: Towards a standardized engineering framework for distributed, collaborative product realization. In: Proceedings of the ASME Design Engineering Technical Conference (DETC 2003), pp. 1–11 (2003)
25. Nakajima, T., Ishikawa, H., Tokunaga, E.: Technology challenges for building Internet-scale ubiquitous computing. In: Proceedings of the Seventh IEEE International Workshop on Object-Oriented Real-Time Dependable Systems (2002)

A Descriptive Review and Classification of Organizational Information Security Awareness Research

Gershon Hutchinson[1] and Jacques Ophoff[1,2(✉)] [iD]

[1] University of Cape Town, Cape Town, South Africa
HTCGER001@myuct.ac.za, jacques.ophoff@uct.ac.za
[2] Abertay University, Dundee, UK
j.ophoff@abertay.ac.uk

Abstract. Information security awareness (ISA) is a vital component of information security in organizations. The purpose of this research is to descriptively review and classify the current body of knowledge on ISA. A sample of 59 peer-reviewed academic journal articles, which were published over the last decade from 2008 to 2018, were analyzed. Articles were classified using coding techniques from the grounded theory literature-review method. The results show that ISA research is evolving with behavioral research studies still being explored. Quantitative empirical research is the dominant methodology and the top three theories used are general deterrence theory, theory of planned behavior, and protection motivation theory. Future research could focus on qualitative approaches to provide greater depth of ISA understanding.

Keywords: Organizational information security awareness · Literature review

1 Introduction

Information security is still a cause of significant concern for modern organizations despite the variety of technological solutions developed to combat this problem [1] as the literature repeatedly stresses that humans are the weakest link in the information security chain [2, 3]. Information systems (IS) and organizations require the interactions of humans to exist. Humans build systems; humans use networks and services; humans manage organizations; organizations render services to humans; humans attack IS and organizations and not computing devices. With the impact that humans have on organizations and IT, it should be of no surprise the effect humans can have on information security [4].

Information security ensures business continuity and limits the impact of security incidents which can harm the organization [5]. The importance of human behavior in the context of information security has been recognized [e.g. 6, 7], particularly regarding user compliance to organizational information security policies (ISPs) [8, 9]. ISA is a vital component of information security [10, 11] and consists of general knowledge of information security and cognizance of organizational ISP awareness [9]. Information security challenges can be managed more successfully when the human factor is considered in combination with technological solutions [12].

© Springer Nature Switzerland AG 2020
H. Venter et al. (Eds.): ISSA 2019, CCIS 1166, pp. 114–130, 2020.
https://doi.org/10.1007/978-3-030-43276-8_9

This research aims to descriptively review and classify the current body of knowledge on organizational ISA research to answer the question: *What is the current state of organizational information security awareness research?* Okoli and Schabram [13] argue that literature reviews, per se, can constitute valuable and original work and it can be a starting point for individuals interested in a specific topic. An interpretive research stance was taken, with an inductive approach used to analyze secondary data and identified themes and patterns from the data.

The remainder of this paper is organized as follows: Sect. 2 reviews ISA key concepts and the extant literature in general. In Sect. 3, the research methodology is presented where the approach, philosophy, and methodologies used to carry out the research is explained. The classification and descriptive review provide a detailed analysis of the data in Sect. 4, and in Sect. 5, a discussion on the findings is presented. Finally, the conclusion summarizes the key findings, describes the practical implications, and provides recommendations for future research.

2 Background

ISA is a vital component of an effective information security management program [14]. Kruger and Kearney [15] state that the primary objective of ISA is to ensure that individuals are conscious of threats related to the use of IT and comply with the organization's policies and procedures. This definition recognizes a cognitive state of mind whereby the user's perception concerning secure information practices within the organization is pertinent and framed by ISPs [6]. Bulgurcu et al. [9] note that to have ISA, you should not only be information security conscious (understand that passwords are a necessary precaution) but also ISP conscious (understand the organizational requirements for passwords).

Due to its social nature, there is no general approach, definition, or method to ISA [16, 17]. Many studies consider ISA to be a cognitive state of mind which knows and understands information security risks, threats, organizational processes, policies, security objectives [9, 10, 18]. Bulgurcu et al. [9] and Parsons et al. [3] define ISA as the staff's cognizance of information security and ISPs of their organization. Rhee et al. [19] define ISA as alertness in understanding the different security threats and one's exposure to these threats, which contrasts with Tsohou et al. [20] who consider the procedural aspect to ISA, i.e. the process required to achieve secure information practices. One can define ISA as a process which changes user perceptions, behavior, norms, habits, attitudes and organizational culture and structure towards information security practices [21].

Defining a measurable criterion for a security conscious person is an important and challenging component for assessing ISA [11]. Based on the above definitions of ISA, we define ISA as an individual's general knowledge of information security and cognizance of their organization's ISPs. This definition is suitable as it contains both a cognitive state of mind where users know and understand the security mission of their organization [9] and the importance and significance of information security [3].

2.1   Measuring Information Security Awareness

IT has evolved to a point where actual behavioral monitoring of individuals is possible. However, researchers still find it difficult to conduct such studies due to factors such as company buy-in, legal ramifications, and community relations [7]. Most studies on ISA therefore use self-reporting measures, such as surveys, to measure perceptions of risk. The advantages of self-reporting measures are that they are easy to develop, distribute, and analyze. The disadvantages are that they are prone to demand effects and well-known biases such as demand bias, common methods bias, subjectivity bias, and social desirability bias [22].

2.2   Information Security Awareness Antecedents

Organizations recognize that staff can either be a risk or an asset in the fight against information security threats [9]. Awareness remains a vital issue of information security. Increasing individuals ISA through training and awareness programs could lead to safer technology use. However, such solutions are often overlooked by organizations [23]. Tsohou et al. [24] conclude that training and awareness programs are not efficient due to inadequate investments by organizations. Khan et al. [25] mention several recommended solutions which can be used to improve ISA such as computer-based training, video games, newsletters, information sessions, posters, and messages. They consider group discussion as the most effective method for measuring ISA as it enables two-way communication whereby each user can share experiences and knowledge.

Individual Antecedents. This level focuses on factors originating from the individual. Individuals with higher levels of ISA usually had prior security training or has a higher level of education [9]. Haeussinger and Kranz [16] noted that previous negative experiences with information security, such as malware or phishing attacks, are also likely to increase individuals' levels of ISA.

Organizational Antecedents. This level focuses on factors originating from the organization. This includes formalization of work procedures which identifies that security awareness controls exist and heightens individuals ISA [21]. Top management support is a crucial factor in ensuring staff compliance with ISPs [26] and organizational culture change [27]. Merete Hagen et al. [28] exclusively looked at non-technological solutions for information security and found ISPs to be a vital and critical component for the success of these solutions. The importance of ISPs has been established by several sources [9, 29, 30]. Another crucial antecedent is awareness campaigns such as security education, training and awareness (SETA) programs which strengthen individuals ISA [31]. SETA programs ensure the sustainability of ISPs by educating individuals of their importance and necessary precautions [29]. Other solutions include procedures [32], guidelines [29], campaigns, incentive programs [33], and fear appeals [34].

2.3   Theoretical Perspectives

Studies on behavior have stemmed from the disciplines of psychology and sociology which have been used and adapted by criminology. Information security researchers have often adapted criminology theories [35, 36] for investigating information security [e.g. 6, 25]. Reasons to use behavioral theories include a more profound consideration and understanding of the behavior problem and solutions to address the problem [6]. However, the main aim of behavioral research in information security is to understand why only specific individuals adhere to organizational ISPs [36]. Lebek et al. [36] conducted a theory-based review of security awareness in behavioral research and identified 54 theories. Below, the three most used theories in ISA research are summarized.

General Deterrence Theory. General Deterrence Theory (GDT) in relation to information security comes from the discipline of criminology, which is used as a deterrent mechanism by heightening the perceived threat of penalties or punishments for IS misuse [29]. Classic deterrence theory posits that individuals will be deterred from illicit acts with greater certainty, severity, and celerity of sanctions [37].

Theory of Planned Behavior. A literature review conducted by Sommestad et al. [38] and Lebek et al. [36] on contributing factors of security compliance and information security behavior, found the Theory of Planned Behavior (TPB) to be the most used theory by researchers. TPB is an extension of the Theory of Reasoned Action (TRA), and posits that human behavior is moved by three forms of beliefs: behavioral, normative, and control. Humans are prepared to behave a certain way if it is favorable unto them or if they perceive social pressure from important others. The necessary extension of TPB would be the perception of control over the behavior [39, 40]. In addition, if humans assess behavior as positive (attitude), or they believe that influential others would like them to perform the behavior (subjective norms) this should lead to higher intentions and they would be inclined to perform a behavior [41].

Protection Motivation Theory. Protection Motivation Theory (PMT) originated in health psychology and explains the coping procedure towards possible threats by considering various protective behaviors [36]. There are two main parts to the theory: threat appraisal and coping appraisal. Threat appraisal relates to the individual's assessment of risk for misuse of IS. Perceived vulnerability and perceived severity are the two main components of threat appraisal. The coping appraisal is the individual's ability to deal with the potential threat or risk [42].

3   Methodology

An interpretive approach was used for this study as the purpose of this research was to review and classify the literature. Interpretive research starts with the assumption that access to reality is shaped by social construction such as shared meanings, language and consciousness [43]. The research attempted to make sense of the publications being reviewed by analyzing secondary data and identified themes and patterns from the data.

King and He [44] state that there are four main approaches to reviewing literature namely, narrative review, descriptive review, vote-counting, and meta-analysis. The purpose of a descriptive review is to explore the literature to find propositions and interpretable patterns in data. The descriptive review is positioned on the qualitative-quantitative continuum and an appropriate method for achieving the research objective.

The descriptive review's main component is qualitative. However, quantitative elements are present in specific processes, e.g. statistical analysis [44].

3.1 Grounded Theory Literature-Review Method

The research strategy followed a five-stage approach, referred to as the Grounded Theory Literature-Review Method (GTLRM), developed by Wolfswinkel et al. [45]. While this is not a grounded theory study, aspects of the grounded theory method were used in the coding and classification process.

The first (Define) stage of the GTLRM consists of the inclusion and exclusion criteria, as well as the scope of the review for articles in the data set. In step one, the criteria for inclusion or exclusion of articles is defined, such as determining a time frame for the publication, as an example, the last five years. In step two appropriate research fields are stipulated, step three involves the selection of appropriate database sources, and in step four the possible search terms, methods, and criteria are identified.

The second (Search) stage consists of the search process using the criteria defined in the first stage. The search process can be long and tedious, with possible outcomes ranging from many to few. It may transpire that specific synonyms required to complete the search are missing and that the first stage needs to be revisited. New search terms may possibly be found during this process. Documentation of searches, sources used, and results is important for the transparency and replicability of the study.

In the third (Select) stage, qualifying sample articles get selected. This process involves the removal of duplicates and confirming that the selected articles meet the requirements. This can be accomplished by reviewing the title, abstract, introduction, full text and by executing a forward and backward citation for additional articles. If new articles are found the process is repeated.

The fourth (Analyze) stage is where the fundamental principles of grounded theory are implemented. The researcher starts reading articles individually and performs three steps of coding in a systematic process. The three stages of coding which is used are open, axial and selective coding. Open coding utilizes a bird's eye view of the data collected to abstract high-level classes from sets of variables or concepts. This can be in the form of a word, statement or paragraph. Next, axial coding identifies the interrelationships between categories and their subcategories. Finally, the categories identified will be integrated and refined in the selective coding process; categories and subcategories can evolve during the reading and analyses of excerpts.

Finally, the fifth (Present) stage, presents the research findings and the documented steps taken to acquire these findings. This empirical data can be exhibited using various methods such as diagrams, tables, graphical representations.

3.2 Sampling and Data Collection

This study utilized theoretical sampling, which is a form of purposive sampling. Theoretical sampling pursues theoretical lines of enquiry for the identification of core themes, relationships or processes on which to focus the research. Theoretical saturation occurs when the collected and analyzed data stops producing new properties which are relevant to a category and where the relationships among classes have been verified [46].

For practical purposes the sample range was over a period of ten years, ranging from 2008 to 2018. Initially, this research study was restricted to the basket of 8 IS journal databases which are listed by the Association for Information Systems. However, due to an insufficient number of articles which were found in the journal databases, the search source criteria had to be amended. The inclusion of two specialized information security journals namely, 'Computers & Security' and 'Information & Computer Security' were added to the list of AIS basket of eight journals as this was not only an IS study but also an information security study and these journals contained relevant articles on the topic. 'Information Management & Computer Security' or 'Information & Computer Security' was selected as it is listed in the Google Scholar Top 20 publications for information security, and it was from an IS field. 'Computers & Security' is a highly ranked information security journal in Google Scholar and SCImago Journal & Country Rank.

Only peer-reviewed academic journals were considered for this research. Non-peer-reviewed articles, publications not written in English, books, working papers or conference proceedings were excluded. Articles which were not in an organizational setting (such as home users) or only marginally included ISA (such as studies focused on specific systems such as email, BYOD, or malware) were excluded. The pre-defined search terms that were used to conduct the literature search for relevant articles were: Information Security Awareness, awareness program, security education, information security cognizance, information security behavior, information security knowledge, security awareness. The search terms were split, combined and the use of Boolean operators was used under the search options of the journal databases. Table 1 lists the journal databases used, and total articles found in the initial search.

Table 1. Journal database and initial search count

Journal database	Initial search count
Journal of Information Technology	341
Journal of Association for Information Systems	107
European Journal of Information Systems	684
Journal of Strategic Information Systems	70
Journal of Management Information Systems	530
Information Systems Research	799
Information Systems Journal	333
MIS Quarterly	469
Computers & Security	688
Information & Computer Security	532

A total of 4553 articles were found. Using the select stage of the GTLRM and the exclusion criteria above, the final sample was brought down to 59 articles which were used for the data analysis.

3.3 Analysis

The coding methods from stage four of the GTLRM was used to analyze the sample collected. The first step was open coding, which utilizes a bird's eye view of the data collected to abstract high-level classes from sets of variables or concepts. In the next step, axial coding was used to identify the interrelationship between categories and their subcategories. The categories identified was integrated and refined in the selective coding process [45]. NVivo 12 Pro was the Computer-Aided Qualitative Data Analysis Software (CAQDAS) used to assist with the analysis process. The collected sample was added to the NVivo project, and the data was analyzed, classified and developed into themes.

4 Classification and Descriptive Review

The classification and descriptive review consists of two sections. First, a detailed breakdown of the classification framework which was developed through the analysis process is provided. Second, a further breakdown of the articles and categories are explored in the descriptive review.

4.1 Classification

A classification framework was developed through the analysis process of open, axial and selective coding as recommended by Wolfswinkel et al. [45]. The rereading of articles ensured the effectiveness and relevancy of the framework. Themes and categories were highlighted and extracted from the articles which have also led to the formation of subthemes and subcategories.

The results of the analyses' resulted in four top-level categories and eight subcategories. The top-level categories which were developed from the full-text review of the 59 articles are 'Behavior', 'Antecedents', 'ISP' and 'Theory Development'. The 'Behavior' category focuses on the behavior of insiders within the organization, while the 'Antecedents' category looks at how individuals and organizations can increase or improve their levels of ISA. The 'ISP' category focuses on the compliance and violations of ISPs within the organization. 'Theory Development' use existing theories, extends theories or proposes new theories, frameworks or technologies to improve or understand behavior.

The subcategories were derived by assigning individual articles according to their specific research interest. Many of the themes and views expressed in the articles were similar, and it is more than likely that articles could contribute to more than one subcategory. However, by utilizing only one subcategory for each article, the classification of the main categories and subcategories of ISA Research is simplified, structured and the relationships between the two are conceptualized.

Behavior. This category focuses on the human attributes of the individual/s towards secure information security practices within the organization. These attributes can consist of perceptions, attitudes, behavior, knowledge, work habits and values [47]. The success or failure of the organization's approach to information security ultimately lies in the way employees conduct themselves [48, 49].

Analysis. This subcategory covers articles focusing on research studies attempting to understand the behavior of individuals. The motivation behind the behavior of Individuals towards secure information security practices can vary from individual to individual, and there seems to be no one-size-fits-all approach to address the problem currently. Öıütçü et al. [50] used data collected from surveys to rate behavior on a four-scale system, which are: Risk Perception Scale (RPS), Exposure to Offence Scale (EOS), Conservative Behavior Scale (CBS) and Risky Behavior Scale (RBS). Snyman and Kruger [51] exploratory investigation found behavioral threshold analysis to be feasible for constructing ISA programs.

Culture. The articles listed in this subcategory focuses on the habitual practice of doing things by the organizations and its individuals. The way things are done around here is the common theme found in the articles about organizational culture [48, 52]. The way things are done around here to protect organizational information assets is the common theme to describe information security culture [48, 53, 54]. Da Veiga and Martins [55] state that organizations with a strong security culture have higher compliance with ISPs and regulatory requirements by employees.

Future Research Areas. This subcategory consists of two articles which discuss future directions for information security behavioral research. Crossler et al. [7] found that future research should focus on: separating insider deviant behavior from insider misbehavior; behavioral research; approaches to understand cyberattacks and to improve ISP compliance.

Antecedents. This category contains articles which focus on ways in which organizations can increase or improve their levels and the levels of their employees ISA. The effectiveness of information security requires the participation and commitment of all parties [28].

Non-technological. This subcategory has the highest article count and provides non-technological solutions to prevent Information Security threats or improve ISA. The human element within the organization is the central theme. Adequate SETA programs are the most effective non-technological solution for both staff and the organization [31, 55, 56].

Information Security Policies. Articles in this category focus on the compliance and non-compliance of ISPs and covers how ISP effectiveness can be achieved or increased. Theories used in criminology, social psychology and other related disciplines are referenced extensively for testing user ISP compliance/non-compliance [9, 34, 57, 58]. Many techniques used by security managers are listed such as SETA programs [29], guidelines and policies [9]. Other techniques such as positive reinforcement strategy (reward), negative enforcement strategy (punishment) [57] and campaigns [33] were also used.

Compliance. This subcategory examines approaches for ensuring ISP compliance. It looks at various strategies for management to consider such as stick vs carrot approach [57]. Sommestad et al. [38] conducted a review of 29 quantitative studies dealing with individual ISP compliance/non-compliance and found that factors such as self-efficacy, subjective norms, response cost, perceived severity and certainty of sanctions can be used to identify compliant behavior. Perceived severity of security breaches, perceived probability [30] and habits are also antecedents of ISP compliance [58].

Violation. This subcategory contains articles discussing the non-compliance of ISPs by staff. Like the compliance subcategory above, researchers try to understand the rationale behind information security policy violations. Findings reveal that employees are not the same and that individuals have different reactions to information security interventions [34].

Theory Development. This category consists of articles which use existing, extends, or proposes new theories, frameworks or technologies to improve our understand employee behavior.

Application of Existing Theory. The articles listed in this in this subcategory use existing theories or technologies to understand, explain or deter behavioral traits. Thomson and van Niekerk [59] use goal-setting theory from social sciences to encourage employees to contribute to good information security practices.

Advancement in Research. This subcategory contains the second largest article count dealing with new or extended theories, frameworks or technologies. Johnston et al. [33] created an Enhanced Fear Appeal Rhetorical Framework as they felt that the current fear appeal rhetorical framework was inadequate. Liang and Xue [49] developed the Technology Threat Avoidance Theory (TTAT) to understand users' IT threat avoidance behavior using elements from cybernetic theory and coping theory.

4.2   Descriptive Review

The map in Fig. 1 displays the article count by the first author's country. The USA had the highest article count with 20 articles (34 %). South Africa had nine articles (15 %). Norway and Finland had four articles (7%) while Greece, Australia, England and Sweden had three articles (5%). Canada and Germany had two articles (3%) with Malaysia. Austria, Qatar, Ireland, Turkey and China only having one article (2%).

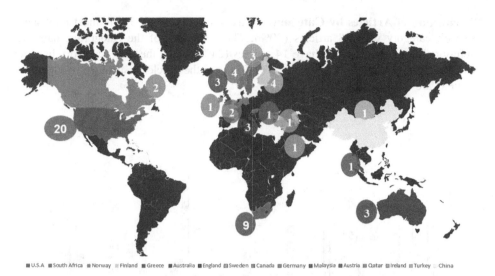

Fig. 1. Distribution of articles by the first author's country

Distribution of Articles by Year. Figure 2 displays the distribution of articles published from the year 2008 to 2018. From 2011 to 2013 there was a decline in the number of articles published. From 2014 to 2018 the number of published articles increased with the highest published article count being for the year 2017, which had 12 articles. The sudden increase in published articles for 2017 could possibly be related to stricter privacy/regulatory laws such as the General Data Protection Regulation (GDPR) which was adopted in April 2016. Due to data collection occurring in the second quarter of 2018, only five articles were recorded for the year. Therefore, this is not a complete list of articles for the year 2018.

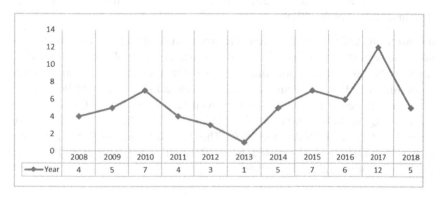

Fig. 2. Distribution of articles per year

Distribution of Articles by Category. 'Theory Development' is the most published research category with 18 articles (30%). The remainder of the categories, namely, 'Behavior' and 'Antecedents' have 14 articles (24%) while, the 'ISP' category has the lowest article count with 13 articles (22%). In Fig. 3 the articles distributed by category per year are displayed.

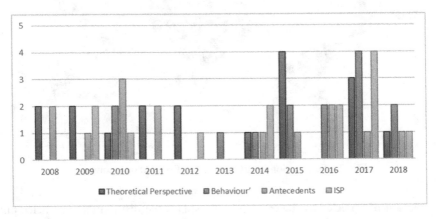

Fig. 3. Distribution of articles by category per year

The category 'Antecedent' research articles appear throughout the review period, except for 2012 and 2013 which had no articles. The 'Theory Development' category was prevalent throughout the review period except for 2012, 2013 and 2016 where no articles were recorded. From the year 2013 to 2018, the research articles for the 'Behavior' category appeared each year, and before this, except for two articles in the year 2010, no other articles were listed. The years' 2010, 2014, 2017 and 2018 features all the main categories appearing together with 'Antecedents' being the dominant category for the year 2010, 'ISP' for 2014, 'Behavior' and 'ISP' for 2017 and 'Behavior' the dominant category for 2018.

Distribution of Articles by Applied Research Methodologies. The chart in Fig. 4 displays the research methodologies used throughout the publications. Four different research methodologies were identified, namely, literature review, empirical research, proposed model/method and action research. 'Empirical Research' clearly stands out as the dominant applied research methodology with 42 articles (71%) of which 30 articles (72%) were 'Quantitative', nine articles (21%) were 'Qualitative', and three articles (7%) used a 'Mixed Methods' approach. This was followed by 'Literature Review' eight articles (13%) and 'Proposed Model/Method' eight articles (14%). 'Action Research' was only used in one article.

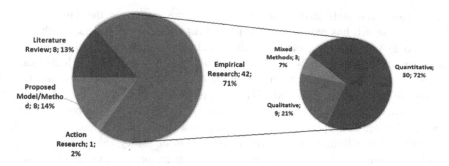

Fig. 4. Applied research methodologies

Theories Used in Articles. Twenty-six different theories were used in the research articles. Some theories were combined to form a new one, while other theories were extended. The most commonly used theories in the reviewed articles were: General Deterrence Theory in eight articles (14%); Theory of Reasoned Action or Theory Planned Behavior in seven articles (12%); and Protection Motivation Theory in six articles (10%). Other theories, appearing once each, were: Actor-Network Theory; Theory of Cognitive Moral Development; Theory of Contextualism; Control Balance Theory; Elaboration Likelihood Model; Fairness Theory; Health Belief Model; Information Foraging Theory; Theory of Interpersonal Behavior; Theory of Motivational Types of Values; Neutralization Theory; Organizational Justice Theory; Rational Choice Theory; Reactance Theory; Regret Theory; Self-Determination Theory; Theory of Self-Regulation; Social Bond Theory; Structuration Theory; Technology Threat Avoidance Theory; Unified Model of Information Security Policy Compliance; Universal Constructive Instructional Theory; and Value-Based Compliance Theory.

5   Discussion

Although 26 theories were identified during the data analysis most of these theories were only used once except for GDT, TRA/TPB and PMT which were the dominant three applied theories. GDT is the most applied theory in the articles for this research study as with the case of D'Arcy and Herath [37] who found GDT to be the most widely applied theory in IS security research. While GDT, TRA/TPB and PMT provides essential insights for behavioral IS security studies, some researchers have doubts regarding their effectiveness. D'Arcy and Herath [37] argue that deterrence theory in the context of IS security provides inconsistent and sometimes contradictory findings while, Johnston et al. [33] found the conventional PMT to be inadequate due to its focus being on individual's things (e.g. data) instead of physical self, as is the case in the healthcare context. Bulgurcu et al. [9] note that a problem with TPB is that nearly an infinite number of variables can affect the performance or non-performance of any behavior. This would explain why 'Theory Development' is the number one category in this research study as researchers are still using theories from other fields to try and understand this phenomenon.

Behavioral research studies seem to be on the rise over the last few years. Behavioral research has mainly used self-reporting measures to understand the factors leading to ISA [22]. These factors such as individuals' attitudes, satisfaction, motivations or intentions are only verifiable through self-reporting [36] which makes it unsurprising that most empirical studies in the reviewed publications used quantitative methods. Johnston et al. [33] and Menard et al. [60] state that the use of intentions rather than actual behavior is the biggest challenge for behavioral information security research. Crossler et al. [7] emphasize that this is a challenge that researchers need to overcome as it is a limitation to theory development or theory validation.

This research study looked at antecedents from an organizational perspective to include everything operating within the organization setting such as technology, staff and managers. At the organizational level, management's understanding and identification of the factors influencing ISA is required for effective ISA training and ISA programs. Management ISA support and commitment to information security are positive attributes to increased staff ISA. The most crucial non-technological security management practices, protecting the organization and increasing staff ISA, are the provisioning of ISPs and SETA programs. At the individual level, higher education or security training, prior negative experiences with information security or previously reprimanded for security violations have found to increase individual's ISA.

6 Conclusion

This research presented a review of organizational ISA research. A total of 59 articles which met the search criteria were used for the data analysis, which resulted in four high-level categories and eight subcategories. The review revealed that ISA research is evolving with theory development having the highest research focus. The top three theories used for ISA research are GDT, TPB, and PMT. Various approaches are used to ensure ISP compliance ranging from sanctions to campaigns, of which SETA programs are the most common.

Like most academic studies, this descriptive review and classification has limitations. First, only articles that were published in English were considered for this review. Furthermore, this study used a predefined list of search terms which was not refined as new search terms arose during the search or analysis process. Second, non-peer-reviewed journals and other potential sources of information such as whitepapers, conference proceedings and books were excluded. These limitations may put this study at a disadvantage of presenting a complete picture of the ISA research landscape. Future studies could include all relevant IS journal databases, specialized information security journals, and other relevant potential sources of ISA research such as books, whitepapers or conference proceedings. Also, search terms should be refined as new terms arise and the use of backward and forward citations should also be considered to increase the sample size.

Acknowledgements. This work is based on the research supported wholly/in part by the National Research Foundation of South Africa (Grant Numbers 114838).

References

1. Grant, K., Edgar, D., Sukumar, A., Meyer, M.: Risky business: perceptions of e-business risk by UK small and medium sized enterprises (SMEs). Int. J. Inf. Manag. **34**(2), 99–122 (2014). https://doi.org/10.1016/j.ijinfomgt.2013.11.001
2. Arachchilage, N.A.G., Love, S.: Security awareness of computer users: a phishing threat avoidance perspective. Comput. Hum. Behav. **38**, 304–312 (2014). https://doi.org/10.1016/j.chb.2014.05.046
3. Parsons, K., Calic, D., Pattinson, M., Butavicius, M., McCormac, A., Zwaans, T.: The Human Aspects of Information Security Questionnaire (HAIS-Q): two further validation studies. Comput. Secur. **66**, 40–51 (2017). https://doi.org/10.1016/j.cose.2017.01.004
4. Metalidou, E., Marinagi, C., Trivellas, P., Eberhagen, N., Giannakopoulos, G., Skourlas, C.: Human factor and information security in higher education. J. Syst. Inf. Technol. **16**(3), 210–221 (2014). https://doi.org/10.1108/JSIT-01-2014-0007
5. Kruger, H.A., Drevin, L., Steyn, T.: A vocabulary test to assess information security awareness. Inf. Manag. Comput. Secur. **18**(5), 316–327 (2010). https://doi.org/10.1108/09685221011095236
6. Bauer, S., Bernroider, E.W.N.: From information security awareness to reasoned compliant action. ACM SIGMIS Database: DATABASE Adv. Inf. Syst. **48**(3), 44–68 (2017). https://doi.org/10.1145/3130515.3130519
7. Crossler, R.E., Johnston, A.C., Lowry, P.B., Hu, Q., Warkentin, M., Baskerville, R.: Future directions for behavioral information security research. Comput. Secur. **32**, 90–101 (2013). https://doi.org/10.1016/j.cose.2012.09.010
8. Bauer, S., Bernroider, E.W.N., Chudzikowski, K.: Prevention is better than cure! Designing information security awareness programs to overcome users' non-compliance with information security policies in banks. Comput. Secur. **68**, 145–159 (2017). https://doi.org/10.1016/j.cose.2017.04.009
9. Bulgurcu, B., Cavusoglu, H., Benbasat, I.: Information security policy compliance: an empirical study of rationality-based beliefs and information security awareness. MIS Q. **34**(3), 523–548 (2010)
10. Siponen, M.T.: A conceptual foundation for organizational information security awareness. Inf. Manag. Comput. Secur. **8**(1), 31–41 (2000). https://doi.org/10.1108/09685220010371394
11. Bitton, R., Finkelshtein, A., Sidi, L., Puzis, R., Rokach, L., Shabtai, A.: Taxonomy of mobile users' security awareness. Comput. Secur. **73**, 266–293 (2018). https://doi.org/10.1016/j.cose.2017.10.015
12. Parsons, K., McCormac, A., Butavicius, M., Pattinson, M., Jerram, C.: Determining employee awareness using the Human Aspects of Information Security Questionnaire (HAIS-Q). Comput. Secur. **42**, 165–176 (2014). https://doi.org/10.1016/j.cose.2013.12.003
13. Okoli, C., Schabram, K.: A guide to conducting a systematic literature review of information systems research. In: Working Papers on Information Systems, vol. 10, no. 26, pp. 1–51 (2010). https://doi.org/10.2139/ssrn.1954824
14. Prasetio, A., Sari, P.K., Ramadhani, D.P.: Electronic Word-of-Mouth (EWOM) Adoption Model for Information Security Awareness: A Case Study in University Students, pp. 154–159 (2015) (2016)
15. Kruger, H.A., Kearney, W.D.: A prototype for assessing information security awareness. Comput. Secur. **25**(4), 289–296 (2006). https://doi.org/10.1016/j.cose.2006.02.008

16. Haeussinger, F., Kranz, J.: Understanding the antecedents of information security awareness - an empirical study. In: Proceedings of the Nineteenth Americas Conference on Information Systems, (Section 6), pp. 1–9 (2013)
17. Tsohou, A., Kokolakis, S., Karyda, M., Kiountouzis, E.: Investigating information security awareness: research and practice gaps. Inf. Secur. J. **17**(5–6), 207–227 (2008). https://doi.org/10.1080/19393550802492487
18. Straub, D.W., Welke, R.J.: Coping with systems risk: security planning models for management decision making. MIS Q. **22**(4), 441–469 (1998). https://doi.org/10.2307/249551
19. Rhee, H., Ryu, Y., Kim, C.-T.: I am fine but you are not: optimistic bias and illusion of control on information security. In: ICIS, pp. 381–394, April 2005
20. Tsohou, A., Karyda, M., Kokolakis, S., Kiountouzis, E.: Managing the introduction of information security awareness programmes in organisations. Eur. J. Inf. Syst. **24**, 38–58 (2013)
21. Jaeger, L.: Information security awareness: literature review and integrative framework. In: 51st Hawaii International Conference on System Sciences, vol. 9, no. 3, pp. 4703–4712 (2018)
22. Anderson, B.B., Kirwan, C.B., Eargle, D.: Using measures of risk perception to predict information security behavior: insights from using measures of risk perception to predict information security behavior: insights from electroencephalography (EEG). J. Assoc. Inf. Syst. **15**(April 2013), 679–722 (2014)
23. Scholl, M.C., Wildau, T., Fuhrmann, F., Scholl, L.R.: Scientific knowledge of the human side of information security as a basis for sustainable trainings in organizational practices. In: Hawaii International Conference on System Sciences, vol. 9, p. 10 (2018)
24. Tsohou, A., Karyda, M., Kokolakis, S., Kiountouzis, E.: Analyzing trajectories of information security awareness. Inf. Technol. People **25**(3), 327–352 (2012). https://doi.org/10.1108/09593841211254358
25. Khan, B., Alghathbar, K., Nabi, S., Khan, K.: Effectiveness of information security awareness methods based on psychological theories. Afr. J. Bus. Manag. **5**, 26 (2011)
26. Puhakainen, P., Siponen, M.: Improving employees' compliance through information systems security training: an action research study. MIS Q. **34** (2010). https://doi.org/10.2307/25750704
27. Posey, C., Roberts, T.L., Lowry, P.B.: The impact of organizational commitment on insiders motivation to protect organizational information assets. J. Manag. Inf. Syst. **32**(4), 179–214 (2015). https://doi.org/10.1080/07421222.2015.1138374
28. Merete Hagen, J., Albrechtsen, E., Hovden, J.: Implementation and effectiveness of organizational information security measures. Inf. Manag. Comput. Secur. **16**(4), 377–397 (2008). https://doi.org/10.1108/09685220810908796
29. D'Arcy, J., Hovav, A., Galletta, D.: User awareness of security countermeasures and its impact on information systems misuse: a deterrence approach. Inf. Syst. Res. **20**(1), 79–98 (2009). https://doi.org/10.1287/isre.1070.0160
30. Herath, T., Rao, H.R.: Protection motivation and deterrence: a framework for security policy compliance in organisations. Eur. J. Inf. Syst. **18**(2), 106–125 (2009). https://doi.org/10.1057/ejis.2009.6
31. Chen, C.C., Medlin, B.D., Shaw, R.S.: A cross-cultural investigation of situational information security awareness programs. Inf. Manag. Comput. Secur. **16**(4), 360–376 (2008). https://doi.org/10.1108/09685220810908787
32. Karjalainen, M., Siponen, M.: Toward a new meta-theory for designing information systems (IS) security training approaches. J. Assoc. Inf. Syst. **12**(8), 518–555 (2011)

33. Johnston, A.C., Warkentin, M., Siponen, M.: An enhanced fear appeal rhetorical framework: leveraging threats to the human asset through sanctioning rhetoric. MIS Q. 39(1), 113–134 (2015). https://doi.org/10.25300/MISQ/2015/39.1.06

34. Johnston, A.C., Warkentin, M., McBride, M., Carter, L.: Dispositional and situational factors: influences on information security policy violations. Eur. J. Inf. Syst. 25(3), 231–251 (2016). https://doi.org/10.1057/ejis.2015.15

35. Lebek, B., Uffen, J., Breitner, M.H., Neumann, M., Hohler, B.: Employees' information security awareness and behavior: a literature review. In: Proceedings of the Annual Hawaii International Conference on System Sciences, pp. 2978–2987 (2013). https://doi.org/10.1109/HICSS.2013.192

36. Lebek, B., Uffen, J., Neumann, M., Hohler, B., Breitner, M.: Information security awareness and behavior: a theory-based literature review. Manag. Res. Rev. 37(12), 1049–1092 (2014). https://doi.org/10.1108/MRR-04-2013-0085

37. D'Arcy, J., Herath, T.: A review and analysis of deterrence theory in the IS security literature: making sense of the disparate findings. Eur. J. Inf. Syst. 20(6), 643–658 (2011). https://doi.org/10.1057/ejis.2011.23

38. Sommestad, T., Hallberg, J., Lundholm, K., Bengtsson, J.: Variables influencing information security policy compliance: a systematic review of quantitative studies. Inf. Manag. Comput. Secur. 22(1), 42–75 (2014). https://doi.org/10.1108/IMCS-08-2012-0045

39. Dang-Pham, D., Pittayachawan, S., Bruno, V.: Why employees share information security advice? Exploring the contributing factors and structural patterns of security advice sharing in the workplace. Comput. Hum. Behav. 67, 196–206 (2017). https://doi.org/10.1016/j.chb.2016.10.025

40. Sparks, P., Ajzen, I., Hall-box, T.: Perceived behavioral control, self-efficacy, locus of control, and the theory of planned behavior, pp. 665–683 (2002)

41. Safa, N., von Solms, R.: An information security knowledge sharing model in organizations. Comput. Hum. Behav. 57, 442–451 (2016). https://doi.org/10.1016/j.chb.2015.12.037

42. Safa, N., Sookhak, M., von Solms, R., Furnell, S., Ghani, N.A., Herawan, T.: Information security conscious care behaviour formation in organizations. Comput. Secur. 53, 65–78 (2015). https://doi.org/10.1016/j.cose.2015.05.012

43. Myers, M.D.: Qualitative Research in Business and Management. SAGE Publications Ltd., London (2013)

44. King, W.R., He, J.: Understanding the role and methods of meta-analysis in is research. Commun. Assoc. Inf. Syst. 16(October), 654 (2005)

45. Wolfswinkel, J.F., Furtmueller, E., Wilderom, C.P.M.: Using grounded theory as a method for rigorously reviewing literature. Eur. J. Inf. Syst. 22(1), 45–55 (2011). https://doi.org/10.1057/ejis.2011.51

46. Saunders, M.N.K., Lewis, P., Thornhill, A.: Research Methods for Business Students. Pearson Education Limited, London (2015)

47. Tsohou, A., Karyda, M., Kokolakis, S.: Analyzing the role of cognitive and cultural biases in the internalization of information security policies: recommendations for information security awareness programs. Comput. Secur. 52, 128–141 (2015). https://doi.org/10.1016/j.cose.2015.04.006

48. Da Veiga, A., Eloff, J.H.P.: A framework and assessment instrument for information security culture. Comput. Secur. 29(2), 196–207 (2010). https://doi.org/10.1016/j.cose.2009.09.002

49. Liang, H., Xue, Y.: Avoidance of information technology threats: a theoretical perspective. MIS Q. 33(1), 71–90 (2009). https://doi.org/10.2307/20650279

50. Ölütçü, G., Testik, Ö.M., Chouseinoglou, O.: Analysis of personal information security behavior and awareness. Comput. Secur. 56, 83–93 (2016). https://doi.org/10.1016/j.cose.2015.10.002

51. Snyman, D., Kruger, H.A.: The application of behavioural thresholds to analyse collective behaviour in information security. Inf. Comput. Secur. **25**(2), 152–164 (2017). https://doi.org/10.1108/ICS-03-2017-0015
52. Connolly, L., Lang, M., Gathegi, J., Tygar, D.J.: Organisational culture, procedural countermeasures, and employee security behaviour: a qualitative study. Inf. Comput. Secur. **25**(2), 118–136 (2017). https://doi.org/10.1108/ICS-03-2017-0013
53. D'Arcy, J., Greene, G.: Security culture and the employment relationship as drivers of employees' security compliance. Inf. Manag. Comput. Secur. **22**(5), 474–489 (2014). https://doi.org/10.1108/IMCS-08-2013-0057
54. Da Veiga, A., Martins, N.: Defining and identifying dominant information security cultures and subcultures. Comput. Secur. **70**, 72–94 (2017). https://doi.org/10.1016/j.cose.2017.05.002
55. Da Veiga, A., Martins, N.: Improving the information security culture through monitoring and implementation actions illustrated through a case study. Comput. Secur. **49**, 162–176 (2015). https://doi.org/10.1016/j.cose.2014.12.006
56. Merete Hagen, J., Albrechtsen, E.: Effects on employees' information security abilities by e-learning. Inf. Manag. Comput. Secur. **17**(5), 388–407 (2009). https://doi.org/10.1108/09685220911006687
57. Chen, C.C., Ramamurthy, K., Wen, K.-W.: Organizations' information security policy compliance: stick or carrot approach? J. Manag. Inf. Syst. **29**(3), 157–188 (2012). https://doi.org/10.2753/MIS0742-1222290305
58. Tsohou, A., Karyda, M., Kokolakis, S., Kiountouzis, E.: Managing the introduction of information security awareness programmes in organisations. Eur. J. Inf. Syst. **24**(1), 38–58 (2015). https://doi.org/10.1057/ejis.2013.27
59. Thomson, K., van Niekerk, J.: Combating information security apathy by encouraging prosocial organisational behaviour. Inf. Manag. Comput. Secur. **20**(1), 39–46 (2012). https://doi.org/10.1108/09685221211219191
60. Menard, P., Bott, G.J., Crossler, R.E.: User motivations in protecting information security: protection motivation theory versus self-determination theory. J. Manag. Inf. Syst. **34**(4), 1203–1230 (2017). https://doi.org/10.1080/07421222.2017.1394083

Theorising Information Security Policy Violations

Indren Govender$^{(\boxtimes)}$ and Bruce Watson$^{(\boxtimes)}$

Stellenbosch University, Stellenbosch, South Africa
{ieg, bwwatson}@sun.ac.za

Abstract. Information system security threats perpetuates organisations in spite of enormous investments in security measures. The academic literature and the media reflect the huge financial loss and reputational harm to organisations due to computer related security breaches. Although technical safeguards are indispensable, the academic literature highlights the 'insider threat'. Organisational employees pose a significant threat, considering, they already have access to the organizations' information systems. It's a matter of how they use/abuse it. This article explores the theoretical foundation in the domain of information systems security policy violations. The academic databases are queried for key theories in computer compliance/non-compliance. These theories are examined for theoretical development. A problem area is identified and subsequently, a theoretical model is proposed in an attempt to explain: Why employees violate information systems security policies?

Keywords: Insider threat · Computer security policy · Computer security compliance · Computer abuse · Neutralisation theory · Self-control theory

1 Introduction

Information security issues persists in organizations in light of continued data breaches, systems outages, and malicious software [1]. Organizations have addressed the growing list of security threats through a combination of technical, administrative, and physical controls, but despite these efforts, information security breaches persists in organizations. As a result, information security has become a focal area for practitioners and academics [2]. Posey et al. [3] claim that organizations employ a myriad of approaches to protect organizational information assets from security threats; inclusive of a wide spectrum of artefacts and efforts: firewalls, intrusion detection systems, disaster recovery, business continuity planning and security, education, training, and awareness (SETA) programs, etc. Crossler et al. [4] claim that the scope of Information Security (IS) research includes technical, behavioural, managerial, philosophical, and organizational approaches that address the protection and mitigation of threats to information assets. They advance that information security was primarily focused on technical issues concerning the design and implementation of security subsystems, such as advanced technical approaches to prevent intrusion into organizational systems, detection of denial of service attacks and more advanced solutions for firewall protection.

H. Venter et al. (Eds.): ISSA 2019, CCIS 1166, pp. 131–144, 2020.
https://doi.org/10.1007/978-3-030-43276-8_10

Crossler et al. [4] confer that although the technical, externally focused efforts are of significance, a predominant weakness in properly securing information assets is the individual user within an organization [5]. This is of detriment to organisations, considering, researchers estimate that nearly half of intrusions and security violations occur from within an organization by organizational insiders [6]. Numerous studies highlight the huge financial and reputational costs brought upon by organisations due to information security breaches caused by the insider threat [7, 8]. Willison and Warkentin [9] confer external factors (external hackers, natural disasters) as a significant threat to the security of an organization's information and technology resources, but also assert that employees pose a greater security risk. Crossler et al. [4] assert that Behavioral Information Systems Security research is a subfield of the broader Information Systems Security field that focuses on individual behaviours related to protecting information and information systems assets; inclusive of computer hardware, networking infrastructure, and organizational information. Security-related behaviour is defined as the behaviour of employees in using organizational information systems (including hardware, software, and network systems etc.); taking into cognisance that such behaviour may have security implications [10].

Posey et al. [3] defines behavioural information security research as the systematic examination of human actions that impacts on the confidentiality, integrity, and availability of information and information systems. They advance that although technology is pivotal to protecting organizational information systems assets, insiders' behaviour ultimately determine the success of security initiatives since technology extends protection only so far before the control of information is entrusted to insiders [11]. They assert that research indicates that managers who oversee security projects overemphasize the use of technology to the detriment of recognizing the importance of human behaviour and organizational structures and policies. Cram et al. [12] argue that pivotal to addressing these risk factors of insiders is the adoption of information security policies. Consequentially, there has been an increase in the IS security academic research community publishing papers on the design, implementation, and effectiveness of security policies in Organizations [12]. Bulgurcu [13] define information security policy as a "statement of the roles and responsibilities of the employees to safeguard the information and technology resources of their organizations". They advance that information security policy (ISP) establishes rules to address specific security issues by providing explicit instructions to employees on how to interact with the information and technology resources of the organization. Studies have emphasised that employees' compliance with organisational rules, guidelines and requirements as stated in their ISP is a useful mechanism for influencing employee's behaviour towards how information resources are used [13].

The literature surveyed provides overwhelming evidence of widespread violation of information systems security policies. Bulgurcu [13] advances that both, empirical and anecdotal evidence highlight the increase in computer related incidents in organisations, despite the increase in investment in technology-based solutions; articulating that effective information security in organizations is dependent on both, technical and socio-organizational resources. The shift in mind set of information security towards individual and organizational perspectives led to employees' compliance with ISP evolving as a pivotal socio-organizational resource [14]. However, with security technical controls in place, security policies implemented and consequences of non-compliance explicated, together with security awareness and training programmes in place, adherence with security policies is still an issue of serious concern (15). The literature surveyed establishes that employees' failure to comply with information systems security policies is of grave concern [16]. Information security policy abuse is defined as any act by employees using computers that is against the established rules and policies of an organization; inclusive of unauthorized access to data and systems, unauthorized copying or transferring of confidential data and selling confidential data to a third party, among others [17]. Guo [10] assert that characteristics of security policy abuse include:

- it is intentional
- the employee most likely has malicious motives
- it does not require any specific computer knowledge and skills
- it may be committed by either end users or IS professionals
- it is not for the purpose of doing the employee's job
- it will likely cause direct damage to the organization's security
- it requires employees' action

Research indicates that even though most organisations have ISPs in place, a substantial number of employees that knowingly and routinely disregard these ISPs is of a huge proportion [19, 20]. The information systems security literature has seen a growing interest in investigating insider behaviour that may have security implications. Despite the advancement of theoretical development contributed by this body of research, inconsistent findings are evident, especially the divergent conceptualizations of security-related behaviour [10]. Guo [10] assert that the information systems (IS) security literature highlights and exhibits a growing interest in investigating the issue of employee behaviour that may have security implications in organizations [15]. This body of research focused on the antecedents of the behaviour; referred to as security-related behaviour. Although this area of research has made significant contribution to behavioural issues in IS security management, many inconsistent findings were found [10].

Siponen et al. [23] concluded that the IS security field has not matured as other IS disciplines have, pointing to a lack of growth in terms of the levels of empirical research, a paucity of theory, and an over-emphasis on technical as opposed to more social and behavioural topics. In light of this, this paper examines Information Security Policy (ISP) violations in organisations from a theoretical perspective. Searches were conducted on the academic databases for scholarly work on information security compliance/non-compliance to make sense of the terrain, in an attempt to offer conceptual clarity on ISP violations. Subsequently, this paper contributes to theory by proposing a theoretical model to investigate information security policy violations. This paper proceeds as follows: The next section explores the theoretical landscape in the context of ISP compliance/non-compliance. The following section identifies and explicates the theoretical gap, together with a critique of the key theories explicated. Finally, a theoretical model is developed and proposed, aligned to the problem statement: Why do employees violate information systems security policies?

2   Theoretical Landscape: Information Security Compliance/Non-compliance

A plethora of studies in the information systems (IS) ethics literature have used ethical behavioural models to predict various unacceptable, inappropriate and illegal uses of IS in the workplace [21]. These studies have explored the theory of reasoned action, theory of planned behaviour, and theories of moral reasoning and development, along with additional individual and situational characteristics [12]. In the IS security literature, various individual and workplace factors associated with ISP compliance were investigated. Much of this work is grounded in the rational view of human behaviour, such that ISP compliance is based on a cognitive evaluation of costs and benefits associated with compliance [18]. D'Arcy and Lowry [18] advance that studies in this realm have drawn from several rationality-based behavioural theories (such as Deterrence Theory, Protection Motivation Theory, Rational Choice Theory, and theory of Planned Behaviour [18]. Boss et al. [22] affirm that among the theoretical approaches recently used for security compliance includes Deterrence Theory, Rational Choice Theory and Protection Motivation Theory. The key theories are discussed below.

2.1   Deterrence Theory

Siponen et al. [23] review of the Information Systems (IS) Security literature revealed deterrence theory as the most cited theory in Information security policy (ISP) compliance/non-compliance. D'Arcy and Herath [2] affirm Deterrence theory as one of the most widely applied theories in IS security research, more especially in behavioural IS security studies. Negative computing behaviours refers to the intentional disruption to IS security and these studies have focused on the predictive influence of disincentives or sanctions rooted in deterrence theory [12]. Deterrence theory is based on the rational choice view of human behaviour; predicting that unethical behavior can be controlled by the threat of sanctions that are certain, severe and swift. IS scholars have used deterrence theory to predict user behaviours that are both, either supportive or disruptive of IS security [2]. Classic deterrence theory focuses on formal (legal) sanctions, claiming that the greater the perceived certainty, severity and celerity (swiftness) of sanctions for an illicit act, the more individuals are deterred from such acts [2]. However, new findings revealed inconsistent and even contradictory findings with respect to deterrence theory in the security context. This was substantiated by D'Arcy and Herath [2] who found contradictory results on the effects of deterrent factors on employee behaviour. Notwithstanding the contradictory findings in utilising deterrence theory, this theory is held in high esteem in praxis, especially regarding the widely adopted international security management standard: ISO/IEC 27002. This standard draws from deterrence theory in recommending security policies, guidelines and awareness programmes [24].

2.2   Rational Choice Theory

D'Arcy and Lowry [18] assert that pivotal to Rational Choice Theory is that individuals perform a mental cost-benefit analysis when deciding whether to engage in a particular behaviour. Because of its narrow focus on costs and benefits, Rational Choice Theory has been merged with other rationality-based theories of human behaviour to delineate a pathway from the expected costs and benefits of ISP compliance to the performance of this behaviour. D'Arcy and Lowry [18] integrated Rational Choice Theory together with the Theory of Planned Behaviour for their theoretical model rather than other rationality-based behavioural theories that have been applied to ISP compliance (i.e. Deterrence Theory and Protection Motivation Theory), arguing that Deterrence Theory is a subset of Rational Choice Theory that pertains to the perceived-cost portion of the rational decision process (cost-benefit analysis), hence their model subsumes aspects of both theories. Bulgurcu [13] also proposed and empirically tested a combined Rational Choice Theory - Theory of Planned Behaviour model of ISP compliance. Rational choice theory is apt to the organisational compliance context since, just as criminal acts, violations of organisational policies are subject to sanctions (such as disciplinary measures by organisational management for irregular practices) [25]. Moreover, this theoretical integration is aligned, given that the Theory of Planned Behaviour constructs are regarded as drivers of rational behaviour [18].

D'Arcy and Lowry [18] assert that the Theory of planned behaviour literature highlights normative influences in terms of subjective and descriptive norms [26]. Psychological research indicates that both types of norms are powerful determinants of human behaviour [27]. In the theoretical model proposed by D'Arcy and Lowry [18], they use subjective norms to represent the degree to which employees believe that other key personnel at their organisation want them to comply with the ISP, whereas descriptive norms refers to the degree to which employees believe other key personnel at their organisation are actually performing the behaviour prescribed by the ISP [28].

2.3   Protection Motivation Theory

Boss et al. [22] assert that contemporary Information Systems security literature on compliance resulting from sanctions, threats, or fear is due to a move from earlier Deterrence Theory-based approaches to a stronger emphasis on Protection Motivation Theory [4]. Moreover, they justify that this shift was the consequence of Deterrence Theory and Rational Choice Theory being viewed as command and control, while Protection Motivation Theory uses persuasive messages that warn of a personal threat and describe countervailing measures that encapsulates protective behaviour. Protection Motivation Theory is used to understanding insiders' motivation to engage in protective behaviours [3]. Protection Motivation Theory incorporates the threat and coping appraisal process. These two appraisals (threat and coping appraisal) are the two core components of Protection Motivation Theory that shape protective intentions [3, 22]. This was originally used in preventive medicine to explain individuals' protective responses following the communication of health threats via fear appeals. Protection Motivation Theory is now widely used as a general theory of motivation to explain individuals' actions regarding any threat [3].

3 Theoretical Gap

Guo [10] differentiates two broad categories of security-related behaviour i.e. desirable behavior such as information security policy (ISP) compliance as compared to ISP abuse/security policy violation. He argues that although the two categories of behaviours are related, evidence suggests that a better approach is to treat them as distinct constructs, advancing that ISP violation and policy compliance are conceptually and empirically different. Furthermore, the International Federation for Information Processing (IFIP) Working Group 8.11/11.13 on Information Systems Security Research have deliberated over the future direction of Behavioural information security research and amongst other categories, have identified "Separating insider deviant behaviour from insider misbehaviour" and "Improving information security compliance" as two key areas that future studies should explore [4]. This research article addresses these two factors. The motive for the category "Separating insider deviant behaviour from insider misbehaviour", is to conduct more focussed studies on each component i.e. non-compliance, but non malicious intentions (failing to log off, delayed backups) from non-compliance with malicious intentions (sabotage, data theft) [4].

Willison and Warkentin [9] argue that IS security managers must identify and mitigate a wide range of threats which may originate from sources that are within the organization itself (internal) or from external entities, and they may be from human perpetrators or non-human phenomena (Fig. 1). They extended the Loch et al. [29] threat taxonomy to include greater granularity, especially for the "insider threat." as depicted in Fig. 1.

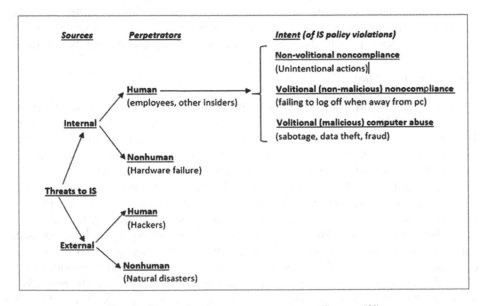

Fig. 1. IS security threat vector taxonomy (Source: [9])

The 'Threats to IS' refers to the source/s of the threat, which could be internal or external to the organization. The perpetrators of both, the internal and external threats could be either human or non-human. The external human threats (hackers) are generally person/s that use various means to infiltrate the organisation while the external Nonhuman threats (natural disasters) refers to outside factors not directly targeted by person/s. Internal Nonhuman threats (hardware failure) refers to threats derived inside the organisation but not directly by person/s. The area of significance in Fig. 1 is the internal human threat or commonly referred to as the 'insider threat'. Willison and Warkentin [9] categorised this threat along a continuum on the basis of intent regarding IS policy violation. 'Non-volitional noncompliance', is unintentional behaviour, where employees may simply forget to do what they are supposed to do, while 'Volitional (but non malicious) noncompliance' is intentional behaviour without malice. The third type, 'Volitional (malicious) computer abuse' presents the most serious problem, where the insider causes deliberate harm to the organisation. This article is located in this area. Guo [10] uses 'motive' as a dimension to describe whether an employee's behavior is malicious or non-malicious. Willison and Warkentin [9] affirm that the IS security community has responded to the serious threat of insiders as reflected in studies of compliance or noncompliance with policies; however, the focus has not been on the third category: 'Volitional (malicious) computer abuse'. This is of grave concern considering [18] report that over half of all information security breaches results from deliberate ISP violations committed by users [30].

Willison and Warkentin [9] extended the widely cited and established 'Straub and Welke's (1998)' security action cycle (Fig. 2) to expound on the insider threat. They outline four areas of implementation to mitigate risks (Fig. 2): Deterrence, Prevention, Detection and Remedies. Henceforth, organizations first attempt to deter the risks posed by insiders by deterring potentially dishonest staff. Failure in this area, leads to preventive measures for computer abuse, followed by efforts for detection, and finally addressing remedies.

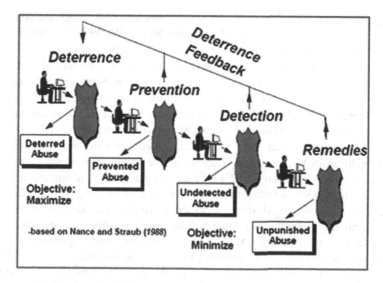

Fig. 2. Straub–Welke security action cycle (Source: [9], page 4)

They emphasise that the objective of organizations should be to maximize deterrence and prevention efforts, thereby minimizing the need for detection and remedy. Moreover, they argue for moving beyond the security action cycle by encompassing the phenomena that temporally occurs prior to deterrence [9], specifying the need to take cognisance of the thought processes of the potential offender and the organizational context. Subsequently, they propose the general extension to the Straub–Welke security action cycle, referred to as the 'extended security action cycle' (Fig. 3) which depicts the events which occur prior to deterrence and focus on the "pre-kinetic" events (T^{-4}).

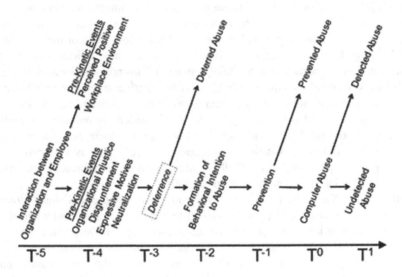

Fig. 3. Extended security action cycle (Source: [9], page 5)

Along the timeline in Fig. 3, T^0 depicts the key moment where the offender has successfully perpetrated some form of computer abuse. Working backward along the timeline (left), is 'Prevention' (T^{-1}),' where research has been conducted, focusing on the offender behavior in the organizational context [9]. To the left of prevention is 'Behavioral intention' (T^{-2}), wherein researchers have combined a number of theories to understand those factors which together form behavioural intention. One of these factors is Deterrence (T^{-3}), which has been the focus for several ISP researchers and as stated earlier, is one of the most studied area of employee computer abuse. Willison and Warkentin [9] accentuate that there is a paucity of research in this phenomena which exist temporally prior to deterrence. They argue for recognition of phenomena which temporally occur prior to deterrence (T^{-4}) as of significance; advancing the need to consider the relationship between the thought processes of the potential offender and the organizational context. Moreover, this could impact the efficacy of IS security controls, specifically deterrence safeguards. This research article draws on Willison and Warkentin [9] Extended Security Action Cycle framework, and is specifically grounded in the Pre-Kinetic Events (T^{-4}) 'thought process of the potential offender'. Neutralisation Theory (T^{-4}) is proposed in developing the theoretical model in an attempt to explain 'Why employees violate Information Security Policies?'". Neutralization uses cognitive techniques to rationalise/justify criminal/deviant behaviour [31].

3.1 Neutralisation Theory

Theory and research in criminology indicates that individuals embody 'internalized norms' [31] which can deter individuals from engaging in criminal behavior. They state that individuals can use neutralisation to dissipate internalized norms and social censure (i.e. the 'self-deterring' mechanisms). Neutralisation theory asserts that those who obey the law and those who defy the law, generally believe in the norms and values of society [31], but those who exhibit deviant behaviour could have found ways to justify their actions. The originators of Neutralisation theory [31] claim that people use psychological reasoning to commit aberrant acts by applying neutralisation techniques. These neutralisation techniques are narrative mechanisms that make it possible to justify a deviance from the norm whilst at the same time adhering to the normative system in force, and to avoid a feeling of guilt due to infringement of the norm [31]. Neutralisation techniques allow one to render existing norms inoperative and rationalise their behaviour when defying these norms [15]. This allows the offender to engage in a criminal act without feelings of guilt and shame. As an example, one may perform an illegal action and justify their behaviour as no damage was caused together with no harm/injury was sustained; thereby eluding shame and guilt. Sykes et al. [31] assert that in neutralising their own behaviour, perpetrators can maintain their 'clean image' and fluctuate between criminal and non-criminal behaviour.

Siponen and Vance [15] used Neutralisation Theory to explain why employees violate ISP. Although studies in ISP noncompliance have been traditionally conducted through the lens of Deterrence Theory, extant research reveals that deterrent sanctions may not be the most suitable influencer of employee ISP violation [32]. Siponen and Vance [15] advance that employees rationalise their deviant behaviour, to overcome the effects of deterrence when deciding whether or not to violate security policies. Consequently, this rationalisation/justification process is often stronger than sanctions in predicting employee behaviour [32]. Employees try to reduce their guilt or shame for violating ISP by using neutralisation/rationalisation techniques, as a result, organisational security, education, training and awareness programs (SETA) directed towards policies or sanctions may not be effective enough in mitigating policy violations [32]. Siponen and Vance [15] studied the rationalising process using neutralisation theory for violating ISP which converges to inform this article. Their findings reflect that "neutralisation is an excellent predictor of employees" intention to violate IS security policies" [15]. This was the first study in the domain of security policy violation using neutralisation whereas Deterrence theory was the theory of choice in studying security policy noncompliance. Studies subsequent to [15] findings provided further evidence that neutralisation techniques are strong predictors of IT security violations [9]. Consequently, the attributes of the key theories mentioned (Rational Choice Theory, Theory of Planned Behaviour, Deterrence Theory and Protection Motivation Theory) maybe ineffective, in the presence of Neutralisation Theory. This will apply more especially to individuals who are good at rationalising/justifying their deviant behaviours.

Consequently, this research article draws on neutralisation theory but does not just call for a replication of Siponen and Vance [15] theoretical model. It expands on it by interrogating the theory of Neutralisation. If Neutralisation theory is successfully tested to explain ISP violations, what engenders neutralisation? The study therefore goes beyond advocating neutralisation theory, but explores the source of neutralisation, in an attempt to advance the knowledge claims in the behavioural ISP domain. Marcoulides and Saunders [33] assert that if a study's finding is important, researchers generally elaborate on it or extend it by defining moderators, boundary conditions etc. Sykes et al. [31] make two claims that are key informants for the development of the proposed theoretical model: Firstly, they assert, "as more information is uncovered concerning techniques of neutralization, their origins, and their consequences", more light could be shed on defiant behaviour. Secondly, they argue, "certain personality structures can accept some techniques of neutralization more readily than others, but this question remains largely unexplored". The current research is informed by Sykes et al. [31] two assertions, thereby integrating personality traits to examine neutralisation.

3.2   The General Theory of Crime (Self-control)

Warkentin et al. [34] assert that researchers should probe to understand the distant antecedents of intention (probing deeper) to investigate the root cause in dealing with the behavioural intention. They call for a focus on the offender and applying appropriate theories to provide insight into factors which influence intention. In an attempt to explain neutralisation theory, the General Theory of Crime is investigated. Gottfredson and Hirschi's [35] General Theory of Crime, commonly referred to as self-control theory is one of the most influential theoretical developments in criminology. After the release of their publication on the General Theory of crime, they emerged as the two most cited authors in the top three criminology journals.

Gottfredson and Hirschi [35] self-control theory suggests that low self-control is a Personality trait; a relatively time-stable individual difference. The originators of this theory claim that persons with low self-control are impulsive, insensitive, action-oriented, negatively tempered risk takers who tend to fail to meet the responsibilities of school, work, and family. Gottfredson and Hirschi [35] argue that the origin of self-control is in early childhood socialisation. They claim that children will develop self-control to the degree that their parents set clear rules, monitor children's behaviour, recognise rule violations and consistently sanction such violations. They argue that early parental socialisation promotes or hinders the development of self-control equally across the cultural context.

Rebellon et al. [40] conducted a large scale study to test the reliability and validity of self-control measures to the relationship between parenting and self-control in the six continents incorporating thirty two countries. Their findings were consistent with Gottfredson and Hirschi [35], indicating that self-control theory is cross-cultural. Rebellon et al. [40] recommend that cross-cultural researchers incorporate the contributions of self-control theory in further studies taking cognisance of its generalizability. Gottfredson and Hirschi [35] self-control theory was a plausible theory to explain digital piracy, software (movie) piracy, music piracy [36]. This research article draws on self-control theory, integrating it in a conceptual model to investigate ISP violation.

4 Proposed Theoretical Model

This study adopts a deterministic perspective, using variance theory to propose a theoretical model in an attempt to explain and predict information security policy violations by employees. This is in line with behavioural IS research that generally uses the variance model paradigm, in which the aim is to conceptualise models that attempts to explain or predict a dependent variable. In this study, that dependent variable (intention to offend) refers to information security policy (ISP) violation. Hirschi and Gottfredson's [39] theory of low self-control (individual propensity) emerged as a strong predictor for criminal/deviant behaviour. Subsequently, the conceptual model (Fig. 4) proposes low self-control as a strong predictor of ISP violations.

In line with theory development, the proposed model also integrates neutralisation into the theoretical model. Jackson et al. [37] emphasise that prior studies are lacking in multiple theories. Integrating theories encompasses fusing theories to yield an integrated model in an attempt to elevate the explanatory power than that derived from a single theory. The literature review evidenced neutralisation as a strong predictor of security policy violation. Furthermore, in an attempt to understand the intentions to violate security policies, this article argues that the events which occur prior to deterrence; i.e. the "pre-kinetic" events need to be investigated (See T-4 of Fig. 3); hence, the conceptual model incorporates neutralization.

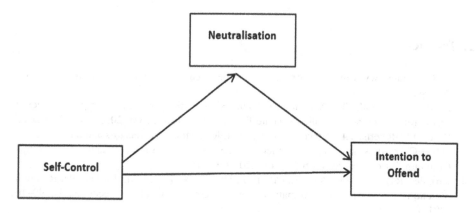

Fig. 4. The proposed theoretical model

Hirschi and Gottfredson's [39] assert that the effect of low self-control on crime may not be independent of other influences or theories. Moreover, they emphasise the interaction between self-control and opportunity. Malin and Fowers [41] describe self-control as an individual's ability to resist temptation when the opportunity arises. The proposed theoretical model integrates neutralization as the opportunity factor. Consequently, this study also proposes low self-control as a strong predictor of ISP violations but mediated through an opportunity factor (neutralisation) to form a theoretical model to test IS security policy violation behavior (Fig. 4). An integrative perspective, more so, incorporating mediator variables provides a more complete account of the causal mechanisms underlying relationships and unique insights that cannot be obtained with a single theory driven model [37]. The proposed theoretical model positions Neutralisation as a mediator in the theoretical model outlined above. Moreover, Olbrich et al. [38] argue that "a correspondence between a variance theory showing correlation of initial states with outcome states and a substantive theory showing the particular dynamics/mechanism or processes by which such initial states move to particular outcomes can form a much more powerful understanding of the phenomenon than without this correspondence". The mechanism of neutralisation (mediator) is influenced by an independent personality trait factor which is internal to the individual (low self-control). The theoretical model for this research project is illustrated in Fig. 4.

5 Conclusion

This article highlights the insider threat that perpetuates in organisations. It then explores the theoretical foundation in security policy compliance/non-compliance, in an attempt to offer conceptual clarity. Subsequently, a theoretical model is proposed to investigate information security policy violations. The proposed variance model, with Self Control as the exogenous antecedent construct and Neutralisation as the endogenous construct; more specifically as a mediator, has not been investigated before.

References

1. PwC. http://www.pwc.com/gx/en/issues/cyber-security/information-security-survey.html. Accessed 21 Nov 2018
2. D'Arcy, J., Herath, T.: A review and analysis of deterrence theory in the IS security literature: making sense of the disparate findings. Eur. J. Inf. Syst. **20**(6), 643–658 (2011)
3. Posey, C., Roberts, T.L., Lowry, P.B., Bennett, R.J.: Multiple indicators and multiple causes (MIMIC) models as a mixed-modeling technique: a tutorial and annotated example. Commun. Assoc. Inf. Syst. **36**(11), 179–204 (2015)
4. Crossler, R.E., Johnston, A.C., Lowry, P.B., Hu, Q., Warkentin, M., Baskerville, R.: Future directions for behavioral information security research. Comput. Secur. **32**(1), 90–101 (2013)
5. Warkentin, M., Willison, R.: Behavioral and policy issues in information systems security: the insider threat. Eur. J. Inf. Syst. **18**(2), 101–105 (2009)
6. Richardson, R.: CSI/FBI Computer Crime and Security Survey. Computer Security Institute (2011). http://www.gocsi.com/survey
7. PwC. http://www.pwc.com/gx/en/consulting-services/information-security-survey/download.jhtml. Accessed 23 Sept 2017
8. SpectorSoft. https://www.sans.org/reading-room/whitepapers/analyst/insider-threats-fast-directed-response-35892. Accessed 23 Sept 2017
9. Willison, R., Warkentin, M.: Beyond deterrence: an expanded view of employee computer abuse. MIS Q. **37**(1), 1–20 (2013)
10. Guo, K.H.: Security-related behavior in using information systems in the workplace: a review and synthesis. Comput. Secur. **32**, 242–251 (2013)

11. Stanton, J.M., Stam, K.R., Mastrangelo, P.M., Jolton, J.A.: Behavioral information security: an overview, results, and research agenda. In: Zhang, P., Galletta, D.F. (eds.) Human Computer Interaction and Management Information Systems: Foundations, pp. 262–280. M. E. Sharpe, Armonk (2006)

12. Cram, W.A., Proudfoot, J.G., D'Arcy, J.: Organizational information security policies: a review and research framework. Eur. J. Inf. Syst. **26**(6), 605–641 (2017)

13. Bulgurcu, B., Cavusoglu, H., Benbasat, I.: Information security policy compliance: an empirical study of rationality-based beliefs and information security awareness. MIS Q. **34** (3), 523–548 (2010)

14. Siponen, M., Pahnila, S., Mahmood, A.: Employees' adherence to information security policies: an empirical study. In: Venter, H., Eloff, M., Labuschagne, L., Eloff, J., von Solms, R. (eds.) SEC 2007. IIFIP, vol. 232, pp. 133–144. Springer, Boston, MA (2007). https://doi.org/10.1007/978-0-387-72367-9_12

15. Siponen, M., Vance, A.: Neutralization: new insights into the problem of employee information systems security policy violations. MIS Q. **34**(3), 487–502 (2010)

16. Siponen, M., Mahmood, M.A., Pahnila, S.: Employees' adherence to information security policies: an exploratory field study. Inf. Manag. **51**(2), 217–224 (2014)

17. Hu, Q., Xu, Z., Dinev, T., Ling, H.: Does deterrence work in reducing information security policy abuse by employees? Commun. ACM **54**(6), 54–60 (2011)

18. D'Arcy, J., Lowry, P.B.: Cognitive-affective drivers of employees' daily compliance with information security policies: a multilevel, longitudinal study. Inf. Syst. J. **29**(1), 43–69 (2019)

19. Dell. https://software.dell.com/whitepaper/insider-threat-spotlight-report890546/. Accessed 23 Sept 2017

20. Goel, S., Chengalur-Smith, I.N.: Metrics for characterizing the form of security policies. J. Strateg. Inf. Syst. **19**(4), 281–295 (2010)

21. Cronan, T.P., Douglas, D.E.: Toward a comprehensive ethical behavior model for information technology. J. Organ. End User Comput. **18**(1), 1–11 (2006)

22. Boss, S.R., Galletta, D.F., Lowry, P.B., Moody, G.D., Polak, P.: What do systems users have to fear? Using fear appeals to engender threats and fear that motivate protective security behaviors. MIS Q. **39**(4), 837–864 (2015)

23. Siponen, M., Willison, R., Baskerville, R.: Power and practice in information systems security research. In: International Conference on Information Systems, pp. 1–13. Association for Information Systems, Paris (2008)

24. Theoharidou, M., Kokolakis, S., Karyda, M., Kiountouzis, E.: The insider threat to information systems and the effectiveness of ISO17799. Comput. Secur. **24**(6), 472–484 (2005)

25. Tyler, T.R., Blader, S.L.: Can business effectively regulate employee conduct? The antecedents of rule following in work settings. Acad. Manag. J. **48**(6), 1143–1158 (2005)

26. Ajzen, I.: The theory of planned behaviour: reactions and reflections. Psychol. Health **26**, 1113–1127 (2011)

27. Rivis, A., Sheeran, P.: Current psychology: developmental, learning, personality, social. Fall **22**(3), 218–233 (2003)

28. Herath, T., Rao, H.: Protection motivation and deterrence: a framework for security policy compliance in organisations. Eur. J. Inf. Syst. **18**(2), 106–125 (2009)

29. Loch, K.D., Carr, H.H., Warkentin, M.E.: Threats to information systems: today's reality, yesterday's understanding. MIS Q. **16**, 173–186 (1992)

30. The cyber security experience: Cyber security pros from Mars; users from Mercury. http://www.meritalk.com/cybersecurityexperience. Accessed 23 Oct 2017

31. Sykes, G.M., Matza, D.: Techniques of neutralization: a theory of delinquency. Am. Sociol. Rev. **22**(6), 664–670 (1957)
32. Barlow, J.B., Warkentin, M., Ormond, D., Dennis, A.R.: Don't make excuses! Discouraging neutralization to reduce IT policy violation. Comput. Secur. **39**, 145–159 (2013)
33. Marcoulides, G.A., Saunders, C.: PLS: a silver bullet? MIS Q. **30**(2), iii–ix (2006)
34. Warkentin, M., Willison, R., Johnston, A.C.: The role of perceptions of organizational injustice and techniques of neutralization in forming computer abuse intentions. In: AMCIS (2011)
35. Gottfredson, M.R., Hirschi, T.: A General Theory of Crime. Stanford University Press, Palo Alto (1990)
36. Ingram, J., Hinduja, S.: Neutralizing Music Piracy: An Empirical Examination. Deviant Behav. **24**(4), 334–366 (2008)
37. Jackson, J.D., Mun, Y.Y., Park, J.S.: An empirical test of three mediation models for the relationship between personal innovativeness and user acceptance of technology. Inf. Manag. **50**(4), 154–161 (2013)
38. Olbrich, S., Frank, U., Gregor, S., Niederman, F., Rowe, F.: On the merits and limits of replication and negation for IS research. AIS Trans. Replication Res. **3**(1), 1–19 (2017)
39. Hirschi, T., Gottfredson, M.: Commentary: testing the general theory of crime. J. Res. Crime Delinq. **30**(1), 47–54 (1993)
40. Rebellon, C.J., Straus, M.A., Medeiros, R.: Self-control in global perspective: An empirical assessment of Gottfredson and Hirschi's general theory within and across 32 national settings. Eur. J. Criminol. **5**(3), 331–361 (2008)
41. Malin, J., Fowers, B.J.: Adolescent self-control and music and movie piracy. Comput. Hum. Behav. **25**(3), 718–722 (2009)

An Institutional Trust Perspective of Cloud Adoption Among SMEs in South Africa

Kenneth Ayong[(✉)] and Rennie Naidoo[(✉)]

University of Pretoria, Private Bag X20 Hatfield, Pretoria 0028, South Africa
ayongkenneth@gmail.com, rennie.naidoo@up.ac.za

Abstract. The purpose of this paper is to identify the major institutional trust mechanisms that facilitate the adoption of cloud services among South African SMEs. By drawing from Giddens' (1990) institutional trust theory and the existing IT trust literature, we developed a conceptual model to improve our understanding of the role of institutional trust between SMEs and cloud service providers. The model was also deployed as a sensitizing framework to deepen our understanding of how institutional trust factors influence SME cloud service adoption decisions. A qualitative field study based on 12 semi-structured interviews of SMEs and cloud service providers in South Africa suggests that the insights gleaned from concepts, such as *design faults* and *operator failure,* can be translated into useful policy guidelines for cloud service providers, state institutions and regulatory bodies that are working to improve the trustworthiness of the cloud ecosystem. Despite the belief held by experts that there is a need to strengthen institutional mechanisms in the cloud ecosystem, the relative advantage of cloud over alternative technology remains the primary motivational factor of SME adoption. The SMEs in this study were unaware of the risks involved in cloud adoption and are content to mimic the behavior of their peers when adopting cloud services. Other social actors in society will have to play a prominent role in evaluating and strengthening institutional trust in the cloud ecosystem.

Keywords: SME · Adoption · Cloud services · Institutional trust · Abstract systems · Relative advantage

1 Introduction

The South African Government considers SMEs to be a critical element for economic growth and a main source of employment [1]. In South Africa, SMEs make up about 56% of the private sector and contribute about 36% to the gross domestic product [2]. Information technology plays a crucial role in the survival and growth of SMEs. Cloud computing is a mechanism of delivering Information Technology (IT) services either as a software, platform or infrastructure through the internet. In this study, cloud computing is defined as information technology services delivered through the Internet to enable business processes. Like traditional utilities, these services are deployed as an on-demand and pay-as-you-use method, making it an attractive investment for an SME because it allows them to focus their efforts on their core business functions [3]

© Springer Nature Switzerland AG 2020
H. Venter et al. (Eds.): ISSA 2019, CCIS 1166, pp. 145–157, 2020.
https://doi.org/10.1007/978-3-030-43276-8_11

The slow rate of adoption among developing countries has been confirmed by the IDC (IDC, 2013) when compared to developed economies, such as Denmark (38%) and Finland (51%) [4, 5].

Despite cloud technologies providing benefits such as cost savings, flexibility, and, increased collaboration, it also has a number of challenges such as security concerns, data ownership concerns, lock-in, service availability, and the requirement for enforceable regulations [6]. The fact that many developing economies have weak institutional mechanisms to regulate the cloud service provisioning environment compared to developed economies provides an important explanation for this lagging adoption rate [7]. Examples of strong institutional instruments include the GDPR privacy regulation that protects European citizens' personal data anywhere in the cloud as well as the Patriot Act of the USA.

Though a substantial increase in scholarly research on the role of trust in inter-organisational transactions, such as cloud service transactions, has been recorded in recent years, these studies have been found to be highly disjointed [8]. Trust has appeared to be a dominant theme in understanding the relationships between organisations thus stressing the need to develop a deeper understanding of the nature of this construct [9]. Trust is emerging from various studies as a mechanism that organisations use to deal with uncertain relationships [10, 11].

Most trust literature has focused on the processes of trust building between individuals [12] and organisations as well as inter-organisations [13]. There has been a preference by researchers to focus on individual trust rather than structural trust [14]. This leaves a gap in understanding the role of institutional structures and mechanisms in these relationships, especially in instances where one party has more power than the other. For example, the cloud service provider generally has more power than the SME cloud user. Hence the study of institutional trust is important in these types of relationship.

This study focuses on the institutional mechanisms that facilitate trust between organisations, where one party has more knowledge and power than the other. The purpose of this article is to develop a conceptual framework that can improve our understanding of the role of institutional trust in cloud adoption among SMEs. This study explores the following research question: *What are the institutional trust factors that facilitate the adoption of cloud computing among South African SMEs?*

The rest of this paper is organised as follows. First, we provide a brief literature review of inter-organisational trust, cloud security risks and institutional trust theories as the foundation of the conceptual model. Then we present the conceptual model. The research methodology is described, then the data collection process and analysis results are reported. We then argue, using semi structured interviews, that trust in the cloud ecosystem mediates the path between privacy and security risks towards its adoption. We further discuss key findings, theoretical and practical implications. The study concludes with a few suggestions for future research work on institutional trust in cloud computing.

2 Conceptual Foundations

Trust is arguably one of the most important social phenomena in cloud computing. Many scholars maintain that trust is necessary for understanding new technology adoption decisions and economic exchanges [15]. Empirical literature suggests that trust has a favourable impact on consumer purchase intentions [16]. According to Gefen, [17] trust is a contributory factor in the adoption of Internet technologies. According to Morgan and Hunt [18], creating and maintaining trust in technology interface services, such as cloud computing, will attract new customers and maintain existing ones.

Bachmann, [19] explains that trust requires accepting dependency, reliability, and a relationship with another that can create an outcome that is otherwise not available. SME decision makers, due to their lack of technical knowledge and resources, assume that most privacy and security risks have been assured by the institutional mechanisms within the cloud ecosystem. Hence, in instances where these mechanisms are perceived to be weak, adoption rates will be slow compared to environments where they are strong.

Giddens' theory of structuration and modernity was chosen to develop theoretical insights about the role of institutional trust in cloud computing adoption among SMEs (See Table 1). We adopt Giddens' [20] insights on the crisis of trust in the contemporary society. In the process of the transformation from tradition to modernity, the trust issue has become increasingly significant both in day-to-day experiences and in theory. Giddens' account of trust recognises the transformation from traditional to modern systems. Modern systems are becoming increasingly complex for the end-user to understand, thus creating more uneasiness and anxiety. On the other hand, trust helps to create a sense of certainty about modern systems.

Table 1. A Giddens conception of institutional trust

Concept	Description	Example in cloud computing
Abstract capacity	Trust is based upon a vague and partial understanding of a system	The customer has confidence in the vendor's ability despite the remoteness of the vendor
Expert system	Technical systems that organise the social environments in which we live	Cloud-Based Expert System (CBES) model for decision making in various facets of modern society assisting cloud customers in areas such as health, transport, education, analytics, robotics and artificial intelligence
Structure	Structure refers to resources and guidelines for social practices and fulfilling the demands of users	The limited resources of SMEs to meet their business objectives requires them to adopt cloud computing due to the competitive global nature of business influencing their decisions

(continued)

Table 1. (*continued*)

Concept	Description	Example in cloud computing
Agency	This refers to human actors whom through their knowledge and capability of doing things use their cognitive skills [21]	Cloud computing service providers use their skills to facilitate business processes through technology on behalf of cloud users to achieve their business goals
Time-Space distanciation	This means that social actors can act without being physically present in the situation	Cloud users can establish a relationship with the cloud service provider and start transacting without a physical presence, even when the two parties are at different geographical locations
Ontological security	Identifying the validity of values incorporated in an institution and the assumption that this modern life makes satisfactory sense to a high number of people to motivate their ongoing active support for the institution and the compliance with its rules	The confidence that most cloud users have in the continuity of their existence and constant reliance on surrounding technological changing environments
Facework commitments	Personal trust is considered to facework commitment where there is mutual and an intimate personal relationship	When cloud service providers sell their products through presentations to gain trust and understand the specific needs of the users. Most cloud providers don't have a personal relationship with the users
Faceless commitments	Trust in expert system where ignorance and dependency drives trust	The more ignorant cloud users can depend on expert systems, such as a cloud technology that does not fail, the more they trust it. Just like users trust Google and the internet today
Design faults	The design of abstract systems may lead to malfunction and not meet the consumers' expectations, leading the consumer to deviate away from their projected benefits	Cloud technology is designed to be robust, secure and prevent human error but due to bad design the service is sometimes out of service, vulnerable to hackers, etc.
Operational failures	Abstract systems are operated upon by humans and humans can make mistakes or errors leading these systems to fail to meet the consumers' expected benefits. This is possible despite the quality of the design of such a system	Cloud technology, as a form of expert systems, is operated upon by the cloud service provider's technical resources who can make mistakes or errors leading to SMEs consuming these services to not achieve the expected benefits

Giddens' definition of trust considers the capacity of dealing with a lack of knowledge when he states that trust is "made based on a "leap into faith" which brackets ignorance or lack of information" [21]. Trust is inherently risky, and a trusting decision is a leap of faith [14]. There are two types of trust to be considered, traditional and institutional trust [22]. When organisations consider their experiences and the protection from institutions, trust is gained quicker [22]. According to Giddens [20], trusted expert systems adopted by social actors can be described as abstract systems. For example, the judicial, banking systems and air traffic control systems which have a combination of technical mechanisms, procedures, professional expertise and other structures enable them to function effectively and thus to be trusted.

Cloud technology is a combination of technical mechanisms (physical servers, applications, operating systems), procedures (service access procedures), and professional expertise (cloud brokers, cloud architects). SMEs adopt this technology with confidence in the absence of technical knowledge of how they function and no contact with its structures Using the air traffic control system as an analogy, the SME owner is similar to the traveler who is unaware of the air traffic control system (expert system). The traveler does not understand how this system functions but trusts that they will travel to their destination safely. Similarly, the SME owner focuses on the core needs of their business while relying on the cloud technology partner to perform as promised. Gollmann [23] supports this notion that users trust in complex technologies emerges through experience and not necessarily through understanding.

Social actors trust these abstract systems and act with confidence in the absence of personal technical knowledge of how these systems function and without contact with its structures but continue to use them without the detailed knowledge of how they work. Similarly cloud computing as a new technology, allows users to consume it through the internet without knowledge of how it works, hence it can be categorised as a modern abstract expert system

According to Giddens [20], abstract systems can prevent users from achieving their goals since they do not control these systems and cannot fully predict its future behaviour. The two factors, according to Giddens [20], that lead to the unpredictability or erratic character of abstract systems is *design fault* and *operation failure*. Following Giddens [20], an SME cloud user adopts an abstract system, such as cloud technology based on the following:

- *Faceless* commitments with the cloud vendor
- No *personal* trust relations with the cloud vendor
- Without the *physical co-presence* of cloud provider
- Confidence in the continuity of cloud services as a social practice

These risky features of abstract systems are sustained by high levels of trust, and more importantly institutional trust. The complexity of cloud technology requires its design to be embedded with robust mechanisms to prevent failures that will compromise the objectives of the user. If these embedded designs are not implemented into the technology as expected by the customer, there is a risk of design faults which creates various risks to the customer, such as security risks. We highlight a few security risks that arise because of failures in the design of this complex technology. Table 2 below highlights what the cloud service provider can do to prevent security vulnerabilities by better embedded designs.

Operational failures refer to the failure of abstract systems due to human error. This is possible despite the quality of the design of such a system. The better the design of these abstract systems the lower the possibility of operational failures. Cloud users do not have sufficient knowledge to assess the design quality of the cloud technology they seek to adopt, neither do they have contact with those operating on these systems.

Table 2. Security risks as a result of failure in design of cloud technology

Security risk	Vulnerability	Mitigation by CSP in technology design
Brute force attacks Dictionary attacks	Weak password policy Weak encryption or authentication	CSP implements password policy in the technology design that is consistent with industry standards such as 27001, CoBIT
Management interface compromise	Remote access System or OS vulnerabilities	CSP embed security designs to prevent penetration of systems
Data loss or Manipulation	Loss of physical control of the data and poor integrity or backup controls	Backup procedures defined, and how long data is kept
Cross - VM attack	Multi-tenancy	Media Access Control (MAC) spoofing, Address Resolution Protocol (ARP) should be protected
Denial of Service	Inadequate resource filtering Weak policies for resource capping	Controls are implemented to manage external and internal attacks, such as distributed denial of service

Cloud technology is a complex system which is operated and maintained by the provider on behalf of the customer. Though the customer has confidence that these operators are technical experts and professionals, they are just humans who can make mistakes and errors during the process. If the technology is not robustly designed, it is more prone to errors or if the operators are not well trained, they are prone to mistakes. We have listed in Table 3 below the risks that arise in instances of cloud providers" operators making mistakes that create operational failures. The power imbalance between the cloud consumer and cloud service provider also add to the possible failures of these abstract systems. Wherever there is human intervention, Giddens claims that there will be unintended consequences beyond the control of the user, especially when there is an imbalance of power and technical knowledge of these systems. Governments have the monopoly power to make and enforce laws that regulate the cloud universe in the interest of all its consumers including SMEs. Giddens' defines trust as "confidence in the reliability of a person or system", regarding a given set of outcomes or events, where that confidence expresses a faith in the probity, or in the correctness of abstract principles "technical knowledge" [20, p. 33].

From this definition of trust by Giddens, we can extend this to the relationship between the SME cloud service adopter or prospective adopter's confidence in the cloud system with the belief that the relationship will yield the desired benefits and trusts the correctness of the abstract principles surrounding the cloud ecosystem. This trust in the abstract principles is also based on the belief that there are institutional mechanisms in place protecting its interests. The conceptual model is based on this definition of trust and the role of institutional mechanisms in mitigating the risks surrounding the relationship between an SME cloud adoptor and the cloud provider.

Table 3. Security vulnerabilities of cloud technology

Security risk	Vulnerability	Mitigation by CSP in operating cloud technology
Service compromise	Hypervisor vulnerabilities Lack of resource isolation	CSP can isolate multitenant applications and data to mitigate cloud services from being compromised
Insider treat	Weak encryption or authentication Insiders on the provider side	Due diligence mechanisms in place for hiring employees with access to sensitive customer data and administrative rights
Physical threats due to theft or vandalism	Unreachable data storage location Weak physical security measures	Background checks done on cloud provider employees with physical access to cloud facilities done
Man-in-the-Middle data leakage	Communication encryption vulnerabilities Weak authentication mechanism	Customer VMs encrypted to prevent vulnerability
Cookie manipulation	Lack of hashes to protect the cookie	Cloud service provider to enforce code of ethics for employees
Fraudulent resource consumption	Exploitation of the Cloud Pricing Model	Cloud service provider to enforce code of ethics for employees on how long security logs are retained and who has access to such logs
Non-compliance poor Governance	Unclear roles and responsibilities and Lack of standard technologies and solutions	Employees must be certified and accredited with industry bodies

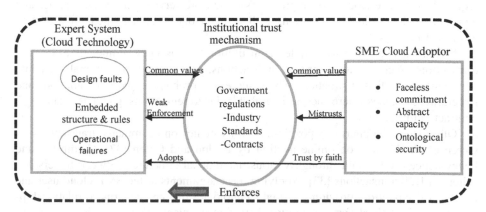

Fig. 1. An institutional-trust model of Cloud Adoption

The proposed research model and propositions are shown in Fig. 1. The characteristics of an SME cloud adopter as per Fig. 1 identifies faceless commitment towards the cloud service provider, since the SME does not have the technical knowledge to assess the design quality of the cloud technology and an ontological security for survival in the modern global economy for the SME. These characteristics of the SME within the South African economy slows adoption because the institutional trust mechanisms expected to be put in place by government and industry bodies are weak or unenforceable.

The cloud user will trust that a cloud service provider has the required expertise to embed the necessary structures and rules in place to prevent design faults, thereby ensuring reliable service [24]. Both the cloud service provider and the cloud user have common values which are the laws governing cloud technology provision, the industry standards and contracts signed between the parties. Though these values are known, the SME cloud user does not trust government institutions to enforce these values. Cloud consumers nevertheless trust this technology for its existence and the fact that its complexity expects the provider to have the required expertise to embed the necessary structures and rules within its design and operations to minimize or eliminate failures. Trust is required for SME ontological security and for the continuity of their existence, they therefore must rely on new technological changing environments [25]. Similarly, [26] suggest that inter-organisational trust is a fundamental factor in enabling and maintaining economic transactions between organisations.

Institutional trust factors such as government regulations, contracts and standards are important trust mechanisms in creating trust in impersonal or faceless economic environments where there is no sense common values [27, 28]. Guarantees and safety nets such as state laws, certifications and SLAs and other performance structures embody institutional trust and assure the trustor that the relationship can be trusted [29]. The common values and beliefs about the behaviour and goals of trusting parties increase the trust between them [18, 30]. The SME cloud user believes that the cloud service provider will work in their interest since they have a reputation to keep and as a legal business will respect the laws of the state. SMEs do not have the resources required to manage cloud service providers if there are service performance issues and hence put their trust in the institutions such as regulatory bodies and the judicial system to protect them [31].

McKnight and Chervany [15] define institution-trust as a key component of Internet transactions, such as cloud services transactions, and classify institutional trust into situational normality in situations where success is probable in normal situations and structural assurances where success is probable due to regulations, guarantees and legal contracts in place [15].

Other studies support this position, such as studies on ecommerce transactions by Gefen et al. [17] and on online auction by Pavlou and Gefen [32]. Credibility and benevolence can be built through various institutional structures between buyers and sellers in B2B transactions [33]. Applying these arguments to the SME cloud user and cloud service provider providing virtual technologies that enables trusted relationships requires built-in third party institutional trust mechanisms such as legislation, rules, escrow and certifications that improved the SMEs trusting belief in the relationship

[15, 17, 28]. Without these institutional safeguards, first time cloud users such as SMEs will be reluctant to adopt such technology.

Another perspective of institutional trust is concerned with routines and controlling mechanisms including external regulators in a business ecosystem such as cloud service [34]. Cook, Hardin and Levi [35, p. 196] suggest that "Societies are essentially moving away from trust relationships toward externally regulated behaviour". Government regulatory bodies fall short of their responsibility of enforcing regulatory and legislative mechanisms on expert systems such as cloud technology sometimes due to lack of technical knowledge. These lapses weaken the institutional trust embodied in these types of expert systems, making vulnerable users such as SMEs cautious in adopting these modern technologies, thereby reducing the adoption rate as compared to other developed economies.

According to Bachmann [19], this third-party guarantor performs a function that ensures trust between the trustor and the trustee that would otherwise not be possible because the institutional arrangements, such as legal regulations, certifications, professional code of conduct, corporate reputation, can reduce the risk that a trustee will behave untrustworthily. This allows a potential cloud service adopter such as an SME to make a leap of faith and invest trust in a relationship with a cloud service vendor. Institutions appear as formal institutional arrangements if they are based on explicit rules of behaviour. These practices are grounded on legal rules, practices of regulatory guidelines, certification bodies' principles, industry associations' standards, service level agreements and contracts creating an institutional arrangement leading to stable trusted relationships [21]. SMEs will generally have faith in the cloud service ecosystem if there are promises, contracts, regulations, and guarantees in place [15].

3   Method

The goal of this research is to more fully understand and describe the process by which SME adoption decisions about cloud services are motivated by institutional trust factors. This type of research relies on qualitative data. Adoption decisions are best understood by analysing informants' social constructions through language and shared meanings. Fieldwork based on semi-structured interviews lasting 30 to 60 min were used to collect the data. A set of 12 interviews was conducted as a primary data collection method. Interviews were recorded with the permission of the participants and transcribed for further analysis. These nine informants were categorised into three main groups. These were SMEs that had already adopted cloud computing services, SMEs that intended to adopt cloud computing services in the next three years and SMEs that did not intend to adopt cloud computing services soon. For better triangulation of findings, this data was supplemented with three interviews of SME cloud service providers. Thematic analysis was adopted as the qualitative data analysis strategy. The authors read the data sets multiple times and worked independently to generate a set of thematic categories. Finally, we selected exemplars to show the link between the data and the thematic analysis. The thematic findings show the four interrelated themes about institutional trust emerged from the data.

4   Findings

Mimicking the behavior of partners and competitors. Four SMEs stated that they fear going 'extinct' if they do not adopt cloud technology. Cloud computing is seen to be important due to their future competitiveness and hence has a significant influence on their adoption decision. An important influence in the adoption decision is the behavior of partners, such as suppliers and competitors in the industry. SMEs are more likely to trust cloud service if their partners and competitors have already adopted it.

Relative advantage mitigates the risk of poor institutional mechanisms. Some SMEs (T04, T06, T07, T08) were of the view that they have no choice but to trust the cloud providers, as the relative advantage outweighs the risk it has over traditional IT. Others indicated that security and privacy is a serious concern because they are responsible for their customers' data which is handed over to a third-party cloud service provider. However, five SMEs (T02, T04, T05, T07, and T08) say since large organisations are adopting this technology, they too feel that they can adopt it and benefit from the advantages promised. Some SMEs said *"Not really. It has always worked and is working for bigger companies why worry. Though I don't know much about cloud computing systems, but it seems to be working well for us ".* There is a perception of ownership that the service provider gives the customer. One cloud service provider (T09) says *"the fact that I am running the customer job doesn't mean I have access to them. I can perform backups but cannot log in and access your data except ... the customer gives me access, I will be logged out".*

Lack of technical knowledge in SMEs creates reliance on the Cloud Provider expertise. The design faults in cloud technologies make them vulnerable to hackers. This can create mistrust and uncertainty among SMEs. The lack of technical knowledge by SMEs also creates reliance on the expertise of cloud service providers to ensure the service is secure, protected and available when required. Four of the SMEs (T05, T07, T09, and T10) disclosed that they do not have the technical ability, due to the technical nature of this type of technology, to verify if the promised security features have been implemented by the cloud service provider. The SMEs that adopted cloud services trust cloud service providers and the institutional mechanisms around various role players within the cloud ecosystem.

Assuming sufficiency of institutional trust mechanisms. Most of the uncertainty was about the enforcement of laws governing the cloud service providers. SMEs (T01, T02, T04, T06, and T08) were of the opinion that it is the responsibility of government to ensure that consumers of cloud services are protected against any abuse, though also concede that there exists some breaches in the past that proves that governments do not fully have control over what cloud services providers do. For example, an SME said *"Is ICASA not also controlling these service providers? I think this is part of communications".* Another SME said: *"If they were not regulated, they will not be providing such services in South Africa".* Most cloud service providers are self-regulated due to the global nature of their customer base and operations. Service provider T09 was of the opinion that *"Data sovereignty is often an issue for customers. That is where your data is stored is sovereign to that country. We stick to Microsoft ethical practices. We are regulated by Microsoft practices and rules. We are driven by the clients' specific regulations"* This is contrary to other institutional trust research (e.g. [19, 28, 32], which proposes standardised rules and regulations that create certainty and structure. Some SMEs are not sure who is enforcing the rules or whose role it is to enforce these rules, one (T01) said "*I am not entirely sure exactly who is controlling these companies. What I know is that because they use Visa and Master card they are controlled by regulatory bodies as they have to settle using a local account*". Another SME is also very skeptical on the role of government agencies in enforcing regulations, "*I don't know exactly all the role players. I am sure government plays a part and maybe some international partners in regulating these providers, but I don't think they are doing a great job at it. If they were, we will not be hearing a lot of about breaches in big companies like Sony and even governments like USA government. Remember the guy who downloaded top secrets from the US government and exposed them. Imagine the US government with all the technology. I know there may be many players in the space of cloud computing, but I am not sure what roles they play in protecting us consumers*". The power of the cloud service provider in the relationship with the cloud user is real. Some SMEs (T02, T03, T05, T07, T08) are aware of the power of the cloud service provider with one saying that "*We depend on the cloud service provider to maintain our accounts and data. They back-up our data and we trust that our systems can be recovered in case it falls over*". This is consistent with existing research that says, trust is not completely independent of inter-organisational relationships and other power relation structures due to complex interrelationships between cloud users and cloud service provider [36].

Adopters noted that they do not have the technical expertise to monitor the contracts and SLAs they sign with cloud providers, making them vulnerable to abuse and non-compliance. Strangely, the SMEs who adopted cloud services seem to think that government institutions and industry bodies have put mechanisms in place to govern cloud service providers and enforce these mechanisms to protect their interests.

5 Conclusion

The results of this study highlight how SMEs socially construct their perspectives of institutional trust in cloud services and explore how these constructions could be influencing SME cloud adoption decisions. Our study finds that in order to survive, some SMEs merely mimic the behavior of larger organizations, their partners and competitors when making the adoption decision. As predicted by the diffusion of innovation theory [37] the perception of the greater relative advantage of Cloud services also seems to mitigate the high risk of poor institutional mechanisms among SMEs. As predicted by Giddens [20], the lack of technical knowledge by some SMEs creates greater reliance on cloud provider expertise. Finally, we found that SMEs simply assume the sufficiency of institutional trust mechanisms in Cloud ecosystems. Since SMEs do not have the capacity to evaluate cloud service innovations effectively, other social actors in society will have to play a prominent role in evaluating and strengthening these institutional trust mechanisms. The empirical literature on the strength of institutional trust of cloud computing services and other new platforms in South Africa and other developing markets is sparse. Design faults and operator failure can be useful conceptual tools for the development of policy guidelines by global and regulatory bodies responsible for the cloud ecosystem. Improvements to the trustworthiness of the cloud ecosystem will safeguard the interests of SMEs that appear to be naïve about the risks of cloud computing. Since SMEs lack the requisite technical knowledge and are often less powerful than CSPs, enforceable institutional mechanisms will be required to protect their interests.

We recommend that future research examine the strength of these institutional mechanisms in safeguarding the interest of SME cloud users in developing economies.

References

1. Berry, A., von Blottnitz, M., Cassim, R., Kesper, A., Rajaratnam, B., van Seventer, D.: The economics of SMMEs in South Africa. TIPS-Trade Ind. Policy (2002). http://www.tips.org.za/files/506.pdf. Accessed 22 Apr 2019
2. Fatoki, O., Smit, A.: Constraints to credit access by new SMEs in South Africa : a supply-side analysis. Afr. J. Bus. Manag. **5**(4), 1413–1425 (2011)
3. Alshamaila, Y., Papagiannidis, S., Li, F.: Cloud computing adoption by SMEs in the north east of England: a multi-perspective framework. J. Enterp. Inf. Manag. **26**(3), 250–275 (2013)
4. European-Commission, "ICT – Information and communication technologies, European," European Commission (2013)
5. Giannakouris, K., Smihily, M.: Cloud computing - statistics on the use by enterprises. Eurostat (2014). http://ec.europa.eu/eurostat/statisticsexplained/index.php/Cloud_computing_-_statistics_on_the_use_by_enterprise
6. Venkatraman, S., Wadhwa, B.: Cloud computing a research roadmap in coalescence with software engineering. Softw. Eng. Int. J. (SEIJ) **2**(2), 2 (2012)
7. Paik, S.: Supply management in SMEs: role of SME size. Int. J. Supply Chain Forum **12**(3), 10–21 (2011)
8. McEvily, B., Perrone, V., Zaheer, A.: Introduction to the special issue on trust in an organizational context. Organ. Sci. **14**(1), 1–4 (2003)
9. Zaheer, A., Harris, J.: Interorganizational Trust (2006)
10. Lumineau, F., Quélin, B.V.: An empirical investigation of interorganizational opportunism and contracting mechanisms. Strateg. Organ. **10**(1), 55–84 (2012)
11. Rousseau, D.M., Sitkin, S.B., Burt, R.S., Camerer, C.: Not so different after all: a cross-discipline view of trust. Acad. Manag. Rev. **23**(3), 393–404 (1998)
12. Jap, S.D., Anderson, E.: Safeguarding interorganizational performance and continuity under ex post opportunism. Manag. Sci. **49**(12), 1684–1701 (2003)
13. Koza, M.P., Lewin, A.Y.: The co-evolution of strategic alliances. Organ. Sci. **9**(3), 255–264 (1998)
14. Lewis, J., Weigert, A.: Trust as a social reality. Soc. Forces **63**, 967–985 (1985)
15. McKnight, D., Chervany, N.: What trust means in e-commerce customer relationships: an interdisciplinary conceptual typology. Int. J. Electron. Commer. **6**(2), 35–53 (2002)
16. Jarvenpaa, S., Tractinsky, N.: Consumer trust in an internet store: a cross-cultural validation. J. Comput.-Mediated Commun. **5**(2), JCMC526 (1999)
17. Gefen, D., Karahanna, E., Straub, D.: Trust and TAM in online shopping: an integrated model. MIS Q. **27**(1), 51–90 (2003)
18. Morgan, R., Hunt, S.: The commitment-trust theory of relationship marketing. J. Mark. **58**(1), 20–38 (1994)
19. Bachmann, R.: Understanding institutional-based trust building processes in inter-organizational relationships. Organ. Stud. **32**(2), 281–301 (2011)
20. Giddens, A.: The Consequences of Modernity. Stanford University Press, Palo Alto (1990)

21. Giddens, A.: The Constitution of Society: Outline of the Theory of Structuration. Polity Press, Cambridge (1984)
22. Child, J., Möllering, G.: The development of contextual based trust in the Chinese context. Judge Institute of Management, University of Cambridge (2000)
23. Gollmann, D.: Why trust is bad for security. Electron. Notes Theor. Comput. Sci. **157**(3), 3–9 (2006)
24. Kumar, N.: The power of trust in manufacturer-retailer relationships. Harvard Bus. Rev. **74**(6), 92–106 (1996)
25. Ganesan, S.: Determinants of long-term orientation in buyer-seller relationships. J. Mark. **58**(1), 1–19 (1994)
26. Bachmann, R., van Witteloostuijn, A.: Analyzing inter-organizational relationships in the context of their national business systems: a conceptual framework for comparative research. Eur. Soc. **11**, 49–76 (2009)
27. Giddens, A.: Risk, Trust, Reflexivity, pp. 184–197. Polity Press, Cambridge (1994)
28. Zucker, L.: Production of trust: institutional sources of economic structure, 1840–1920. Res. Organ. Behav. **8**(1), 53–111 (1986)
29. Shapiro, S.: The social control of impersonal trust. Am. J. Sociol. **93**(3), 623–658 (1987)
30. Heide, J., John, G.: Alliances in industrial purchasing, the determinants of joint action in buyer-supplier relationships. J. Mark. Res. **37**(1), 24–36 (1990)
31. Reichheld, F.F., Schefter, P.: E-loyalty: your secret weapon on the web. Harvard Bus. Rev. **78**(4), 105–113 (2000)
32. Pavlou, P.A., Gefen, D.: Building effective online marketplaces with institution-based trust. Inf. Syst. Res. **15**(1), 37–59 (2004)
33. Pavlou, P.: Institutional trust in interorganizational exchange relationships: the role of electronic B2B marketplaces. J. Strateg. Inf. Syst. **11**(4), 105–143 (2002)
34. Sztompka, P.: Trust: A Sociological Theory. University Press, Cambridge (1999)
35. Cook, K., Schilke, O.: The role of public, relational and organizational trust in economic affairs. Corp. Reput. Rev. **13**, 98–109 (2010)
36. Mizrachi, N.D.I., Anspach, R.: Repertoires of trust: the practice of trust in a multinational organization amid political conflict. Am. Sociol. Rev. **72**, 143–165 (2007)
37. Rogers, E.M.: Diffusion of Innovations, 4th edn. Simon and Schuster, New York (1995)

Data Privacy Compliance Benefits for Organisations – A Cyber-Physical Systems and Internet of Things Study

Ntsako Baloyi[1,2](✉) and Paula Kotzé[2](✉) (iD)

[1] Council for Scientific and Industrial Research, Pretoria, South Africa
nbaloyil1@gmail.com
[2] Department of Informatics, University of Pretoria, Pretoria, South Africa
paula.kotze@gmail.com

Abstract. The protection of people's privacy is both a legal requirement and a key factor for doing business in many jurisdictions. Organisations thus have a legal obligation to get their privacy compliance in order as a matter of business importance. This applies not only to organisations' day-to-day business operations, but also to the information technology systems they use, develop or deploy. However, privacy compliance, like any other legal compliance requirements, is often seen as an extra burden that is both unnecessary and costly. Such a view of compliance can result in negative consequences and lost opportunities for organisations. This paper seeks to position data privacy compliance as a value proposition for organisations by focusing on the benefits that can be derived from data privacy compliance as it applies to a particular subset of information technology systems, namely cyber-physical systems and Internet of Things technologies. A baseline list of data privacy compliance benefits, contextualised for CPSs and IoT with the South African legal landscape is proposed.

Keywords: Internet of Things · Cyber-physical systems · Data privacy · Privacy compliance benefits · POPI act

1 Introduction

Privacy is a multi-dimensional and multi-discipline concept that is not always easy to define. This paper focuses on a specific form of privacy, which is information or data privacy, also referred to as privacy of personal information [1]. In this paper, data privacy refers to control over one's personal information [2, 3]. Such control allows one to decide what may or may not be done with your personal information in cases where the law does not place any restrictions on such control.

Worldwide, organisations are under siege from regulatory authorities for violations of people's privacy [4, 5]. The increased focus on data privacy and the enactment of the General Data Protection Regulation (GDPR) [6] by the European Union (EU) has led to a worldwide rush of enacting data privacy legislation [7]. South Africa is among the countries that have enacted privacy legislation in the form of the Protection of Personal Information Act 4 of 2013 (POPI Act) [8]. The significance of privacy as an important

© Springer Nature Switzerland AG 2020
H. Venter et al. (Eds.): ISSA 2019, CCIS 1166, pp. 158–172, 2020.
https://doi.org/10.1007/978-3-030-43276-8_12

area of focus for organisations can therefore hardly be challenged. Ignoring data privacy can have dire consequences for organisations.

An earlier study [9] found that organisational readiness for data privacy compliance in South Africa was still a concern. Organisations should ensure their compliance to data privacy laws by leveraging organisational processes and structures to create an environment for data privacy to thrive. However, data privacy need not only be seen as a problem, but should also be seen as a value adding tool or opportunity for an organisation and its stakeholders.

Furthermore, technologies that process personal information are privacy prone, thereby affecting organisations that own or use them. Data privacy compliance is therefore also an important consideration for the processing of personal information through modern information technologies. This paper specifically focuses on cyber-physical systems (CPSs) and Internet of Things (IoT) technologies that collect and process personal information (and excludes those that do not). One of the strengths of CPSs and IoT technologies is their ability to capture or record vast amounts of information, some of which may be personal information. This strength is a double-edged sword as it is also a source of possible privacy risks and concerns. Data privacy has therefore been identified as one of the challenges that have to be addressed for CPSs [10] and IoT [11], since these technologies could have peculiar privacy risks and concerns, not typical of traditional information technology systems. These privacy concerns are due to data collection and processing methods that involve the use of sensors and advanced data processing (e.g. data mining) techniques or algorithms. The uniqueness of privacy concerns is also as a result of the possible covert nature of data collection, which may not involve meaningful data subject participation or informed consent.

Organisations are core to the advancement of data privacy in CPSs and IoT technologies. However, privacy compliance for organisations, like any other compliance requirements, is often seen as an extra burden that is both unnecessary and costly. Such a view of compliance can result in negative consequences and lost opportunities for organisations. Cavoukian and Dixon [12] have proposed the identification of information security and privacy compliance benefits as a useful exercise for justifying investment.

Privacy compliance benefits, however, is an area that that remains largely unexplored. There are many publications that focus on benefits or applications of data, CPSs and IoT for individuals, organisations and nations [13–21]. It is customary to focus on the value that technologies themselves can bring, as has been evidenced and is further corroborated by the work of Carroll [22] on cloud computing and virtualization benefits. The value of data as well as technologies like CPSs and IoT is significant and well-articulated. Interestingly, not much literature exist that focus on value that could result from compliance in general, and privacy compliance specifically. Such a position does not provide organisations with much incentive for compliance other than being legally abiding and responsible corporate citizens.

Contextualised within the South African legal landscape, this paper focuses on such privacy compliance benefits, with a view to bring to light the value that organisations can derive as a result of data privacy compliance, specifically as it relates to CPSs and IoT. The list of baseline privacy compliance benefits for organisations are not necessarily limited to CPSs and IoT, but could also find relevance for other technologies and domains with privacy implications.

Section 2 provides background on CPSs, IoT and privacy. Section 3 outlines the research methodology followed in compiling the list of benefits. Section 4 discusses the findings and presents a proposed list of privacy compliance benefits. Section 5 comments on the use of the benefits while Sect. 6 concludes the paper.

2 Background

2.1 Cyber-Physical Systems and Internet of Things

There are no standard definitions for both CPSs and IoT. This paper views a CPS as highly automated physical systems or processes with computing and networking [14]. An alternative definition views CPSs as electronic control systems that control physical machines, such as, controlling motors and valves in an industrial plant [23]. The typical characteristic of CPSs are physical component cyber-capability, multi-scale networking, dynamic reorganisation, self-configuration, high automation, cyber-physical adaptation, self-management and dependable operation [24].

Two distinctions are made to the definition of IoT, namely, small and large IoT deployments or applications [25]. The Institute for Electrical and Electronics Engineers (IEEE) definition for small deployments of IoT focuses on the interconnectedness of things to the Internet and their remote management [25]. The IEEE's definition for large deployments of IoT focuses on complex systems that possess self-adaptive, high-automation and physical-to-digital capabilities. Large IoT deployments are sometimes referred to as Industrial Internet of Things (IIoT) [26]. In this paper, IoT shall refer to the interconnection of things to the Internet and the ability to remotely manage them, in line with the definition for small scale deployments. The large-scale deployment of IoT, i.e. IIoT, shall be referred to under the umbrella concept of CPSs.

Examples of IoT applications include an individual's interconnected devices, smart homes, etc. [18]. CPSs' applications areas could include power grids, vehicular transportation, smart buildings, eHealth, smart manufacturing, etc. [14, 19].

2.2 Privacy and the Protection of Personal Data

At least 108 countries and regions were reported to have enacted data privacy legislation by 2016 [27]. South Africa has enacted privacy legislation in the form of the POPI Act [8] to address privacy for both natural and juristic persons. Examples of privacy legal instruments enacted by other countries and regions include the European Union's GDPR [6], United Kingdom's Data Protection Act [28] and the African Union's Convention on Cybersecurity and Personal Data Protection [29].

Privacy legal instruments are underpinned by principles or conditions for the lawful processing of personal information. These principles or conditions are largely a variation of the five fair information practices (FIPs) introduced by the United States Department of Health, Education and Welfare in 1973 [30]. The FIPs are transparency, use limitation, access and correction, data quality and security.

The POPI Act [8] is premised on the right to privacy which is provided for in Section 14 of the Constitution of the Republic of South Africa of 1996 [31]. The POPI Act is concerned with regulating the processing of personal information and therefore does not only apply to CPSs and IoT but to all processing of personal information. Processing is an all-encompassing term that covers anything that can be done with personal information, including collection, retrieval, storage, alteration, destruction, transmission, etc. [8].

The POPI Act [8], however, does not define the term privacy. Data privacy in this paper refers to privacy over personal information, giving data subjects control over their personal information [2, 3]. Personal data is defined as information relating to an identifiable, living natural person or existing juristic person [8, 32]. A data subject is a person whose identifying personal data is the subject of collection or processing [8].

Sections 8–25 of the POPI Act [8] lays down eight conditions for the processing of personal information, as provided in Table 1.

Table 1. Conditions for the lawful processing of personal information [8].

Privacy condition	Description
Accountability	To ensure that all the conditions and relevant provisions of the POPI Act are complied with, when processing personal information
Processing limitation	To ensure that only minimal personal information is processed and such processing is lawful and conducted in a reasonable manner. Further that personal information is collected directly from data subjects and primarily based on informed consent, unless certain conditions apply
Purpose specification	To specify and communicate the purpose for the processing of personal information. Responsible parties, may, in certain circumstances be required to retain or restrict the processing of personal information
Further processing limitation	To ensure that personal information is only processed for specified or compatible purposes unless there are other valid legal grounds for further processing, such as informed consent
Information quality	To ensure that personal information is accurate, complete, not misleading and updated where necessary
Openness	To ensure that responsible parties maintain documentation of processing activities and communicate details relevant for data subjects to exercise their rights
Security safeguards	To ensure that responsible parties take appropriate and reasonable technical and organisational measures to secure the integrity and confidentiality of personal information within their control or possession
Data subject participation	To ensure that data subjects are able to request access, correction, deletion and other actions to their personal information

3 Research Methodology

The primary objective of this paper is to assist organisations to embed data privacy into their organisational culture with an appreciation of the value that data privacy compliance can bring. The focus is specifically on privacy compliance benefits for organisations that use or develop technologies for CPSs and IoT to address the paucity of organisational data privacy compliance benefits for these technologies and empower them to view data privacy compliance as a value adding exercise.

A design science research (DSR) approach was followed to conduct the research to compile the benefits, allowing for knowledge generation and contribution through iterations or circumscriptions. The variant of DSR followed is that by Vaishnavi, Kuechler and Petter [33], with five activities, namely, awareness of the problem, suggestion for a solution, development, evaluation and conclusion. The list of privacy compliance benefits was developed in two DSR development iterations followed by a refinement process.

During the first development cycle, a literature study and content analysis (of legal instruments) were conducted to identify privacy compliance benefits with likely significance for organisations with respect to CPSs and IoT. This iteration resulted in an initial list of 14 privacy compliance benefits. The second development iteration, to review and refine the initial list of privacy compliance, included an expert review process that used interviews and questionnaires. The panel of 23 experts, with 202 years of combined experience, included specialists from eight different domains, including CPSs/IoT, data privacy law, data privacy, management, enterprise risk, human resources, information security and enterprise architecture. They were asked to review the provided benefits, suggest exclusions of any of the listed benefits and inclusion of new benefits. This cycle resulted in changes to the phrasing of some benefits and the addition of three new benefits, resulting in a total of 17 benefits.

As an evaluation exercise for factual accuracy and coverage, the 17 organisational privacy compliance benefits for CPSs and IoT were reviewed by another panel of 21 specialists from similar domains to the development panel, also with at least 202 years combined experience. The reviews were conducted in the form of interviews guided by an open-ended questionnaire. The guiding question was to determine whether the presented benefits highlight the most important benefits of data privacy compliance for organisations in relation to CPSs and IoT. The respondents were requested to substantiate their responses. The proposed list of data privacy-related benefits for organisations in the context of CPSs and IoT were found to be representative of the most important benefits that organisations can derive from privacy compliance. One additional benefit was suggested for inclusion and included in the final list of 18 benefits. The review formed part of the evaluation for a broader project focusing on developing a data privacy framework for CPSs and IoT for IT professionals [34].

The usefulness and relevance of the benefits was also demonstrated on a real-world IoT project being deployed at an organisation in South Africa [34]. Many of the benefits were found to be directly relevant to the project and the context of the project.

4 Privacy Compliance Benefits for Organisations Using or Developing CPS and IoT Technologies

Organisational data privacy compliance benefits refer to the value that an organisation can derive as a result of privacy legal compliance, with particular focus on CPSs and IoT domains. The ability to avoid, mitigate or transfer certain privacy risks can also be seen as privacy compliance benefits. Privacy compliance benefits are meant to assist organisations to appreciate the value that data privacy compliance can bring to an organisation, in order to build a case for spending resources on data privacy compliance beyond the need for legal compliance.

In total, this paper proposes a non-exhaustive list of 18 organisational privacy compliance benefits. These are potential privacy compliance benefits that organisations may derive as a result data privacy compliance for CPSs and IoT technologies. Each of these benefits are discussed in more detail in the remainder of this section.

4.1 Legal Compliance

The primary organisational benefit emanates from being able to demonstrate respect for the rule of law through legal compliance. The ability to demonstrate privacy compliance is essential not only for regulatory authorities, but for various other stakeholders as well such as data subjects, investors, etc. Data privacy compliance, in this instance, means compliance with the law (or legal obligations) [35]. In the South African context, this primarily means complying with the POPI Act [8] and secondarily with associated domestic and international privacy laws. Legal compliance is a benefit as it has the potential to protect organisations from legal sanctions and adverse public action. Data privacy compliance is an advantage for organisations in that they conduct their operations knowing that they are in compliance with the law and are providing value to their clients and other stakeholders.

4.2 Data Subject Trust and Confidence

Data subjects, as active or inactive participants in CPSs and IoT technology-related processing activities, should be able to trust the product or service and the intentions of the organisations involved, and have confidence that the organisations will treat their personal information in line with the law. However, the nature of CPSs and IoT is such that people may become data subjects without their knowledge. CPSs and IoT are often not geared for an opt-in mechanism as opt-in may sometimes be difficult to effect for these technologies. An example of this could be in a smart city environment where various types of sensors that process personal information may be deployed across a city. Sometimes data subjects may not even have full appreciation of the extent of the data collected or the data processing activities, even where such information may be readily available. In such situations, organisations responsible for the CPSs and IoT technologies have an even greater responsibility to ensure that they are data privacy compliant because of the nature of their CPSs and IoT related activities.

Data privacy compliance and respect for people's data privacy have the potential to increase levels of trust and confidence in organisations [1, 35, 36]. An effort by an organisation to comply with data privacy laws can boost people's perceptions about the organisation and their willingness to use or participate in the organisation's CPSs and IoT related activities or initiatives. Data subject trust and confidence in organisations is thus a benefit that organisations can derive from ensuring data privacy compliance when dealing with personal data, especially in areas such as CPSs and IoT.

4.3   Data Subject Retention

Data privacy breaches and an apparent lack of systems to safeguard people's privacy can result in people losing confidence in organisations and deciding to boycott their products and services [37]. It follows that evidence of data privacy protection mechanisms can contribute towards data subject retention, which is in the best interest of organisations [35]. Loss of data subjects may imply a loss of customers or important participants for CPSs and IoT initiatives, which could be detrimental to such programmes. Data subjects may be more likely to continue participating in or using CPSs and IoT related projects, systems or solutions when they are aware that there is no immediate danger to themselves as could result from data privacy violations. The value that organisations can derive could be increased data subject retention as the risk of flight would be mitigated.

4.4   Public Trust

Public trust in an organisation is important for the organisation's brand, services and financial sustainability. One of the factors that can affect an organisation's bottom line is how people perceive an organisation, which has a direct bearing on the level of trust that they apportion to that organisation. Dissatisfaction by one member of the public could result in serious consequences for an organisation due to the ease with which people can disseminate their frustrations to increased networks of people. Privacy related frustrations are not an exception and can in fact solicit even higher levels of rage from the public. Organisations therefore need to jealously and actively guard as well as manage the trust that the public has on them. Privacy is one area that organisations should ensure that they are not left vulnerable as it could result in the erosion of public trust on the entire organisation and its products or services. Data privacy protection is but one of many areas that can bring about greater public trust in organisations [38, 39], and has been posited as one of the factors that can increase confidence in organisations [35]. Public trust in organisations with CPSs and IoT technologies has the potential to encourage or enable CPSs and IoT technology uptake and confidence by the public.

4.5   Consumer Trust and Confidence

The strength and sustainability of any commercial organisation hinges on its customer base, natural or juristic. Organisational customer trust and confidence, or lack thereof, can have serious financial implications. Consumer trust and confidence also have a direct impact on customer perceptions of the organisation's brand and may influence how customers speak about the organisation to others [1, 36]. Consumers who trust or have confidence in organisations or particular brands often remain loyal customers and can confidently introduce others to the same organisation or brand. This makes consumer trust and confidence in organisations and their brands an essential element for their growth and survival. Consumer action and public outrage has proven to be effective in getting organisations to review practices detrimental to consumers [40].

Consumer trust and confidence is an area that could have a bearing on customer satisfaction and continued willingness to engage with the organisation, or its services and products, especially those most likely to affect their privacy. All the organisation's stakeholders, including customers and employees, should have confidence in how the organisation handles data privacy. Customer trust (including that of employees) over an organisation's data privacy practices and processes is essential for CPSs and IoT project buy-in and support [35].

4.6 Respect for Consumer Privacy

Organisations are often criticised for pursuing profits at the expense of human rights abuses and other societal effects [41]. Data privacy compliance can be one way to practically demonstrate that an organisation are is concerned about and does have respect for consumers, their privacy and by extension their human rights [36]. This is one way to demonstrate organisational customer-centricity, especially for potentially invasive technologies like CPSs and IoT.

4.7 Improved Service Provision

Access to personal information is important for the provision of services to individuals and is beneficial for statistical and research purposes. CPSs and IoT sensors can be great sources for personal information related to service provision. Lawful processing of personal information by organisations can benefit both organisations and data subjects as it can result in better service provision [35]. Compliance with data privacy laws empowers organisations to legally process personal information in the furtherance of their objectives, which could in turn result in improved service provision for the organisation's clients.

4.8 Reducing Organisational Reputational Risk

An organisation's reputation affects its ability to do business in an optimal manner. Data privacy violations, or lack of data privacy compliance, can be a contributing factor to an organisations' reputational damage. Data privacy compliance can, therefore, reduce the exposure of the organisation to reputational risks resulting from CPSs and IoT operations [38, 39]. Organisations can in turn be spared from data privacy-related law suits, prosecutions, public outcry, regulatory sanctions, etc. A good name remains one of the important attributes that organisations need and anything, including privacy-related risks, that could adversely affect it has the potential to threaten their very existence.

4.9   Improved Risk Management

Incorporating privacy into an organisation's risk management processes strengthens an organisation's internal risk controls. Conducting a privacy risk assessment is a legal requirement in terms of Sections19(2) and 109(3)(g) of the POPI Act [8]. Organisations can improve their risk management procedures by incorporating personal data related risks, specifically those relating to CPSs or IoT. This would result in them satisfying the requirement for risk assessments of personal information and consequently be making inroads toward data privacy compliance. Data privacy compliance can strengthen internal risk management in organisations [1].

4.10   Data Privacy Risk Minimisation

Organisations are increasingly exposed to privacy-related risks, especially in the form of data breaches. Data privacy breaches could include information security breaches, unlawful processing, inability to provide data subject access to personal information where applicable, etc. The minimisation of data privacy risk is an advantage as it reduces an organisation's risk exposure. The volume and sensitivity of personal information that organisations manage increase their risk of data breaches. Putting systems in place to ensure that an organisation is data privacy compliant can greatly minimise potential data privacy breaches [38]. Compliance with the eight conditions for the lawful processing of personal information [8] (see Table 1) could minimise organisations' exposure to data privacy-related risks. CPSs and IoT devices have particularly been identified as high-risk targets for information security breaches and likewise data privacy breaches [10, 11].

4.11   Reduction of Complaints and Disputes

It is in the best interest of any organisation to ensure that there is minimal stakeholder dissent or dissatisfaction resulting from the use of CPSs and IoT to process personal information. With Section 24 of the POPI Act [8] empowering data subjects to dispute the accuracy of collected personal information or lawfulness of the processing and request its correction or deletion, organisations need to be privacy compliant and prepared to support data subjects. Furthermore, Section74 of the POPI Act empowers any person to lay a complaint with the Information Regulator [42] where they feel that there has been interference with their right to protection of personal information.

Compliance with data privacy laws can greatly reduce privacy-related complaints or disputes and/or assist with their speedy resolution [38, 39]. Data privacy compliance may also reduce the risk of infringement by organisations and enforcement action by the Information Regulator [39]. Reduced data privacy-related complaints and disputes may save an organisation valuable resources and increase confidence [39].

4.12   Public Perception of Transparent Practices

In business, just as in life, perceptions are everything. Organisations need to be seen to be transparent with people's personal information by being open and clear about their

CPSs or IoT data processing activities. Demonstrating that an organisation is transparent can boost its image in society and with its customers, which can in turn result in greater public confidence [35, 43]. Automated decision-making (Section 71 of the POPI Act [8]) and data subject access (Sections 18 and 23 of the POPI Act) are some of the areas where data subjects can witness an organisation's transparency or lack thereof. In terms of Sections 17–18 of the POPI Act, the openness condition stipulates that organisations or responsible parties should document details about their processing operations and disclose certain information to data subjects. Organisations therefore need to ensure that they are favourably perceived by the public as this can improve their reputation. Privacy compliant practices can aid with this purpose.

4.13 Reduced Risk of Collateral Intrusion

CPSs and IoT technologies present a risk of capturing large amounts of information about people indiscriminately. This risk is known as collateral intrusion as data subjects other than those targeted can be affected, and even those targeted may not have consented to the processing of their personal information. CPSs and IoT could lead to the collection and processing of vast amounts of personal information that could result in adverse inferences towards data subjects. Compliance with data privacy conditions or principles may reduce the risk of collateral intrusion [44]. This is made possible through mechanisms such as data minimisation, de-identification and others. The perceived reduced risk of collateral intrusion is a benefit as it could lead to better acceptance of CPSs and IoT technologies and a reduced likelihood of legal action as a result of data privacy breaches.

4.14 Regulated Data Sharing

Data is central to the benefits associated with CPSs and IoT. It is also the main focus of privacy laws. Organisations have a need to process data, some of which may be personal information. It may also be in the nature of an organisation's business to have to share personal data. Compliance with personal data privacy laws can be an enabler for lawful sharing, whilst the opposite may directly limit an organisation's operations. Information may be lawfully shared in compliance with the POPI Act's [8] eight conditions for lawful processing of personal information (see Table 1). It may also be shared by relying on the further processing limitation condition, as per Section 15 of the POPI Act. Transborder transfer or sharing is regulated by Section 72 of the POPI Act. Requests for access to personal information, which results in the sharing of personal information, may also emanate from the process as set out in the Promotion of Access to Information Act 2 of 2000 [45].

Data privacy compliance can, therefore, enable data sharing where the conditions set out in the POPI Act [8] are met. Data sharing can be one of the advantages that organisations that comply with data privacy laws can legally enjoy, and shared data can accordingly be afforded appropriate protection [39]. Data transfers may be difficult to avoid in CPSs and IoT technologies and should, therefore, be done in privacy compliant ways. It is difficult for organisations to control or monitor what is done with personal information once shared. As a consequence, being able to show that an organisation took all reasonable measures/precautions before sharing personal information can save organisations from liability or reduce their liability.

4.15 Better Data Security/Protection

Information security is very important for CPSs and IoT environments, more so when dealing with personal information of natural and juristic persons. In terms of Sections 19–21 of the POPI Act [8], one of the data privacy conditions or principles (see Table 1) is security safeguards. The security safeguards principle requires organisations to take appropriate technical and organisational measures to protect personal information. A focus on information security measures for personal data, in terms of Section 19 of the POPI Act, can help strengthen an organisation's information security. Information security is very important for CPSs and IoT environments, more so when dealing with personal information of natural and juristic persons.

Many privacy breaches are likely to be as a result of information security breaches. Adequate focus on information security is an advantage with respect to both information security and privacy. Organisations would be less likely to be exposed to privacy breaches, which would in turn expose all their operations to scrutiny. Information security is important to protect the organisation and data subjects, and also to ensure that CPSs and IoT technologies are not hijacked to be used for nefarious purposes.

4.16 Encourage Adoption of CPSs and IoT

Privacy has been identified as one of the challenges that plagues CPSs and IoT technologies and could affect their effective adoption [10, 11]. Data subjects and the public at large are likely to be more amenable to CPSs and IoT technologies when they perceive a level of transparency, are given adequate control over their personal information and realise that an organisation takes their data privacy seriously [46].

This benefit is closely related to consumer trust, since buy-in would not exist where there is no trust. Employee technology buy-in, as a result of clear data privacy respecting practices, was identified as a benefit by some human resource specialists during the development of the benefits. Privacy compliance can therefore support a more enabling environment for the adoption of CPSs and IoT technologies.

4.17 Improved Trade Relations and Investment

Data privacy compliance has been identified as an area that can open up opportunities in the trade space, especially from a transborder perspective, as certain regions or countries prohibit trade when inadequate protection of personal information is present. For example, Article 43 of the GDPR [6] and Section 72 of the POPI Act [8] prohibit the transfer of personal information to third countries or international organisations where there are no appropriate safeguards or adequate levels of protection in place. Having appropriate safeguards or adequate levels of protection could therefore eliminate barriers for organisations doing business across borders, at least relating to data privacy, and may consequently attract investment.

An increase in investment opportunities and investor confidence regarding CPSs and IoT is a possible benefit that could accrue to organisations as a result of data privacy compliance, especially in the age of the fourth industrial revolution, for which these technologies are enablers. Proving that a particular device, product, service, solution or project is data privacy compliant may, together with other factors, inspire investor confidence. It would highlight competitive and compliance aspects that can draw investor support and, thus, investment opportunities for CPSs and IoT initiatives. The opposite could negatively affect investment even for transactions unrelated to personal information; a single area that exposes the organisation to risks can affect unrelated investments.

4.18   Organisational Management Efficiency

An organisation that follows a proper privacy risk management process empowers its management to effectively oversee the implementation of data privacy compliance. A risk assessment report can provide management with a quick overview of what to expect for data privacy compliance, without the need for them to be experts in privacy law. This increased ability to provide more informed oversight is in the best interest of privacy in general and organisations responsible for CPSs and IoT technologies in particular.

5   Using the Benefits

This paper focuses on privacy compliance benefits, with a view to highlight the value that organisations can derive as a result of data privacy compliance in relation to CPSs and IoT. To effectively use the benefits provided, it is necessary to understand organisational strategic priorities and the project scope. The project scope should then lead to the identification of the value that the organisation can derive from the technology and the risks associated with the project. With the understanding of the project scope, technological value, potential privacy risks and the organisation's strategic priorities, one can then identify data privacy benefits relevant for the CPSs or IoT project and the organisation. The benefits can be based on the list of benefits provided for in this paper or could be completely new benefits. This paper simply seeks to stimulate thoughts (consideration) of benefits directly linked to privacy compliance. The use and applicability of the benefits were demonstrated in a proof of concept exercise on an IoT project at a South African organisation [34] and were found to be representative of the benefits that would result from privacy compliance.

6   Conclusion

This paper advocates for the protection of personal information as a human right to privacy and as an exercise that can have potential value for organisations. Organisations are important stakeholders in the data privacy value chain. They therefore cannot remain on the periphery of the privacy discourse and act as mere implementing agents of the law through compliance. Their role has to be a form of active citizenry that respects humanity, the rule of law and people's right to privacy and self-determination. As organisations take on a more active role in the privacy landscape, there is inherent tangible and intangible value that accrues to such organisations. In a world where organisations may be seen as being merely interested in profits, they have a role to play in re-writing the narrative by actively taking steps to protect and show respect for data subjects and thereby protect their own interests and standing in society.

This paper presented a list of 18 data privacy compliance benefits for CPSs and IoT technologies with the aim to highlight the value that organisations can derive from data privacy compliance. The benefit-focused approach followed in this paper goes beyond viewing privacy as a legal compliance obligation into demonstrating the value that an organisation could derive as a result of privacy compliance. The list of data privacy compliance benefits provided is not exhaustive and serves only as guidance to locating the value for organisations through data privacy compliance. It is also clear that many benefits from the list presented are quite generic and could reasonably apply to any technology or data processing initiative.

Future work opportunities include further refinement and testing of the benefits. A closer focus on data subjects and privacy regulatory authorities is another area worth exploring.

References

1. ICO: Privacy impact assessment and risk management. Information Commissioner's Office, Wilmslow (2013)
2. Westin, A.F.: Privacy and freedom. Wash. Lee Law Rev. **25**, 166–170 (1968)
3. Solove, D.J.: Conceptualizing privacy. Calif. Law Rev. **90**, 1087–1155 (2002)
4. Erickson, K., Howard, P.N.: A case of mistaken identity? News accounts of hacker, consumer, and organizational responsibility for compromised digital records. J. Comput.-Mediat. Commun. **12**, 1229–1247 (2007)
5. Cole, D.D.: Assessing the leakers: criminal or heroes. J. Nat. Secur. Law Policy **8**, 107–118 (2015)
6. European Union: GDPR Portal: Site Overview. https://www.eugdpr.org/eugdpr.org.html
7. Baloyi, N., Kotzé, P.: A data privacy model based on Internet of Things and cyber-physical systems reference architectures. In: Proceedings of the Annual Conference of the South African Institute of Computer Scientists and Information Technologists: SAICSIT 2018 – Technology for Change, pp. 258–268. ACM (2018). https://doi.org/10.1145/3278681. 3278712
8. Government of South Africa: Protection of Personal Information Act 4 of 2013. Government Printing Works (2013). www.justice.gov.za/legislation/acts/2013-004.pdf
9. Baloyi, N., Kotźe, P.: Are organisations in South Africa ready to comply with personal data protection or privacy legislation and regulations? In: Cunningham, P., Cunningham, M. (eds.) IST-Africa 2017 Conference, pp. 1–11. IEEE (2017)
10. Babiceanu, R.F., Seker, R.: Big data and virtualization for manufacturing cyber-physical systems: a survey of the current status and future outlook. Comput. Ind. **81**, 128–137 (2016). https://doi.org/10.1016/j.compind.2016.02.004
11. Internet Society: The Internet of Things: An Overview (2015)

12. Cavoukian, A., Dixon, M.: Privacy and Security by Design: an Enterprise Architecture Approach. Information and Privacy Commissioner, Ontario (2013)
13. Aktypi, A., Nurse, J.R.C., Goldsmith, M.: Unwinding Ariadne's identity thread: privacy risks with fitness trackers and online social networks. In: Proceedings of the 2017 on Multimedia Privacy and Security, pp. 1–11. ACM, New York (2017). https://doi.org/10.1145/3137616.3137617
14. Lee, E.A., Seshia, S.A.: Introduction to Embedded Systems: A Cyber-Physical Systems Approach. MIT Press, Cambridge (2017)
15. Lee, J., Bagheri, B., Kao, H.: A cyber-physical systems architecture for Industry 4.0-based manufacturing systems. Manuf. Lett. **3**, 18–23 (2015)
16. Thinakaran, K., Dhillon, J.S., Gunasekaran, S.S., Chen, L.F.: A conceptual privacy framework for privacy-aware IoT health applications. In: 6th International Conference on Computing and Informatics, Kuala Lumpur, pp. 175–183 (2017)
17. Torre, H., Koceva, F., Sanchez, O.R., Adorni, G.: A framework for personal data protection in the IoT. In: Internet Technology and Secured Transactions (ICITST), pp. 384–391. IEEE (2016). https://doi.org/10.1109/ICITST.2016.7856735
18. Atzori, L., Iera, A., Morabito, G.: The Internet of Things: a survey. Comput. Netw. **54**, 2787–2805 (2010). https://doi.org/10.1016/j.comnet.2010.05.010
19. Khaitan, S.K., McCalley, J.D.: Design techniques and applications of cyberphysical systems: a survey. IEEE Syst. J. **9**, 350–365 (2015). https://doi.org/10.1109/JSYST.2014.2322503
20. Stankovic, J.A.: Research directions for the Internet of Things. IEEE Internet Things J. **1**, 3–9 (2014)
21. Wood, A.D., et al.: Context-aware wireless sensor networks for assisted living and residential monitoring. IEEE Network **22**, 26–33 (2008). July/August 2018
22. Carroll, M.: A Risk and Control Framework for Cloud Computing and Virtualization. University of South Africa, Pretoria (2012)
23. Colbert, E.: Security of cyber-physical systems. J. Cyber Secur. Inf. Syst. **5** (2017)
24. Miclea, L., Sanislav, T.: About dependability in cyber-physical systems. In: EWDTS, pp. 17–21 (2011)
25. Minerva, R., Biru, A., Rotondi, D.: Towards a Definition of the Internet of Things (IoT). IEEE (2015)
26. Lin, S., et al.: The Industrial Internet of Things Volume G1: Reference Architecture, Industrial Internet Consortium (2017)
27. Tesfachew, T.: Key challenges in the development and implementation of data protection laws. In: Data Protection Regulations and International Data Flows: Implications for Trade and Development, United Nations, Geneva, pp. 7–22 (2016)
28. Government of the United Kingdom. Data Protection Act 29 of 1998. Government of the United Kingdom (1998). www.legislation.gov.uk/ukpga/1998/29/pdfs/ukpga_19980029_en.pdf
29. African Union: African Union Convention on Cyber Security and Personal Data Protection, African Union (2014)
30. Cate, F.H.: The failure of fair information practice principles. In: Winn, J.K. (ed.): Consumer Protection in the Age of the "Information Economy." Ashgate Publishing, Hampshire (2006)
31. Government of South Africa. Constitution of the Republic of South Africa. Government of South Africa (1996). (ISBN 978-0-621-39063-6), www.justice.gov.za/legislation/constitution/SAConstitution-web-eng.pdf
32. OECD: Guidelines Governing the Protection of Privacy and Transborder Flows of Personal Data (1980)
33. Vaishnavi, V., Kuechler, W., Petter, S.: Design Science Research in Information Systems. http://desrist.org/desrist/content/design-science-research-in-information-systems.pdf

34. Baloyi, N.: A Data Privacy Framework for Cyber-physical Systems and Internet of Things for Information Technology Professionals. University of Pretoria, Pretoria (2019)
35. ICO: Subject Access Code of Practice Information Commissioner's Office, Wilmslow (2014)
36. Weinberg, B.D., Milne, G.R., Andonova, Y.G., Hajjat, F.M.: Internet of Things: convenience vs. privacy and secrecy. Bus. Horiz. **58**, 615–624 (2015). https://doi.org/10.1016/j.bushor.2015.06.005
37. Reuters. Musk Deletes Facebook Pages of Tesla, SpaceX After Challenged on Twitter. https://www.reuters.com/article/us-spacex-musk/musk-deletes-facebook-pages-of-tesla-spacex-after-challenged-on-twitter-idUSKBN1GZ2MZ
38. ICO: Anonymisation: Managing Data Protection Risk Code of Practice, Information Commissioner's Office, Wilmslow (2012)
39. ICO: Data Sharing Code of Practice, Information Commissioner's Office, Wilmslow (2011)
40. Head, T.: Momentum agree to R2.4 m payout for Nathan Ganas' family. https://www.thesouthafrican.com/momentum-agree-pay-ganas-family-why/
41. Baloyi, N., Kotźe, P.: Do users know or care about what is done with their personal data: a South African study. In: Cunningham, P., Cunningham, M. (eds.) IST-Africa 2017 Conference Proceedings, pp. 1–11. IEEE (2017)
42. Kula, S.: Appointment of the Information Regulator for POPI and PAIA. https://www.michalsons.com/blog/appointment-of-the-information-regulator/20059
43. ICO: The Guide to Data Protection, Information Commissioner's Office, Wilmslow (2017)
44. ICO: In the Picture: A Data Protection Code of Practice for Surveillance Cameras and Personal Information Information Commissioner's Office, Wilmslow (2015)
45. Government of South Africa. Promotion of Access to Information Act 2 of 2000. Government of South Africa (2000). www.justice.gov.za/legislation/acts/2000-002.pdf
46. Sinclair, M., Siemieniuch, C., Palmer, P.: The identification of knowledge gaps in the technologies of cyber-physical systems with recommendations for closing these gaps. Syst. Eng. **22**, 3–19 (2019)

Author Index

Printed in the United States
By Bookmasters